VIRGINIA LAND CAUSES

Lancaster County
1795–1848

and

Northampton County
1731–1868

᪥᪥

Compiled by
Stratton Nottingham

᪥᪥

with a
Preface by
Miles Barnes

HERITAGE BOOKS
2011

HERITAGE BOOKS

AN IMPRINT OF HERITAGE BOOKS, INC.

Books, CDs, and more—Worldwide

For our listing of thousands of titles see our website
at
www.HeritageBooks.com

A Facsimile Reprint
Published 2011 by
HERITAGE BOOKS, INC.
Publishing Division
100 Railroad Ave. #104
Westminster, Maryland 21157

Originally published 1931

— Publisher's Notice —
In reprints such as this, it is often not possible to remove blemishes from
the original. We feel the contents of this book warrant its reissue despite
these blemishes and hope you will agree and read it with pleasure.

International Standard Book Numbers
Paperbound: 978-1-55613-438-8
Clothbound: 978-0-7884-8960-0

FOREWORD

The records included in this volume, the land causes of Lancaster and Northampton counties, are in reality chancery suits and contain the same general information as the Accomack Land Causes published in 1930. The value of these records to the researcher is obvious, as they contain in concrete form information it would take months of painstaking research to dig out of the court records. The suits for division of land, ejectment proceedings, &c., trace the various owners of the land, their descendants and next of kin both of the half and whole blood through many generations, often giving birth, death and marriage dates not otherwise obtainable.

The declarations and answers are generally set out fully in the special verdicts of the juries, but depositions showing anything of interest not included in the verdicts are also fully abstracted.

The compiler wishes to acknowledge his appreciation to Mr. Oscar B. Chilton, Clerk of Lancaster, and Mr. George T. Tyson, Clerk of Northampton, and their deputies, for the many courtesies extended him while making these abstracts.

INTRODUCTION

Stratton Nottingham's untimely death at age forty-five robbed Virginia of an indefatigable compiler of genealogical data. Born in 1887 at Eastville in Northampton County on Virginia's Eastern Shore, Nottingham as a young man served as deputy clerk of the Northampton court. About 1920 he removed to Onancock in the adjoining county of Accomack. There Nottingham took up the full-time practice of genealogy and, as a byproduct of his professional research, began the publication of numerous genealogical compilations--marriage bonds, militia rolls, land causes, wills and administrations. His output was prolific. Between 1927 and 1931, he published thirteen volumes of abstracts from the court records of Accomack, Northampton, Lancaster, Mecklenburg, Northumberland, and Westmoreland counties. His work has enjoyed an enviable reputation for accuracy and has saved generations of genealogists countless hours of research. Stratton Nottingham surely would have accomplished more had not appendicitis occasioned a fatal attack of pneumonia. Nottingham died at the home of his parents on King Street, Onancock, on March 30, 1932.

Heritage Books' republication of Stratton Nottingham's work is most welcome. Many of Nottingham's books have long been unavailable, and all were originally printed on inferior paper, now rapidly deteriorating. *Virginia Land Causes*, the third volume to be republished, has been out of print for many years. The volume includes abstracts of chancery suits, land divisions, and ejectment proceedings for Northampton County for the period 1731-1868 and for Lancaster County for 1795-1848. It provides the genealogist and the historian with insights into Virginia kinship patterns, land transfers, and holdings in real, personal, and slave properties. In its painstaking detail, *Virginia Land Causes* is a typical example of Stratton Nottingham's care and discipline.

Brooks Miles Barnes
Onancock, Virginia
11 January 1991

LAND CAUSES 1795-1823

(Lancaster County)

Bartlett James, Mary James, William Kent and
    Elizabeth, his wife, by Charles Leland, their Attorney,
vs. - Suit for recovery of land, slaves &c.
    Lawson Hathaway & Achilles Barnett & Ann, his wife.

Sheriff's return dated 14 March, 1796, executed on Lawson Hathaway, Achilles Barnett is non inhabitant of my Baliwick. In consideration of which the said suit did abate against the said Achilles Barnett and the same continued till the next rules to be held for the said Court, and the complainant's to file their bill against the said defendant Hathaway, which bill is in these words, to-wit: Sheweth unto your worships your orators and oratrixes, Bartlett James, William Kent and Elizabeth, his wife, who was Elizabeth James, and Mary James: That your orator is the brother by the father's side and your oratrix is the sister by the same side of a certain John James who departed this life sometime in the year 1788 without having made any legal disposition of his estate by will or other writing good and valid in law; that the said John James left neither wife nor child, but that Nancy James, a sister of the whole blood who has since intermarried with a certain Barnett, and your orators were his next of kin and the only persons under the law capable of taking his estate; that under the act regulating the course of descents the said Nancy, his sister of the whole blood, is entitled to 2/5 part of the land and personal estate of which the said John James died seized and possessed and no more, and that your orators as being of the half blood are each of them entitled to 1/5 of the same; that your orators upon being well advised that this was the law have made frequent application to the said Barnett, who intermarried with the said Nancy, for their distributive parts of the lands, slaves and moveable estate of which the said John James died seized and possessed, but now so it may please your worships that the said Barnett and Nancy, his wife, combining and confederating together and with a certain William James and Lawson Hathaway, whom your orators pray may be made defendants herein, and divers other persons how to injure and oppress your orators and deprive them of their so just right, and possessed themselves of the whole estate, both real and personal of the said John James without ever accounting with your orators for their parts------------; That the said Barnet and Nancy, his wife, have since by their deed of conveyance of record among the records of Lancaster County Court conveyed the same to the said

1

Lawson Hathaway, insisting that your orators had no claim or interest in any part of the said estate, and setting up a will made by collusion and framed for him, the said John James when he was on his death bed, and if executed by him at all not until a few hours before his death when in the last stages of a confluent smallpox, and in the height of delirium, and at a time when he was entirely bereft of his senses and memory, being obliged to be raised up in his bed by a certain William James (whom your orators charge as prime agent in this fraudulent business, and who together with the said Lawson Hathaway, as your orators believe, contrived the said will) and when raised up your orators charge he was so ill that the said William James was obliged to take his hand and make a mark for him by way of signature----12 March, 1796 - p. 29

That on Tuesday, the 10th day of March, in the year 1802, Doddridge Pitt Chichester, Ellen Sydnor and Fanny Sydnor, an infant under the age of 21 years, by the said Doddridge Pitt Chichester, her guardian, exhibited their bill of complaint unto the worshipfull Court against Samuel G. Sydnor and Richard Sydnor, William Sydnor, Ann Sydnor and Samuel B. Sydnor, infants under the age of 21 years, by Samuel G. Sydnor, their guardian, which bill is as follows: Humbly complaining sheweth unto your worships your orator Doddridge Pitt Chichester, your oratrix Ellen Sydnor, your oratrix Fanny Sydnor, an infant under the age of 21 by the said Doddridge Pitt Chichester, her guardian; that George Sydnor was the son of your oratrix Ellen Sydnor and brother of your orator's wife and your oratrix Fanny Sydnor, and he, the said George, being seized of a tract of land in the county of Lancaster did on the ___ day of March, 1798, depart this life so seized of the land aforesaid, being of lawful age and intestate; that Samuel G. Sydnor, whom your orator and oratrixes pray to be made a defendant hereto, is also a brother of the said George; that William F. Sydnor, the brother of the said George, departed this life on the ___ day of April, 1798, leaving four children, to-wit: Richard Sydnor, William Sydnor, Ann Sydnor and Samuel B. Sydnor, infants under the age of 21, whom your orator and oratrixes also pray to be made defendants hereto by Samuel G. Sydnor, their guardian, that the said Samuel G. Sydnor hath in his own right and as guardian aforesaid, possessed himself of the land aforesaid and refuseth to let your orator, Doddridge Pitt Chichester and your oratrix Ellen Sydnor and your oratrix Fanny Sydnor have any part of the said land, whereas your orator expressly charges that he is justly entitled to 1/5 of the said land for his own life as tenant by the curtesy, he having married the sister of the said George Sydnorby whom he had issue born alive. Your orator further sheweth that his wife survived the said George, and that your orator was after the death of the said George actually seized of all the land aforesaid and continued so seized till very lately when the same came to the seisin of the defendant Samuel G. Sydnor. Your orator and oratrixes do not controvert the right of the said Samuel G. Sydnor to 1/5 of the aforesaid land in his own right, nor do they controvert the right of the other defendants, the children of William F. Sydnor to one other 1/5 part of the said land, that being the part of their deceased father; Your orator and oratrixes further show unto your worships that William Sydnor, the father of your oratrix Fanny, and the grandfather of the defendants Richard, William, Anne and Samuel B. Sydnor, children of William F. Sydnor, and father of the other defendant, Samuel G. Sydnor, did on the __ day of __, 17__ duly make and publish his last will and testament wherein and whereby among other things he devised to his son James Sydnor the land and plantation whereon he, the testator, lived, known by the name of deep creek, together with the land adjoining which the testator had purchased of Robert Mitchell, called Cyrus's, after the death of your oratrix Ellen Sydnor, widow of the testator, to which will reference is here made as part of this bill; that the testator died so seized of the said las mentioned lands on the __ day of __ 1794; that James Sydnor, the devisee in the remainder departed this life on the __ day of March, 1796, an infant under the age of 21 without issue, leaving his brothers Fauntleroy, Moore, George and William Fauntleroy Sydnor and Samuel G. Sydnor, and the following sisters, Caty and Fanny Sydnor; That Fauntleroy departed this life on the __ day of April, 1796, an infant under the age of 21 years intestate and without issue; Moore departed this life on the __ day of November, 1797, having first made and published his last will and testament to which reference is made as a part of this bill, wherein among other things he devised his part of the land which had been devised to James by their father to his, the said Moore's sister Fanny; That George Sydnor departed this life on the __ day of March, 1798, intestate and without issue, but being of lawful age; that William Fauntleroy Sydnor departed this life on the __ day of April, 1798 intestate, and leaving four children, to-wit: Richard, William, Ann and Samuel B. Sydnor, now infants and defendants hereto by the said Samuel G. Sydnor, their guardian; That Caty Chichester, formerly Sydnor, and wife to your orator Doddridge Pitt Chichester, departed this life on the __ day of January, 1801, leaving one child, but which child died soon after it's mother an infant under the age of 21 and without issue, by reason of which promises the said land so devised to James by his father ought now to be divided first into seven equal shares, then one seventh part to be divided into six equal parts, and the one seventh of the whole land together with one sixth part of one seventh to be allotted to your oratrix Fanny as the part of which her brother Moore was entitled to out of the land so as aforesaid devised to James by his father, after deducting or taking off which two parts, to-wit: the seventh part of the whole land and the one sixth part of one seventh, the balance of the land aforesaid to be divided into three equal parts, one part to be allotted to your oratrix Fanny, one other part to the defendant Samuel G. Sydnor and the other one third part to the children of William F. Sydnor &c. - p. 62

3

Martin Carter & John Lunsford, Guardian of Thomas Carter,
    by Ellyson Currie, their Attorney,
vs - Suit for recovery of a negro.
Merryman Chilton.

Jury impaneled and returned the following verdict:

We of the jury find that Thomas Carter died leaving duly executed his will, which said will was proved in the County Court of Lancaster in these words: (Abstract) I give and bequeath to my son John Carter and to his heirs my negro wench named Minon and all her increase, and also her child already born. To my son Edward Carter and his heirs my negro girl Frank and all her increase, also to my son Edward and his heirs my lower plantation with all the land there and the appurtenances thereunto belonging. To my son Thomas and his heirs all the cash I have already paid toward the purchase of 143 acres of land of a certain John Atkins, formerly of Northumberland County, with all writings and deeds I have thereunto concerning the same, also I give to my said son Thomas Carter's son Edward Carter, Jr., and the said Edward's heirs forever, my negro girl named Sue, and all her increase. To son Thomas one half my wearing clothes. To son Rawleigh Carter negro Sarah and her increase; also to my said son Rawleigh my upper plantation where I now live. To my son George Carter and his heirs my negro girl Siller and all her increase. To daughter Judith Chilton and her heirs my negro girl Hannah and all her increase. I have already given my daughter Mellicent Cummings three negroes which is all I intended to give her. To daughter Lucy Smither and her heirs my negro girl Jinny and her increase. To daughter Sarah McTyre an equal share in the division of my estate, she having already received a negro boy named Charles divided in the estate of her first husband, Robert H. Henning, Jr. To daughter Alice Griggs negro boy named Harry and negro girl Esther and all her increase. To grandaughter Ann Hunton negro girl Winny and her increase. To son James Carter the use of my two negroes Mingo and Mark to maintain him during his natural life, and it is my express will and desire that he be under the care of my son Edward Carter unto whom, after the death of my son James, I give all his estate of what nature soever, provided he, the said James, shall live fifteen years from the date of this will, but if not to be equally divided as my other estate. To daughter in law Ann Hunton personalty. To grandson Charles Chilton, the son of my daughter Mary, 40 L current money, having already given his brother Thomas Chilton and paid to him the like sum. To cousin Dale Carter 5 L cash. Balance of estate to be equally divided between my children, to-wit: John, Edward, Rawleigh, George, Judith, Lucy, Sarah, Alice and my grandson Edward Carter, Jr., the son of my son Thomas Carter, and it is my will that my son Edward have my negro man Daniel in this equal division. Sons Edward and Rawleigh Ex'rs. 25 Sept. 1775 - Witt: Dale Carter, Jeduthan James, Rich: Stephens, William Stephens - Probated 19 Dec. 1776.

By which said will the said Thomas Carter bequeathed to a certain James Carter, his son, the use of the negro man Mingo mentioned in the declaration during his life, and provided he, the said James, should life fifteen years from the 25 September, 1775, the date of the said will, then he bequeathed the said negro man Mingo to another son of the said Thomas, the testator, named Edward Carter, which Edward was the father of Martin Carter, one of the plaintiffs, and the grandfather of Thomas Carter, the other plaintiff who sues by his guardian; That the said James Carter did live fifteen years and upwards from the said 25 September, 1775. We find the will of Edward Carter, Sr. in the following words and figures (Abstract) "In the name of God Amen, I Edward Carter of Christ Church Parish in Lancaster County" To wife Catharine my riding chair – Personalty, the use of three negroes, viz: Leety, Pleasant and a boy Jack, and their increase during her natural life, she to have the liberty of disposing of them to any of my children she chooses. To my said wife during her natural life the use of three other negroes, Daniel, Young Harry and Alice and her increase, also the use of my still &c. during her natural life, and after her death I give Young Harry and Alice and her increase to my son Martin and my still &c to my son Martin. To daughter Hannah Hunton and son in law John Hunton during their natural lives the use of six negroes, Martha, Jenny, Charles, Nell, Myma and Martha's child and their increase, which said negroes they now have in possession, and at the death of the said John and Hannah the said negroes and their increase to be divided between the children they shall have by each other. To wife one third part of my chattels, negroes excepted. Balance of my chattels, negroes excepted, to be equally divided between my two sons, Edward and Martin. To my grandaughter Mary Kirk during her natural life the use of my negro girl Sue and her increase, and if my said grandaughter shall have issue I give the said Sue and her increase to her and her lawful heirs forever, and for want of such issue to my daughter Hannah Hunton and her heirs. To grandaughter Catherine Kirk during her natural life the use of a negro girl Jenny, daughter of Tab, and her increase, and if my said grandaughter should have lawful issue I give the said Jenny and her increase to my said grandaughter forever, and for want of such issue to my daughter Hannah Hunton. All my negroes not before named to be divided between my sons Edward and Martin. To son Martin the sum of 1150 L- lawful gold and silver which James Gordon owes me by bond, together with the interest on same to purchase my said son a plantation. Wife Catharine, son Edward and friend Maj. Henry Towles Ex'rs. 1 April 1783 – Witt: James Gordon, William Dunaway – Probated 18 Mar. 1784

We find that Edward Carter, the son of Edward Carter, died intestate prior to the year 1800, leaving issue Thomas, one of the plaintiffs only.

We find that Catharine, the executrix of Edward Carter, Sr., died intestate on or about the __ day of __ 17__ .

We find that the said negro Mingoe was and is in the possession of the defendant Merryman Chilton. We find that Edward Carter the younger left a widow who died on or about the __ day of June, 1799, leaving lawful issue but Thomas, one of the plaintiffs. May – 1800 – p. 77

5

William Newby, administrator of Elizabeth Newby, Susanna Hunton,
     Cyrus Newby and Ann, his wife, who was Ann Hunton, and
     Willliam W. Hunton
vs - Suit for recovery of a negro
Thomas Williams, Alexander Hunton, Ex'r. of Alexander Hunton, dec.

    That sometime in the year __ one Alexander Hunton, of the County
of Richmond, died having prior thereto made his will in writing, which
will is prayed to be made a part of this bill, therein appointing one
Alexander Hunton, son of the testator, and Thomas Williams his
executors; That William Newby, one of the complainants intermarried
with the testator's daughter Betty, and is entitled under the said will
to the negro girl named Judith, as well in the capacity of administrator
as of husband, and that your orators and oratrixes are entitled to a
considerable amount under the residuary clause of the said will, and
also to their respective parts of the money arising from the sale of
land in Albemarle, but now it is that Alexander Hunton and Thomas
Williams, executors of the said will, disregarding the injunctions of
the said will, have wasted and made away with the said estate, both
real and personal, or else refuse to deliver to your orators and oratrixes such parts as they are respectively entitled to-------- In consideration whereof your complainants pray that the said executors may be
made defendants to this bill, and that they may be compelled on oath
to answer the allegations thereof-------- and that they may declare
whether the land in Albemarle devised to be sold hath actually been
sold, and if it has what was the amount of the said sale, and to what
these complainants are individually entitled under the residuary clause
of the said will, which said will is as follows: (Abstract) "I, Alexander Hunton of the County of Richmond and North Farnham parish"
Wife to have whole estate during her widowhood, but if she marry to
have only what the law allows. To son Robert negro girl Pat. To
daughter Mary Hunton negro man Ned during her natural life. To
daughter Betty Hunton negro girl Judy, to her and her heirs forever. To
daughter Susanna Hunton negro woman Frank, to her and her heirs
forever. To daughter Sally Hunton negro James, to her and her heirs
forever. To daughter Nancy Hunton negro Lette, to her and her heirs
forever. To daughter Caty Hunton negro girl Winney, to her and her
heirs forever. To daughter Lucy Hunton negro girl Darkey, to her and
her heirs forever. To son William Hunton negro Tom, to him and his
heirs forever. To son John Hunton negro Dick, to him and his heirs
forever. To son George Hunton negro girl Meina, to him and his heirs
forever. To son Thomas Hunton my plantation where I now live as far
as the road which runs through near the middle of my land, and for
want of heirs to be equally divided between my surviving children. To
son Alexander Hunton the rest of my land from that dividing road
before mentioned to Moratteco branch, and for want of issue to the rest
of my children. Should my daughter Molly continue to be divested of
her reason my son Thomas to keep her and have the use of her estate
as long as she continues in that situation. Should my wife die before
my youngest child arrives to the age of 16 years, that they be suffi-
ciently educated and maintained out of my estate until they come to
the age of sixteen. It is my desire that after the decease of my wife

that my land in Albemarle County be sold and the proceeds divided between all my surviving children except my sons Thomas and Alexander, whom I have already provided with land. Balance of estate to be divided between my children Robert, Mary, Susanna, Betty, Sally, Nancy, Thomas, Alexander, William, Caty, John, Lucy and George Hunton. Wife, son Robert, son Thomas, son Alexander and friend Thomas Williams Ex'rs. 28 Apr. 1789 - Witt: Thomas Williams, James Alderson, Bryant Phillips - Probated 5 Oct. 1789.

The Deposition of George Davenport, taken 16 July, 1803:

That sometime in the year 1794 Elizabeth Hunton, wife of Alexander Hunton died and held the whole of her said husband's estate until her death, and that Elizabeth Newby, daughter of the said Elizabeth Hunton died some years before her mother.

Question by Alexander Hunton: Did Elizabeth Newby leave any issue of her body?

Answer: She did.

Question: Do you know that the Executors of Alexander Hunton, deceased, ever gave up any of the property of the said deceased to William Newby?

Answer: I do not.

Question: Did you see William Newby on his way to this defendant's plantation, and that was your conversation?

Answer: I did, and Newby told this deponent that he had got Brooks opinion and that he was then going to order my negroes home in a few days.

Question: Did you ever see the aforesaid negro Jude at William Newby's?

Answer: I did.

Question: Did you ever hear William Newby say he had the negroes in possession?

Answer: I did, and Jude was now in his possession.

Question: By the Plaintiff: Did you not believe I had a right to go and order the negroes home from what you had heard Williams say?

Answer: I did think you had a right. And further saith not.
23 March, 1804 - p. 93

Thomas Bell, et als,
vs. - Suit for division of land.
Charles Bell

Bill - To the worshipful Court of Lancaster County in Chancery sitting, humbly complaining, show to your worships your orators and oratrixes, Thomas Bell, James Bell, Nathaniel Anderson and Mildred Anderson, his wife, formerly Mildred Bell, Elizabeth Lee, formerly Elizabeth Bell, Ann Gamble, formerly Ann Bell and James Bell. That a certain Charles Bell, dec., made and executed his last will and testament bearing date the 1 day of November, 1780, which was duly proved and recorded in the County Court of Lancaster --------by which will he gave the use of all his estate of every kind to his wife Elizabeth Bell so long as she remained the widow of the said Charles, and by the said will the said Charles Bell gave all his land to his brothers Thomas Bell, not deceased, and the said James Bell to be equally divided between them and their heirs forever; your orators and oratrixes Thomas Bell, James Bell, Mildred Anderson, Elizabeth Lee and Ann Gamble are the children of the said Thomas Bell dec., the said brother of the testator----now your orators and oratrixes just named, together with your orator the said James Bell, the other brother of Charles, the testator, are under the said will entitled to all the lands of which the said Charles Bell died seized, together with Charles Bell, the only remaining child of the said Thomas, dec., after the death of the said Elizabeth Bell - 18 Feb. 1805 - p. 158

Aminidab Seekright
vs. - Trespass
Ferdinand Dreadnought
Jury impaneled and returned the following verdict:
That in the year 1762 William Galloway, Sr., was seized in his demesne as of fee in a tract of land lying in the County of Lancaster on which the trespass in the declaration mentioned is supposed to be committed. That the said William Galloway by deed of indenture acknowledged by him conveyed to John Cundiff in fee simple the said tract containing 100 acres, more or less, said deed dated 20 Aug. 1762, and which land the said William Galloway purchased of Richard Alderson by deed dated 14 Apr. 1757. We find that William Galloway and his wife, Judith, had the use and possession of the said tract of land during the joint lives of the said William and Judith and during the life of the survivor of them; the said William held possession of the said land until his death, and his wife Judith who survived her husband remained in possession thereof until the year 1794 or 1795, the one of the years the said Judith died; we find that the said John Cundiff by deed conveyed to John Heath in fee simple two tracts of land lying in the County of Lancaster, containing 160 acres, more or less, one of which tracts was purchased of Charles Marsh and the other of the said William Galloway, the tract purchased of William Galloway is the 100 acres first within mentioned, which said deed from Cundiff to Heath was dated 6 Mar. 1771. We find that the said John Heath and Judith, his wife, by deed dated 12 Dec. 1774, conveyed the said 100 acres to Nicholas Flood. We find that the said Nicholas Flood died on the ___ day of ___ having first made his last will and testament, proved in the County Court of Richmond County, which said will is in the following words (Abstract) "I Nicholas Flood of the Parish of North Farnham in the County of Richmond - My will is if I happen to die in America and convenient to my place of abode that I be buried at the east end of North Farnham Church on the right hand of my daughter Catharine McCall, and that a vault of either brick or stone be built over our graves large enough to contain also in breadth another coffin on my daughter's left hand for the reception of the remains of my wife. To my wife so long as she remains my widow the use of all the houses which are included within the gardens, grounds &c. except such as shall hereafter be disposed of, and all the said gardens and grounds containing about 20 acres, and also 10 negroe slaves, house

servants & gardiners, also the use of household and kitchen furniture, plate &c. Land in Essex County which I bought of Merrywether Smith and George Clayton to be sold, and that all the slaves and cattle I bought on the said plantation, viz: 24 head of cattle in the year 1767, the year my daughter died, when I intended to have taken the said plantation and negroes and stocks into my own hands, but was persuaded by my wife to leave them for another year or two in the hands of Archibald McCall, be likewise sold by my executor and from the proceeds of my said land and slaves, rents &c. I give one half the interest to my wife. That the beef, pork, salt, tea, sugar &c. laid in for the family's use be inventoried, and that my wife supply herself as long as they shall last or she shall live unmarried, and for the support of my grandaughters if they should come into this country. Should my wife die sometime before my grandaughters come to the age of 21 years, and they shall not have returned to this Colony, and if my executors judge that my household and kitchen furniture shall be in danger of perishing or of being lost or destroyed, then it shall be sold and the money equally divided between my two grandaughters. Grandaughters Elizabeth McCall and Catharine Flood McCall. Leaves his grandaughters china "bought at the sale of my brother's estate". To grandaughter Elizabeth McCall my dwelling plantation and all my lands in Richmond County and one moiety of all my slaves, and for want of issue to her sister Katharine Flood McCall, and for want of heirs to my nephew Nicholas Flood, the second son of my late brother William Flood, and for want of heirs to my nephew William Pinkstant Flood, the eldest son of my said brother, and for want of heirs to Walter Flood Jones, the eldest son of my friend Dr. Walter Jones, and for want of heirs to William Jones, the second son of the said Dr. Walter Jones, and for want of heirs to Elizabeth Flood, the second daughter of my brother William Flood, and for want of heirs to Thomas Griffin Peachy, the second son of my friend and brother in law Col. William Peachy, and for want of heirs to William Travers Peachy, the third son of my said friend Col. William Peachy, and for want of heirs to William Peachy, the eldest son of my friend Maj. Leroy Peachey, and for want of heirs to Leroy Peachey, the second son of Major Leroy Peachey. As soon as my grandaughter Katharine Flood McCall shall attain the age of 21 years, my executors to purchase a good tract or tracts of land contiguous to each other in the Colony of Virginia, to the amount of 2000 L Virginia Currency, which said 2000 L I direct to be paid out of my whole estate, which said tract of land together with the other one half or moiety of my slaves I give and devise to my said grandaughter Katharine Flood McCall, and for want of heirs to her sister Elizabeth McCall. Not signed or witnessed - Proved by Charles McCarty, George Yerby, Benja Bramham, Robert Tomlin, Charles Hammond, who certified that they were well acquainted with the handwriting of Mr. Nicholas Flood &c. Probated 2 Mar. 1778.

We find that the said Nicholas Flood died intestate as to the aforesaid tract of 100 acres purchased of John Heath. We find that Nicholas Flood had one child only, Catharine Flood, who intermarried with Archibald McCall, which said Catharine died before the said Nicholas leaving only two children, to-wit: Elizabeth and Catharine Flood McCall, the lessor of the plaintiff, which Elizabeth died intestate an infant unmarried and without ever having had issue. That the widow of the said Nicholas survived him but died before the institution of this suit. We find that the defendant, Elijah Perciful, is in possession of the said tract of land first mentioned. We find that Catharine Flood McCall aforesaid is the only heir of Nicholas Flood, dec. We find a deed executed by John Heath, Sr., to John Heath, Jr. in fee simple which was regularly proved and recorded in Lancaster County, which was executed to convey the said tract of land, said deed dated 15 August, 1781, and described as "another tract or parcel of land adjoining the same containing by estimation 100 acres, both which said tracts or parcels of land the said Heath purchased of Covey and Cundiff, the latter of which is at present subject to the incumbrance and inconveniences of William Galloway's life, and which said tract or parcel of land was conveyed to a certain Dr. Nicholas Flood in his lifetime by deed efected under duress and imprisonment of the said Heath, the livery of seizen and possession were never delivered the said Flood" &c.

We find that John Heath, Jr. by the name and description of John Heath and Sally, his wife, by deed dated 9 October, 1796, conveyed to Presley Cockrell the said tract of land. We find a deed executed by Presley Cockrell and Jane, his wife, to the defendant Elijah Perciful, said deed dated 20 Jan. 1801, conveying the said tract in fee simple -- 19 Aug. 1805 - p. 160

William Hill, et als,
vs - Suit for dower and division.
Mary Hill, widow of John.
That John Hill sometime in the year ____ died intestate leaving a tract of land, several negroes and other property; that your orators and oratrixes the said William Hill and the said Leroy Pitman and Sally Pitman, the wife of the said William Pitman, the wife Polly, wife of the said Griffin Doggett and Eppa Hall are children and grandchildren of the said John Hill, deceased, the said Leroy and the said Sally being children of Elizabeth, daughter of the said John Hill, deceased; That the said John Hill left besides your orators and oratrixes the following children who are infants under the age of 21 years, to-wit: Lucy Pollard Hill, Thomas Pollard Hill, Milly Hill and Nancy Morris Hill, and also his widow, Mary Hill; that after the dower and thirds of the widow are laid off your orators and oratrixes and the said infant children will be entitled to the residue of the estate of which the said John Hill died seized and possessed &c. - 18 Mar. 1816 - p. 247

Carter, et als,
vs. - Suit for sale of land &c.
Dunnaway
Whereas heretofore, that is to say at a Court held for the said County at the Courthouse on Monday, the 16 day of November, 1818,

Joseph A. Carter, William H. Rogers and Mary P., his wife, Warren Carter, John Lunsford and Lettice Lunsford, his wife, and William H. Carter, Frances M. Carter, John M. Carter and Robert A. Carter (which said William H. Frances M., John M. and Robert A. being infants sue by their brother and next friend, the said Joseph A. Carter) exhibit their bill of complaint into this worshipfull Court against Rawleigh Dunnaway and Frances E., his wife, which said bill followeth in these words, to-wit: Humbly complaining, shew to your worships your orators and oratrixes, Joseph A. Carter, William H. Rogers and Mary P., his wife, Warren Carter, John Lunsford and Lettice Lunsford, his wife, and William H. Carter, Frances M. Carter, John M. Carter and Robert A. Carter (which said William H. Carter, Frances M. Carter, John M. Carter and Robert A. Carter being infants sue by their brother and next friend, the said Joseph A. Carter); that their father made his last will and testament which is of record among the records of this Court and departed this life on the __ day of __ 1813; among other things directed by the said will the testator, the said Joseph, deceased, desired that his children, William Henry, John Miller, Robert Alexander and Fanny, meaning the infants hereinbefore mentioned, should receive as liberal an education as his elder children, Joseph Addison, Warren and Polly, and for that purpose and for support of his widow, Frances E., vested in her, the said Frances E., his whole estate during her life or widowhood, but in the event she married again she was to take one third part of the testator's estate in the same manner she would have done had he died intestate. Your orators set forth that the said Frances E., the said widow, hath intermarried with Rawleigh Dunaway. They further state that the said testator has by his said will directed his land to be sold at the death of the said Frances E., but your orators are of opinion that it would be advantageous to them without producing any injury to the said Frances E. to sell now the tract of land called Harris's containing 178 acres and 25 poles, by which a fund might be raised for the education of the younger children, &c. - p. 264

James Spiller
vs
Susanna Edmonds, et als.
    Bill ---- Humbly complaining, shows to your worships your orator James Spiller; that Benjamin V. Spiller, late of the said County, departed this life on or about the __ day of __ 1801, after having duly made and published his last will and testament which was proved and admitted to record in this court the 20 July, 1801, which said will is prayed to be taken as a part of this bill - Among other things in the said will is the following: "Item: I give unto myson Benedictus Spiller my dwelling plantation whereon I now live, which land I purchased of Mr. Thomas Pinckard, provided that he my said son shall pay unto his brother James Spiller when he shall come of age 250 L &c." Your orator sets forth that he is the James Spiller mentioned as above, and that he is therefore entitled now, and has been since he arrived at age, to the said sum of 250 L, with interest from the 28

December, 1817, which was the day on which he arrived to the age of 21 years. That the said Benedictus Spiller, his brother, died without paying any part of the said sum, and leaving not enough personal estate to pay the debts which he himself contracted, and that there is nothing to which your orator can look from which to receive the money that is due him but the land devised to the said Benedictus by the said will as aforesaid, and which is in consequence of the manner in which the said devise is made charged with the payment of the said sum bequeathed to your orator; That the said Benedictus Spiller died without having disposed of his interest in the said land, which accordingly descended to his mother, brothers and sisters, he having died without children and unmarried; from all the heirs of the said Benedictus Spiller, except William Spiller, a brother of the half blood, Elias Edmonds, late of the said County purchased the said plantation and died intestate seized thereof, leaving a widow and children whose names are as follows: Susanna Edmonds, the widow, Ralph Edmonds, Frances F. Glascock, Janella P. Edmonds who hath since intermarried with Benjamin Waddy, Susanna Edmonds, who hath intermarried with Addison Hall, Elias Edmonds and John W. A. Edmonds, Phillip Edmonds, William Edmonds, Robert Edmonds, Elizabeth Edmonds and Margarett M. Edmonds, the children of the said Elias Edmonds, deceased, the said widow and children, together with the said husbands of the married children aforesaid, and the said William Spiller have been appealed to by your orator either to pay him the said sum of 250 L, with interest as aforesaid or permit the said land and plantation to be sold &c. -- 16 March, 1819 - p. 273

Thomas M. Owens
vs. - Suit for recovery of land
Seth Lunsford, administrator with will annexed of William Blackerby, deceased, Catharine Blackerby, widow of the said William, John Muse and Frances, his wife, Wmson Wiblin and Alice, his wife, John Angell and Sarah, his wife, Elizabeth Blackerby, Catharing Blackerby, Thomas Blackerby, William Blackerby, Joseph M. Blackerby and Richard Blackerby.

Bill - Humbly complaining, shows to your worships your orator, Thomas M. Owens; that Elizabeth How by a deed of indenture bearing date 29 April, 1808, which is of record among the records of Lancaster County, bargained and sold to William Blackerby a tract of land lying in the said County containing 128 acres, more or less; that the said William Blackerby entered into an agreement with the said Elizabeth How which bears even date with the aforesaid deed by which, among other things, the said William stipulated and agreed with the said Elizabeth that if she in her lifetime, or her heirs before the expiration of twelve months after her death, should pay to the said William Blackerby all his claim against the said Elizabeth How, with legal interest thereon, that the said William Blackerby agreed to make to the said Elizabeth How, or her heirs, any deed or deeds for the reconveying to them the said tract of land so as above bargained and sold by the said Elizabeth to the said William------

That the said Elizabeth How made and executed her last will and testament, bearing date the ___day of ___ and departed this life on or about the ___day of ___, and by her said will bequeathed the said tract of land to your orator; that your orator within twelve months after the death of the said Elizabeth offered to pay the said Seth Lunsford, the administrator of the said William Blackerby, the claims due the said William's estate, with interest thereon. The said administrator, knowing that specie has not to be had, demanded that payment should be made in specie, and your orator finding that impracticable, proved two debts against the said William, one due by bond executed by him to Peter Cox, of Baltimore, and the other an execution against the said Seth as administrator of the said Blackerby in the name of James Revere, which issued from the Clerk's Office of this Court for the sum of $62.81, or thereabouts, and he tendered in these two debts and in case the sum of $202.20 to the said Seth Lunsford, administrator as aforesaid, which he was of opinion was more than was justly due from the said Elizabeth to the said William, and at the same time told the said Lunsford that if on a fair settlement more was found due he would pay it if he, the said administrator, would refund if less was found due. The said administrator, however, combining with the widow and heirs of the said William Blackerby, refused to come to any settlement, saying that the land was preferred and that they or all of them did claim the land &c.---- May Term, 1817 - p. 284

John Payne, et ux,
vs - Suit for dower.
Mary Ann Eustace, et als.

Bill - Humbly complaining; shew to your worshipfull Court John Payne and & Harriot, his wife, your orator and oratrix, who was Harriot Eustace, the widow of William Eustace, deceased; That the said William Eustace departed this life on the ___day of ___ in the year___, leaving the following children, John, Mary Ann and William, who are prayed to be made defendants hereto, having first made his last will and testament, which is prayed to be made and taken as a part of this bill, wherein he devised that if your oratrix, his then wife, whould again marry after his decease, instead of the provision therein made for her she should take a full third part of all his estate, both real and personal, and your orator sets forth that he has since intermarried with your oratrix Harriot, and that the real estate of the said William Eustace still remains undivided, and your orator and oratrix are deprived of the enjoyment of their legal rights therein &c. ---- 15 Nov. 1819 - p. 306

Elizabeth Basye and John Cundiff,
vs. - Suit for sale and division.
    Thomas Rock and Nancy, his wife, Samuel Stonham and Betsy,
          his wife and Mary Sampson, John Sampson, Nancy Sampson,
          Elizabeth Sampson, Betsy Sampson, John Sampson and
          Judith Sampson.

    The summons awarded in this case having been returned executed, and it appearing to the Court that Mary Sampson, John Sampson, Nancy Sampson, Elizabeth Sampson, Betsy Sampson and Judith Sampson are infants under the age of 21 years, John Sampson is appointed special guardian to defend them in this suit, and in consideration of the premises the Court doth order and decree that Joseph A. Carter and James Robinson, Jr., be appointed Commissioners, and that they make sale of the lands of which Richard Cundiff died seized and possessed on a credit of twelve months, and take bonds with good and sufficient security payable to the Commissioners of the Court for each of the plaintiffs and defendants respective distributive parts or proportions of the purchase money according to their severel interests therein &c.----- November Term 1824 - p. 57

Thomas M. Locke
vs - Suit for recovery of Land.
Thomas J. Beane, et als.
    We command you to summon Thomas J. Beane, Cyrus Chilton and Leannah, his wife, who was Leannah Beane, and Peter Beane to appear before the Justices of the County Court of Lancaster in the Court House, on the third Monday in May, next, to answer a certain bill in Chancery to be exhibited against them in our said Court by Thomas M. Locke   -------- which subpoena was returned executed by the Sheriff of the said County, and at rules held in the Clerk's Office of said County in the said month of May, in the said year, came the complainant, by his attorney, and filed his bill of complaint, which bill is in the following words:
    Humbly complaining; your orator, Thomas M. Locke, sheweth that Joseph Locke, now deceased, late of this County, being indebted to a certain Peter Beane, Sr., now also deceased, in the sum of ___, to secure the payment thereof the above named Joseph Locke executed a deed of trust bearing date the 1 day of ___18__ , for the sum aforesaid,

together with interest &c., upon a certain tract of land situate, lying and being in the County of Lancaster ---- your orator states that the trustee aforesaid did by virtue of the said deed of trust, sell the above mentioned land and Peter Beane, Sr., before named, became the purchaser, and your orator, who is a son of the said Joseph Locke, being desirous to secure to his father a home during his life agreed with the said Beane to pay him the amount of his debt for which the land aforesaid had been sold to pay, if the said Beane would convey to him, the said Thomas M. Locke, the land aforesaid; in consideration whereof the said Beane did bargain, sell and promise to convey in fee simple to him the said Thomas M. Locke the said tract of land any time after the said Thomas M. should pay to him, the said Beane, the amount he gave for the said tract of land _____ your orator says that he did comply with and discharge the said undertaking which he is ready at any time to shew, and that the said Beane was fully paid in his lifetime the whole amount, but that your orator residing in the City of Baltimore at a great distance from the said Beane no deed was executed to your orator; as a proof that the said Beane considered the land aforesaid not his property he never exercised any ownership over it &c. ---- but so now it is long since the death of the said Peter Beane, Thomas J. Beane, one of the children of Peter Beane aforesaid, and Cyrus Chilton, who married Leannah, a daughter of the said Peter Beane have set up a claim to the before described land as the heirs at law of the said Peter, notwithstanding they are well acquainted with the facts, &c----- 29 Apr. 1829 - p. 134

James Robinson, et als
vs - Suit for sale & division.
James Talley, et als
    Bill - Humbly complaining; sheweth unto your worships your orators and oratrixes James Robinson, George Robinson, Joel Robinson, John and Betsy Robinson, infants under the age of 21 years, and only children of Jeremiah Robinson, deceased, by James Robinson, their guardian and next friend, James Beatty, only child of Betsy Beatty, and who was Betsy Robinson, and Frances, Jane, Edward and John Robinson, infants under the age of 21 years, and only children of John Robinson, deceased, by George Robinson, their next friend, which said James, George and Joel are nephews, and the said infants John and Betsy only children of Jeremiah Robinson, deceased (who was a nephew), the said infants Frances, Jane, Edward and John, only children of the said John Robinson, deceased (who uas also a nephew), and the said James Beatty, only child of the said Betsy Beatty (who was Betsy Robinson, a niece), are the great nephews and nieces of James Robinson deceased, and together with Nancy Tally, the wife of James Tally, who was Nancy Robinson and also a niece of the said James Robinson, deceased, are the next of kin and the only heirs at law of the said James Robinson, deceased. That the said James Robinson, deceased, in his lifetime being seized and possossed of certain real estate, situate, lying and being in the County of Lancaster aforesaid, departed this life in the present year 1832 intestate as to his real estate. Your

orators and oratrixes further show unto your worships that in case the said lands are sold the division of each would not exceed the value of $300., and they believe the interest of all parties concerned would be greatly promoted by a sale and the distribution of the proceeds &c.------ 19 Nov. 1832 - p. 195

Robert N. Chilton, et als
vs - Suit for sale and division.
Richard Mitchell, Administrator, &c., et als.

Bill - Humbly Complaining; sheweth unto your worships your orators &c., Robert N. Chilton and William Yerby and Cordelia, his wife, who was Cordelia Chilton. That Fauntleroy N. Chilton departed this life sometime in the year_____ intestate and possessed of a considerable personal estate and a tract of land lying in the County of Lancaster, supposed to contain about 290 acres, leaving the said Cordelia, a sister, your orator Robert N. Chilton, a brother, and Louisa, Artimesia and Maria Yerby, infants under the age of 21 years, children of Charles J. Yerby and Sally, his wife, which said Sally was also a sister of the said Fauntleroy, but who is now dead, and leaving also Sally Chilton, the widow of him the said Fauntleroy, who has since intermarried with Samuel Gresham, the only heirs and distributees entitled to his estate; that since the death of the said Fauntleroy N. Chilton administration of all his goods, chattels and credits has been granted by the County Court of said County of Lancaster to Richard Mitchell, who has reduced the same into his possession, and as your orators believe has paid off and discharged the debts due and unpaid from his said intestate ----20 Aug. 1832 - p. 198

William Brown, et us,
vs - Suit for sale and division.
Susan Hunton, et al.

Bill - Humbly complaining; sheweth to your worships your orator and oratrix, William Brown, of the County of Westmoreland and Jane, his wife, late Jane Hunton; that the said Jane is the daughter of a certain Thomas Y. Hunton, late of the County of Lancaster, now deceased; that your orator and oratrix were married according to law about the year ____; that the said Thomas Y. Hunton died seized and possessed of a personal estate which has been divided among the heirs of the said Hunton, and a real estate of between two and three hundred acres; That he left a widow and four children, four of whom being since dead your oratrix and a certain Thomas H. Hunton, her brother, are the only children of their father now living---- that the said Susan Hunton is the widow of the said Thomas Y. Hunton and the mother of your oratrix &c.------ 15 Oct. 1832 - p. 203

John F. Christopher,
vs. - Suit for sale & Division.
Achsah Christopher, et als.

Bill - Humbly complaining, shew unto your worships your orator John F. Christopher; that his father, Thomas Christopher, died some time about the year ____ having an interest in a tract of land lying in Fleet's Island, in the County of Lancaster, belonging to the heirs of John Fleet; that at the death of the said Thomas Christopher he left a widow, Achsah Christopher and five children, to-wit; Your orator and George, William, Ellen and Thomas Christopher, which said widow and children are still living; all the children except your orator are infants under the age of 21 years------that there has been a division of the land of the said John Fleet made by virtue of an order or orders of the County Court of Lancaster, and that 13 acres one Rod and thirteen poles have been allotted to the heirs of Thomas Christopher, deceased, aforesaid &c.------ 21 April, 1834 - p. 211

Robert T. Dunaway, Guardian &c.,
vs - Suit for division.
Henry C. Lawson, et ux, et als.

Bill of complaint---- Humbly complaining; shews unto your worships your orator, Robert T. Dunaway, guardian and next friend of Eliza and John Towill; That Thomas Lee died about the year 1809 or 1810, intestate, and possessed of considerable land and personal estate, leaving a widow and three children, namely John, Margaret and Ann; Margaret intermarried with Henry C. Lawson and Ann intermarried with Thomas Towill. That by an order of the County Court of Lancaster William Pollard, Richard Berryman, Joseph Shearman and Samuel M. Shearman as Commissioners, attended by James Alderson as surveyor, divided the said real estate of the said Thomas Lee among his heirs as follows: To the widow 113 3/4 acres; to John Lee 75 1/2 acres; to Henry C. Lawson, in right of his wife who was Margarit Lee, 71 1/2 acres; to Thomas Towill, in right of his wife who was Ann Lee, 71 1/2 acres, and to Lawson & Towill 7 1/2 acres jointly, being woodland as your orator is informed--- that John Lee died under the age of 21 years, without issue and intestate; Thomas Towill is also dead, and the widow of Thomas Lee has also long since died; Ann Towill, who was Ann Lee, the widow of Thomas Towill, intermarried with John Meredith, she the said Ann Meredith, who was Ann Lee, is also dead and left four children by her first marriage, namely Charles, Ann, Eliza and John Towill, and two by her last marriage, namely Margaret and Thomas Meredith; Charles Towill died in the year 1833, of full age but without issue, having made and published his last will, a copy of which is herewith filed; Lawson Hathaway is his administrator. Ann Towill intermarried with Thomas Waters and has since died leaving one child who is an infant by the name of Ann R. Waters; John Meredith, the second husband of Ann Lee has also lately died; That since the first division of the lands of the said Thomas Lee no correct division has taken place &c.---Ann R. Waters not an inhabitant of this Commonwealth - 21 April, 1834 - p. 216

17

Ann S. Meredith
vs - Suit for sale and dower.
Margaret S. Meredith, et als.

Bill of Complaint---- Humbly complaining; shows to your worships your oratrix, Ann S. Meredith, widow of John Meredith, deceased; that your oratrix husband, the said John Meredith, died on or about the___day of___in the present year after having made and published his last will and testament, which is now of record in the County Court of Lancaster County; that the said testator left considerable real and personal estate; his main tract of land he devised to his eldest son, Thomas James Meredith, which said Thomas James qualified as administrator with the will annexed of the said decedent. The said John Meredith, as your oratrix further shows, held a small parcel of land, about 95 acres, which he purchased of Sarah N. Brent, it being part of the tract of land formerly belonging to your oratrix father, Vincent Brent; this small piece of land was not named by the said John Meredith in his will, but passes under the residuary clause in said will to the said John Meredith's three youngest children, namely Margaret Meredith, Thomas Meredith and William V. Meredith, subject to your oratrix dower right in same &c. 15 Sept. 1834 - p. 222

George W. Downman, et al,
vs. - Suit for division.
John B. Downman, et ux, et als.

Bill -- Humbly complaining; sheweth unto your worships your orator and oratrix George W. Downman and Sarah Downman; that James W. P. Downman departed this life sometime in the month of October last, intestate and unmarried & without issue; that the said James W. P. Downman left neither father nor mother living at his death; that he died seized and possessed in fee of a tract of land lying in the County of Lancaster called and known by the name of Morotico; that the said James W. P. Downman left living one brother of the whole blood, to-wit: your orator, George W. Downman, and two sisters of the whole blood, to-wit: your oratrix Sarah Downman, and Harriett Jane, who intermarried with John B. Downman; that he also left the following nieces and nephews, to-wit: Jane E. Downman, an infant and the only child of Joseph B. Downman, deceased, who was a brother of the whole blood of the said James W. P. Downman; Alice Olivia, the only child of Milly Beale, deceased, who was also a sister of the whole blood of the said James W. P. Downman; the said Olivia has intermarried with Thomas M. Edmonds; James F. Ball, an infant, and the only child of Alice Olivia Ball, deceased, also a sister of the whole blood to the said James W. P. Downman; William D. Montague, the only child of Frances Montague, deceased, also a sister of the whole blood of the said James W. P. Downman, and Richard B., Robert, William G., Julius and Littleton D. Mitchell, infants, and only children of Margaret Mitchell, deceased, also a sister of the whole blood of the said James W. P. Downman, deceased &c. ---- 18 November, 1834 - p. 225

Needham Holiday, et ux, et als,
vs. - Suit for sale & Division.
Thomas Robertson, et al.

Bill - Humbly complaining; shew unto your worships your orator and oratrix, Needham Holiday and Amanda, his wife, and Oscar F. Robertson; That sometime in the year __ a certain Thomas G. Robertson, late of the County aforesaid, departed this life, at whose death his heirs were entitled to a tract of land containing about seventy acres, more or less, and that he was possessed of no other land at the time of his death. That the said Thomas G. Robertson left five children which are now living, to-wit: your orator, Oscar F. Robertson and your oratrix, Amanda, who was Amanda Robertson and intermarried with the said Needham Holliday, and Thomas, Lettice and James Robertson, who are infants, &c.---- 17 June, 1733 - p. 232

Feriol Lemoine, et als,
vs - Suit for Division -
Frances B. Lemoine, et als.

Bill of complaint - Humbly complaining; show unto your worships your orator, Feriol Lemoine and your orator and oratrix John H. Harding and Frances J., his wife, who was Frances J. Lemoine; that Feriol Lemoine, the elder, died sometime in the year __ intestate, leaving a widow, Frances B. Lamoine and the following children, to-wit: your orator, Feriol Lemoine, Moreau Lemoine, Frances J., the wife of J. H. Harding, and Louisa, now the wife of A. S. Willis; that since the death of the said Feriol the elder, Moreau Lemoine hath departed this life leaving a widow and two children, to-wit: Frances Ellen and Virginia Lemoine; that the said Feriol died seized and possessed of a certain tract of land lying in the County of Lancaster aforesaid in which the said Frances B. is entitled to dower &c. ---- 21 December, 1835 - p. 270

Benjamin G. George, et ux,
vs. - Suit for division.
Joseph Shearman.

Bill - Humbly complaining; your orator and oratrix, Benjamin G. George and Susan P., his wife, who was Susan P. Shearman, show unto your worships that sometime in the year 18__ Thomas Shearman, of the county of Lancaster, departed this life intestate leaving two children, viz your oratrix, Susan P., now Susan P. George and Joseph Shearman, and that the said Thomas died seized and possessed of a tract of land containing, by estimation, _____ acres, situate, lying and being in the County aforesaid &c. - 18 September, 1837

Hugh Summers, et ux, et als,
vs. - Suit for recovery of land.
Addison Mall, Trustee.

Bill - Humbly complaining; shew to your worships your orators and oratrixes, Hugh Summers and Sarah Ann, his wife, who was Sarah Ann Hammonds, daughter of William and Catharine Hammonds, and William Hammonds, Patsey and Elizabeth, who are all children of the said William and Catharine. that a certain Daniel Pierce and Nancy, his wife, of the County of Lancaster, by deed of record in said office, conveyed to a certain Addison Hall, in trust for the said Catharine Hammonds, and for her only separate use and benefit until the death of her said husband, William Hammonds, a certain tract or parcel of land containing 17 acres, and upon the further trust that after the death of the said William Hammonds, should he die before the said Catharine, his wife, the said Hall should assign, convey or transfer all his right, title and interest in said land to the said Catharine, but should the said Catharine die before the said William, that the said Hall should assign and transfer all his right and interest aforesaid to the children of the said Catharine then living; now your orators and oratrixes set forth that both William Hammonds and Catharine, his wife, have departed this life, leaving the above named children, and that the said Addison Hall has made no transfer or assignment of the said tract of land either to the said Catharine Hammonds, who survived her husband, or to her children since her death &c. ---- 20 August, 1838 - p. 281

Lewis H. Dix
vs. - Suit for Land.

Bill - Humbly complaining; that by virtue of a deed of conveyance entitled a deed of bargain and sale, duly proved and recorded in the Clerk's Office of this County, the children of Thomas Dix by Lucy, his wife, have become entitled to a certain tract of land containing 160 acres, lying in the County aforesaid, near White Marsh Meeting house, and known by the name of Hunter's Square ------ that some short time since the said Thomas Dix died leaving only three children lawfully begotten of Lucy, his wife, to-wit: Catharine E. S., James T. M. and Lewis H. Dix, your orator. The deed aforesaid referred to was made expressly to the aforementioned children by name, and to any others which the said Thomas, now deceased, might after the date of the said deed have by Lucy, his wife------ as the said Thomas Dix after that date had no child by Lucy, his wife, the said Catharine E. S., James T. M. and Lewis H. Dix, your orator, are the only parties interested in the real estate conveyed by the said deed. Your orator has lately attained to lawful age, to-wit: the age of 21 years, the said Catharine E. S. and James T. M., the other children above mentioned are still infants under the age of 21------ 17 June, 1839 - p. 285

Richard B. Mitchell
vs. - Suit for sale and Division.
Samuel Gresham, et ux, et als.

Bill - Humbly complaining; show unto your worships your orator, Richard B. Mitchell; that his mother, Nancy Mitchell, who was Nancy Lansdell, died some years since intestate, seized of a certain piece of land called and known by the name of Pea Vine, situate in the County of Lancaster, containing about 75 acres; that he is one of the children and heirs at law of the said Nancy, and that she left three other children, to-wit: Sally G. Mitchell, who has since intermarried with Samuel Gresham, Athalia A. Mitchell, who has since intermarried with Williamson C. Jones, who has since died, and Mary M. K. Mitchell, who together with your orator are the only children and heirs at law of the said Nancy. That Richard Mitchell, the father of your orator and the husband of the said Nancy, whom he survived, held a life estate in the said tract of land as tenant by the curtesy, and that he has lately died, whereby the said tract or parcel of land has descended to your orator and his three sisters above named, the only heirs of the said Nancy, their mother. That Mary M. K. Mitchell above named is under age   -- 20 April, 1840 - p. 290

Benjamin M. Walker,
vs. - Suit for sale and division.
Judith Carter.

Bill of Complaint - Benjamin M. Walker sheweth unto your worships that a certain Thomas Palmer of the aforesaid County of Lancaster died about the year 1809 possessed of a tract of land lying in the aforesaid County; that the said Thomas Palmer left at the time of his death a widow, namely Judith who subsequently intermarried with a certain Thomas Carter, and the following children, to-wit: Dolly Palmer, Judith Palmer, Thomas Palmer, John Palmer and Chloe Palmer; that 91 acres, 2 Rods and 7 poles of the aforesaid tract of land was allotted to the said Judith Palmer, the widow, as her dower and thirds in the estate of the said Thomas Palmer, and the residue of the said land divided among the above named children of the said Thomas Palmer, deceased; that John Palmer, Thomas Palmer, Jr. and Judith Palmer, three of the children of the said Thomas died intestate and without issue many years since, leaving the aforesaid Dolly Palmer their only sister and heir at law, and that the said Judith, the widow of the said Thomas Palmer the elder, who subsequently intermarried with Thomas Carter, died in the year 1839, possessed of the aforesaid land assigned her as her dower as aforesaid, which is now subject to a division between the heirs of the said Thomas Palmer; That Dale Carter purchased of Dolly Palmer all of her interest in the aforesaid dower land; that the said Dale Carter died about the year 1830, leaving only one child, Judith Carter, and that Chloe Palmer intermarried with Joseph Dale and died some years since (but subsequent to the death of the above named Judith, Thomas and John) leaving the following children, to-wit: Thomas J. Dale, Mildred B. Dale and Elizabeth W. Dale, and that the said Mildred B. hath since intermarried with George W. Booth and Elizabeth W. with Thaddeus C. Stott, of whom your orator claims by virtue of deeds of bargain and sale from the said Thomas J. Dale, George W. Booth and wife and T. C. Stott and wife, conveying all their interest in the aforesaid dower land &c. ---- 20 July, 1840 - p. 292

Robert W. Carter, et als,
vs. - Suit for sale and Division.
William Eustace, et ux.

Bill - Humblying complaining; sheweth unto your worships your orator, Robert W. Carter in his own right and as next friend of Henry R. and Rebecca Dulany, infants and heirs of Fanny Dulany, who was Carter, Mary L. Eliason, who was Mary L. Carter, John A. Carter in his own right and as next friend of Lucy, Maria T. and Fanny D. Tomlin, infants and co heirs of Ann C. Tomlin, who was Ann C. Carter; that they and others are entitled to a certain piece or parcel of land lying in the County of Lancaster, being a part of the tract of which Mrs Frances Garland, formerly _____ died possessed, and estimated to contain 409 acres, and which by recent division has been assigned as their portion as heirs of the late Landon Carter, Sr., deceased; that the said Landon Carter, Sr., died intestate, and entitled in reversion to the said land and left the following children as his heirs at law, viz: Robert W. Carter, Elizabeth L. Carter, now deceased without issue, Ann C. Tomlin, who died leaving the following children, viz: Lucy, Maria T. and Fanny D. Tomlin, and Mary, now the wife of William Eustace; Landon Carter, Jr., now dead without issue, Mary L. Eliason, the widow of William A. Eliason, Fanny Dulany, who has since died leaving two children, viz: Henry R. and Rebecca Dulany, and John A. Carter; that the right of possession in the said land has only accrued since the death of the said Frances Garland, and since the division of the real estate of the said Landon Carter, Sr., deceased &c.-------- 20 July, 1840 - p. 295

James H. Hill,
vs. - Suit for Division.
John M. Hill.

Bill of complaint - Humbly complaining; sheweth unto your worships your orator, James Monroe Hill, by Cyrus Hazzard, his next friend; that about the year 1822 his father, Eppa Hill, departed this life leaving a widow, Mary C. Hill, who has since intermarried with Cyrus Hazzard, and four children, to-wit: John M. Hill, Humprey C. Hill, James M. Hill (your orator), and Milly Hill who has since died; that his said father left a will which was duly admitted to probate and recorded in the Clerk's Office of this Court on the 20 day of January, 1823, a copy of which is filed herewith and prayed to be taken as a part of this bill; that in his will his said father devised to your orator's mother, his said widow, all his land during her natural life, and directed that after her death the same should be sold and that the money arising from the sale thereof should be equally divided between all his children above named; that his mother, who is still alive, and her husband, the said Cyrus Hazzard, have made to your orator, John M. Hill and Humphrey C. Hill, the only surviving children of Eppa Hill, a deed for one tract of the said land, it being a separate and distinct tract, containing 62 acres, and also for an undivided moiety of seven acres more, by which in consideration of the natural love and affection which they bear to your orator, the said John M. Hill and Humphrey C. Hill, they have given, granted, bargained and sold to them all their interest in and to the said tracts of land, which deed bears date 19 August, 1839; that in consequence of the death of Milly Hill he and the said John M. Hill and Humphrey C. Hill have the sole right to the reversion of the said land expectant upon the death of their said mother, which together with the deed before referred to makes them the sole owners of the entire tract of land &c.---- James Monroe Hill made oath that the defendants named in the within bill are not inhabitants of this Commonwealth---October Term, 1839 - p. 300

Lewis Hammonds, et ux,
vs. - Suit for sale and division.
James Lowry, et als.
   Bill - Humbly complaining; shew unto your worships your orator and oratrix, Lewis Hammonds and Lucy, his wife, who was Lucy Lowry, which said Lucy was a daughter of John Lowry, late of the County of Lancaster, but now deceased; That Gawin Lowry by his will bearing date 14 August, 1790, and proved in the Court of said County in the month of September following, bequeathed his real estate as follows: The use of that part of his plantation whereon his nephew Stokely Lowry formerly lived unto his niece Mary Lowry during her natural life, and at her decease he gave the use of the said land unto John Lowry, son of his nephew Stokely Lowry, deceased, during his natural life and at his death to his heirs forever. He also bequeathed the remaining part of his lands not before mentioned unto the said John Lowry during his natural life, and at his decease to his heirs forever. All of which will appear by reference to the said will, a copy of which is hereto annexed as part of this bill; that the said Mary Lowry and John Lowry are both dead; that the said John Lowry died seized and possessed of the said lands so devised to him as above set forth; that the said John Lowry left nine children of whom your orator's wife is one, and the other eight are called James, John, Stokely D., Gawin, David Jeremiah, Polly and Fanny; that the said Polly intermarried, with a certain William Orrel, and Fanny intermarried with one George Nash; that the said James Lowry and John Lowry, William Orrel and Polly, his wife, who was Polly Lowry, are not inhabitants of this Commonwealth; That Gawin, David and Jeremiah Lowry are young and will not be of age for some years to come, &c.---- 15 April, 1839 - p. 304

23

William H. Kirk, et ux,
vs. - Suit for sale and Division.
William H. Harding, et ux, et als.

Bill - Humbly complaining; shew unto your worships your orator William H. Kirk and Elizabeth M., his wife, who was Elizabeth M. Myers, set forth that Charles Rogers, late of this County, deceased, held in right of his wife, Mary Ann, who was Mary Ann Myers, a tract of land containing 105 acres, by estimation; that the said Mary Ann, as well as the said Charles Rogers are dead, leaving no issue, and that the fee simple right in the said tract of land has vested in your orator's wife, of the whole blood, and Lavala Harding, who was Lavala Coles of the half blood, and the children of William Myers, deceased, to-wit: Amanda, Pleasant and William, also of the half blood, who are prayed to be made defendants hereto--that the said Amanda, Pleasant and William Myers are infants and non residents of this Commonwealth   ---- 20 July, 1840 - p. 310

LAND CAUSES.
(1841–1885)

William H. Kirk, et ux,
vs. – Suit for sale and Division.
Amanda Myers, et als.

Bill – Your orator and oratrix, William H. Kirk and Elizabeth M., his wife, humbly complaining, shew that a certain George F. Myers, late of this County, but now deceased, by his last will and testament devised one half of the plantation whereon he lived at the time of his death to his sister, Julia George, to her and her heirs forever, the other one half of the said tract or plantation he disposed of by the following words: I give the other one half of my said plantation upon these terms and conditions, that is to say, if my sister Amanda Coles should have a son to live to the age of 21 years old, then he the son of said Amanda to have the said other half, to him and his heirs forever, but in the event of no such son, then I give the whole of my plantation to my sister Julia George, to her and her heirs forever ------that the above named Amanda departed this life on the ___ day of ___ in the year 18__ without ever having had male issue, and intestate, and that the above named Julia George also departed this life several years previous to the said Amanda, intestate and without issue, and that your orator and oratrix, who was sister of the half blood to George F. Myers, deceased, and Julia George; and Amanda, Pleasant and William Myers, infants, children of William Myers, deceased, (which said Amanda, Pleasant and William are non residents of this Commonwealth and who are prayed to be made defendants hereto), who was a brother of the whole blood to George F. Myers and Julia George, are the only heirs at law of the said George F. Myers and Julia George, and that they, the said William H. Kirk and Elizabeth M., Amanda, Pleasant and William Myers are entitled, and them only, to the above mentioned tract or plantation devised by George F. Myers as aforesaid, &c.----- 18 Jan. 1841 - p. 1

Nelson Robinson, et ux, et al,
vs. – Partition Suit.
Joseph Pursell, et ux.

Bill – Humbly complaining, your orators and oratrix, Nelson Robinson and Frances J., his wife, who was Frances J. Hutchings, Mary E. Hutchings and William R. Hutchings, infants under the age of 21 years, by their next friend, Nelson Robinson, shew that John Hutchings, late of the County aforesaid, deceased, departed this life in the year __ intestate, leaving a widow, Polly Hutchings; that your orators and oratrixes, Frances J., Mary E. and William R. Hutchings are the only children of the said John and Polly Hutchings; that the real estate which the said John Hutchings died possessed of is worth more than $300. to each of his children; that the aforesaid Polly Hutchings, widow and relict of the said John Hutchings, has intermarried with Joseph Pursell &c.---- 16 Aug. 1841 - p. 5

Judith N. Lawson,
vs. - Suit for sale and division.
Alice Brent, et als.

Bill - Humbly complaining; sheweth unto your worships your oratrix, Judith N. Lawson; that Hugh Brent died in the year __ intestate, and that he left the following children his heirs at law, to-wit: Isaac Brent, Hugh Brent, William Brent, Kenner Brent, the two last of whom have since died intestate and without issue, and your oratrix, Judith N. Brent, who intermarried with Thomas L. Lawson, and a widow, Alice Brent; that at the time of his death he was seized of a certain tract or parcel of land containing four acres, three rods and 26 poles, which he purchased of one William Ford, and which at his death descended to his said children and heirs at law, subject to the dower of his widow, the said Alice Brent-- that the said Isaac Brent by deed conveyed his interest in said land to the said Thomas L. Lawson, who has since died intestate leaving two children, to-wit: Elizabeth C. Lawson and Marian L. Lawson his heirs at law who are infants under the age of 21 years; that the said Hugh Brent the younger has by deed conveyed his interest in the said land to the said Alice Brent &c.---- 21 June, 1841

William Walton Headley, et ux,
vs. - Suit for sale and division.
Abner Riveer.

Bill - Your orator and oratrix, William Walton Headley and Juliet, his wife, who was Juliet Riveer, humbly complaining show unto your worships that Cyrus Riveer of this county died in the year intestate leaving two children, viz: your oratrix, the said Juliet, who has since intermarried with the said William Walton Headley, and Abner his only issue living at the time of his death; that the said Cyrus at the time of his death was seized and possessed of a small tract of land containing about 134 acres &c.---- 21 November, 1842 - p. 17

John B. Bramham, et ux,
vs. - Suit for sale and division.
Addison L. Carter, et als.

Bill - Your orators, John B. Bramham and Margaret E. Y. Bramham, his wife, who was Margaret E. Y. Carter, beg leave to set forth that a deed of trust was executed by Elizabeth Selden and Richard Y. Selden to Joseph A. Carter as trustee for the benefit of the children of the said Joseph A. Carter, to-wit; Margaret E. Y. Carter, Addison L. Carter, Marietta E. Carter and W. L. S. Carter (Adelina S. Carter and Althea R. Carter, whom your orators pray may be made defendants to this bill) and which said deed of trust is filed with this bill, marked "A"------ that the aforesaid Joseph A. Carter held the property conveyed in the aforesaid deed of trust during his lifetime in trust for the benefit of the children aforesaid-----that the said Joseph A. Carter departed this life sometime since, and that there is now no trustee----that it is provided in the said deed of trust that the aforesaid trustee should deliver to the aforesaid children their respective parts or portions of the property conveyed in the said deed of trust when they should become of lawful age or when he should see fit------that your oratrix Margaret E. Y. Bramham, who was Margaret E. Y. Carter, has sometime since married your orator John B. Bramham, and has attained to lawful age------that on account of the infancy of all the children except Addison L. Carter she has been unable to obtain her proportionable part of the property aforesaid &c.------ 16 August, 1841 - p. 19

Samuel Downing, et ux, et al,
vs. - Suit for sale and division.
Maria Payne, et al.
  Bill - Humbly complaining, show unto your worships your orators Samuel Downing and Catherine E., his wife, and Richard H. Payne------ that a certain Richard Payne, late of this County, departed this life intestate about the year 1835, leaving a widow and three children, viz: the said Catherine E. and Richard and Maria J; the said Catherine has intermarried with the above named Samuel Downing and the said Maria J. has intermarried with Charles L. Broun; that the said Maria J. has departed this life intestate and under age leaving one child, viz: James P. Broun; that the said Richard Payne left real estate which has been divided according to law, assigning to the widow her dower therein, and the balance between the aforesaid Catherine E., Richard H. and Maria J.------that Maria Payne, the widow of the aforesaid Richard Payne, deceased, is willing to surrender a part of her dower in the said real estate of her deceased husband, viz: the tract commonly known as the "Tan Yard" alias dwelling house tract, containing 197 acres, to the aforesaid Samuel Downing and Catherine E., his wife, Richard M. Payne and James P. Broun, the only child of Maria J. Broun, who was Maria J. Payne above named--that the same cannot be equally divided &c. ---- 20 Feb. 1843 - p. 23

James A. Palmer, et ux,
vs. - Suit for sale and division.
James B. Degges, et us, et als.
  Bill - Humbly complaining; show unto your worships your orators, James A. Palmer & Margaret Ann, his wife, who was Margaret Ann Meredith ------ that about the __ day of __ in the year __ John Towell

27

of this County, a half brother of your oratrix, died intestate in the said County siezed and possessed in fee simple of a tract or parcel of land situate in said County, containing about 300 acres, and that he left as his heirs at law Eliza A. Degges, formerly Towell, who intermarried with James B. Degges, both of whom have removed to the State of Alabama, Ann Rebecca Waters, the infant daughter of Ann Waters, formerly Towell, who intermarried with Thomas Waters, and who has since died; the said Eliza and Ann were sisters of the whole blood to the said John Towell; Thomas W. Meredith and your oratrix, the two latter of whom were a sister and brother of the half blood to the said John Towell &c.---- 19 December, 1842 - p. 27

Nancy Cockrall
vs. - Suit for division.
Martin Sampson, et als.
   Bill - Humbly complaining; shows unto your worships your oratrix, Nancy Cockerrall------that during the year __ her mother, Nancy Sampson, died intestate as to a certain piece or parcel of land lying in this County, containing __ acres, more or less; that she left six children her heirs at law, to-wit: Martin Sampson, George Sampson, Hyram Sampson, Polly Haydon, Judith George and your oratrix; that the said Hiram Simpson is not an inhabitant of this Commonwealth, and that the said land is not worth $300. to each of the parties entitled thereto &c. ---- 17 May, 1841 - p. 30

Nancy Mason
vs. - Suit for sale and division.
John Mason, et als.
   Bill - Humbly complaining; shew unto your worships your oratrix, Nancy Mason--- that Thomas Mason, her father, made and published his last will and testament on the 28 March, 1828, and soon after departed this life, by which said will he devised all his estate, real and personal, to Margaret Mason, his wife, during the term of her natural life, and after her death to his children. That Margaret Mason, the widow of Thomas Mason, has been dead for several years, and that no division of the land and personal estate of the said Thomas Mason has yet been made; that the testator, her father, Thomas Mason, left sons, to-wit: John, William and James, and daughters Margaret and Nancy, your oratrix; that he devised to John 26 acres, to William 26 acres and to James 26 acres, and the balance of his tract to his daughters Margaret and Nancy; that John Mason died in the year ___ leaving three children, to-wit: Thomas, John and Mary; that William died in the year ____ unmarried and without issue and intestate; that James died in the year ___ intestate, unmarried and without issue---- that the above named Thomas Mason, John Mason and Mary Mason children of the aforesaid John Mason, deceased, and your oratrix, Nancy Mason, are the only heirs of the aforesaid William, James and Margaret Mason &c.---- the said Margaret Mason having also died in the year __ unmarried and without issue-- 18 July 1842 - p. 35

William L. Stakes, et als,
vs. - Suit for sale and division.
Betsy Stakes, et als.

Bill - Your orators and oratrix, William L. Stakes, Tyson Dines and Mary S., his wife, who was Mary S. Stakes, Archibald S. Stakes and John F. Stakes respectfully represent to your worships that William Stakes, of the County of Lancaster, departed this life in the year 1843, intestate, and possessed of a small real and personal estate, leaving Betsy Stakes his widow and seven children as his heirs and distributees, viz: your orators and oratrix and Margaret Stakes, George Stakes and Asa Stakes, infants of tender years --- that the real estate of the said William Stakes, deceased, contains only 150 acres, and that it would be impracticable to effect a division &c. ---- 15 January, 1844 - p. 42

John Boyd
vs. - Suit for sale and division.
Mary Boyd, et als.

Your orator, John Boyd, humbly complaining; sheweth unto your worships that in the month of April last Ellen Boyd, of the aforesaid county, departed this life intestate and without issue, possessed of small piece of land, being her undivided one fourth part of the lands of which William Boyd, her father, died seized and possessed, containing about 67 acres, consequently the proportion of said land owned by the said Ellen Boyd contains only 16 3/4 acres----your orator further sets forth that himself in his own right and William Boyd and Mary Boyd, the infants of Thomas Boyd, and Thomas Boyd and Lucy Boyd, the infants of William Boyd, are the only heirs at law and distributees of the said Ellen, deceased------ 17 June, 1844 - p. 61

William S. Doggett, et als,
vs. - Suit for division.
John Kem, et als.

Bill - Humbly complaining; show unto your worships that in the year 1843 David Chilton departed this life intestate and without issue, and that he was possessed at the time of his death of a small tract or parcel of land lying in this County containing, by estimation, about ___ acres; that the said David Chilton had at the time of his death neither father nor mother, nor brother nor sister, nor grandfather nor grandmother, nor uncle nor aunt; that your orator and oratrixes, Joseah Doggett, Jane Doggett, William Doggett, Eliza Doggett, Elizabeth Doggett and Sarah Doggett are the children and only heirs at law of Benjamin Doggett, deceased, who and your orator William S. Doggett were the only children of Hugh Doggett, a maternal great uncle of the said David Chilton; your orators and oratrixes ___Spann, ___Spann and ___Spann, the only children of ___Spann, who was ___Doggett, who with your orators and oratrixes William Doggett, Lucinda Doggett, Margaret Tapscott, wife of Joseph Tapscott, Patsy Forester, wife of

Thadeus Forester, are the only children of Coleman Doggett, another maternal great uncle of the said David Chilton; that your oratrixes Nancy Lunsford, wife of Warner C. Lunsford, Emily Pitman, wife of Thomas Pitman and Mary Doggett are the only children of James Doggett, another maternal great uncle of the said David Chilton, which said Hugh Doggett, Coleman Doggett and __Doggett were maternal uncles of the whole blood of the said David Chilton; that your orator Samuel Doggett is a maternal great uncle of the half blood to the said David Chilton; your oratrix is _____Doggett, the wife of your orator, Hugh Doggett, and your oratrix _____Stephens are maternal great aunts of the half blood to the said David Chilton; that Robert Talley, Sarah Talley and Frances Talley, the children of Polly Talley, deceased, who was Polly Chilton, the daughter of Edward Chilton, and Betsy Chilton who was the daughter of Stephen Chilton, a paternal great grandfather to the said David Chilton, and John Kemm, the son of __Kemm, who was the son of _____Kemm, a maternal great uncle to the said David Chilton, and that your orators and oratrixes aforesaid and the sid Talleys and Kemm are the only heirs at law of the said David Chilton and entitled to the said tract or parcel of land of which he died possessed as aforesaid &c.---- 20 January, 1845 - p. 63

Eustace Conway, et ux, et al,
vs. - Suit for sale and division.
William C. Eustace, et ux, et als.

Bill - Your orator and oratrixes, Eustace Conway and Maria T., his wife, who was Maria T. Tomlin, and Fanny Tomlin, by her next friend and guardian, Eustace Conway, respectfully represent that Mrs Ann C. Tomlin departed this life about the year ____ seized and possessed of a certain mill seat and about 70 acres of land attached thereto, situate in the County of Lancaster, and known by the name of Tomlin's Mill; that at the death of the said Ann C. Tomlin the said mill seat and land descended in parcenary to her children and heirs at law, namely Mary L., Lucy, Maria and Fanny Tomlin; that Mary L. has since intermarried with William C. Eustace, Esq., Lucy with James F. Ball, Esq., and Maria with your orator; that Lucy, the wife of James F. Ball, has departed this life leaving as her heir at law Lucy Olivia Ball, who is an infant of tender years, &c. ---- 17 June, 1844 - p. 68

Thomas Riveer,
vs. - Suit for division.
Alice Bush, &c.

Bill - That in the latter part of the year 1844, or in the early part of the year 1845, Elizabeth Reveer, of this County, who was seized and possessed of a certain tract or parcel of land lying in the upper part of this County, departed this life intestate and without issue; at the time of her death the said Elizabeth had one brother, your orator, Thomas Riveer, and two sisters, Alice Bush and Sarah Muse who survived her, and who are still living, and had had another sister who died before

30

that time, leaving two children, Hiram Hayden and Alice Hayden, the latter of whom has intermarried with Thomas J. Preston &c.---- 15 June, 1846 - p. 73

John E. Blakemore
vs. - Suit for sale of infant's land
Henry L. Biscoe, et ux, et als.

Bill - That in or about the year 1826, William Blakemore, the father of your orator, departed this life seized in fee of a certain tract or parcel of land situate, lying and being in Corrotoman, near Chowning's Ferry, containing 190 1/2 acres; that previous to his death the said William Blakemore made and published his last will and testament, by which he devised the said land to his wife, Tomze Blakemore, during her life or widowhood, and at her death or marriage to his son William, provided he lived to the age of 21 years, which will was duly proved and recorded after the death of the testator--------that the said William the younger lived to the age of 21 years, but that since as his arrival to that age he has died intestate, having three sisters, to-wit: Eliza, who intermarried with Thomas C. Callahan and who has also died since the death of the said William the younger, leaving five children, to-wit: Elizabeth Callahan, Sarah J. Callahan, Ann M. Callahan, William E. Callahan and Thomas C. Callahan, who are all infants under the age of 21 years; Sarah who intermarried with Henry L. Biscoe, and Mary J. who intermarried with Thomas Oldham, all of whom are living, and one brother, namely your orator, and his mother, the said Tomza Blakemore his only heirs at law--that the said Tomza Blakemore is still living and has never married since the death of her husband, the said William Blakemore, the testator, and that she is now and has been from the time of the death of the said William Blakemore, the testator, in possession of the said land pursuant to the provisions of the said will--------that by the arrival to the age of 21 of the said William, the devisee, he took a vested remainder in fee in the said lands, which by his death intestate and without issue descended to his mother, Tomze Blakemore, his said three sisters Eliza, Sarah and Mary and your orator, his brother, his only heirs at law in coparcenary, subject to the life estate of his mother, the said Tomze Blakemore, and that by the death of the said Eliza since the death of the said William Blakemore, the devisee, her portion of the same has descended to her children and heirs at law, the said Elizabeth Callahan, Sarah Jane Callahan, Ann Maria Callahan, William E. Callahan and Thomas C. Callahan; your orator further shows that he has contracted with the said Henry L. Biscoe and Sarah, his wife, and the said Thomas Oldham and Mary J., his wife, to purchase their respective portions of the said land, subject to the life estate of the said Tomze Blakemore, his mother, and that he is anxious to purchase the remaining one-fifth part thereof belonging to the heirs of the said Eliza Callahan &c.------- 18 May 1846 - p. 76

31

William Barnett
vs. - Suit for sale and division of land.
Margaret and Thomas George.

That about twelve or fifteen years ago one Newton George, of the
County of Lancaster, departed this life intestate, seized in fee of a
tract of land adjoining the lands of Louis Hammond and others, containing 130 acres--------the said Newton George left the following
children: James S., Margaret and Thomas George, all of whom except
the first named are infants under the age of 21 years--------On the 27
January, in the year 1847, the said James S. George, the elder of the
said children, sold and conveyed to your orator all his right, title and
interest in and to the said tract--------now your orator shows that
this tract of land is not susceptible of a division in kind &c.--------
19 April, 1847 - p. 85

James W. Gresham
vs. - Suit for sale and division.
Mary Gresham, et als.

Bill of complaint - Humbly complaining; shows unto your worships
your orator, James W. Gresham; that his father, George Gresham,
departed this life many years since, having first made and published
his last will and testament, which was duly proved and recorded in
this Court, by which he devised to your orator his tract of land whereon
he lived at the time of his death, lying in White Chapel, and containing ___ acres after the death of his wife, Mary Gresham, your orator's
mother, to whom he devised the same during her natural life; that
some years after the death of his father, and after all of his children,
to-wit: William Gresham. Betsy Gresham, who had died leaving the said Betsy surviving, and
Charles Palmer, who had died leaving the said Betsy surviving, and
Polly Gresham, who had intermarried with Samuel Harcum, and to
whom, together with your orator the whole estate of their father, the
said George Gresham was devised and bequeathed after the death of
their mother, the said Mary Gresham, had arrived to mature age, he,
your orator, sold the said land to his mother, the said Mary Gresham,
with the approbation and consent of all the said parties, to be paid out
of the estate bequeathed to them in common by their father as aforesaid, to be held by their mother, the said Mary Gresham for and during
her natural life, and at her death to be equally divided among her said
four children, to-wit: William, Betsy, Polly and your orator; that the
same was paid by his mother, the said Mary, out of the personal
estate bequeathed as aforesaid, and that the said land was conveyed to
her pursuant to the sale aforesaid.   That since the sale William
Gresham and Polly, who had intermarried with the said Samuel
Harcum, have died, the said William leaving two children but leaving
a will by which he devised his real estate which he had in possession
to his sister, the said Betsy Palmer, and the balance to be equally
divided between his mother, the said Mary Gresham, your orator and
his sister Polly Harcum and the said Betsy Palmer; that the said
Polly left five children, to-wit: Joseph Harcum, James Harcum,
Emeline L. Harcum, Marrietta Harcum and Willie Ann Harcum and the

said Samuel Harcum, her husband, surviving her; that the said Joseph
is of full age, but that the remaining four are infants &c. ------- 15
November, 1847 - p. 139

Thomas Basye, et al,
vs. - Suit for sale and division.
Harriett C. Basye, et als.
   Bill - Humbly complaining; sheweth to your worships your orators
Thomas Basye and Joseph Basye--------that on or about the __ day
of __, 1840, William Basye, the father of your orators, died seized and
possessed of a certain tract or parcel of land situate and lying in the
said County, containing, by estimation, about 150 acres--------that
the said William Basye, deceased, left at the time of his death a
widow, Harriett C. Basye, and nine children, to-wit: Your orators,
Elizabeth, who intermarried with A. Y. Headley, William, Henry,
Richard F., Lewis O., Novella J. and Mary M. D. Basye, the last six
of whom are infants under the age of 21 years; that Harriet C. Basye
has already been endowed and has no interest in the said tract of land,
and that the interest of no one heir in the said tract of land would be
$300., and that the interest of all parties concerned would be promoted
by a sale &c. -------- 18 Oct. 1847 - p. 142

Robert K. Watts, an infant &c.,
vs. - Suit for sale and division.
Jane Watts, et als.
   Your orator, Robert K. Watts, an infant under the age of 21 years,
who sues by John E. Watts his next friend, shows to your worships
that his father, Joseph L. Watts departed this life intestate leaving a
widow, ____Watts, and four children, to-wit: your orator, Jane Watts,
Elizabeth Watts and David Watts, all of whom are infants under the
age of 21 years, and seized and possessed at the time of his death of
a small tract or parcel of land containing ____acres, which descended
to his children, your orator, his sisters and brother aforesaid, subject
to the dower of his widow, --------that the said ____ Watts, the
widow of the said Joseph L. Watts, has departed this life, and that by
virtue of her death the whole of the said tract or parcel of land is now
owned in coparcenary by your orator, his sisters and brother
aforesaid-------- 18 Sept. 1848 - p. 145

Joseph P. Flippo, et ux, et al,
vs. - Suit for sale and division.
William H. George, et als.
   Your orator and oratrix, Joseph P. Flippo and Eliza P., his wife,
who was Eliza George, shew that Benjamin George, deceased, late of
the County of Lancaster, intermarried with a certain Judith Doggett, by
whom and in virtue of the said marriage the said Benjamin became
entitled during his life to a certain tract or parcel of land, lying and
being in the County aforesaid, containing 150 acres; that the said

Judith died in the year ___ leaving the following named children, viz: Benjamin, your oratrix Eliza, William, Judith Ann, Lamoth Jeter and Eleanor; that since the death of the said Judith two of her above named children, viz: Benjamin and Judith Ann have also died without issue and intestate, leaving as the survivors the aforesaid Eliza, William, Lamoth J. and Eleanor their heirs at law, to whom the aforesaid tract or parcel of land has descended &c. ----- 18 December, 1848 - p. 149

Solomon Bunting, Guardian &c.,
vs. -
Teacle Elicot (Elliot) et als.

Humbly complaining; showeth unto your honours your orator, Solomon Bunting, Guardian of Margaret A., Catharine, William T., and Charles W. and Littleton L. Snead, orphans and heirs at law of Charles S. Snead, deceased; his wife, who will be one of the heirs of the said infants if they die without issue; That the said Charles S. Snead departed this life on the ___day of ___ intestate, leaving a widow, Rachel B. Snead, and the following children, viz: Margaret A., Catharine, William T., Charles W. and Littleton L. Snead his only heirs at law; that the said Charles S. Snead died seized and possessed of the following real estate; a tract of land situate in the County of Lancaster, containing 750 acres on the Rappahannock River, and also the following claves, George, &c. (13), and the following sum of money, $4,947.34, all of which will appear by the inventory of the said Charles S. Snead; that your orators and a certain Louis C. H. Finney, of the County of Accomack, qualified as administrators of the said Charles S. Snead, which they have settled and adjusted-----that upon the death of the said Charles S. Snead your orator is advised that the aforesaid tract of land descended to his children as aforesaid mentioned, his only heirs at law, subject to the dower interest of his widow, Rachel B. Snead, and that his said widow and children are the only distributees of his personal estate; that the said infants have no other estate than the said land and personal estate derived from their father, and that the said Rachel B. Snead would be the heir at law of the said infants if they should die without issue after arriving to the age of 21 years, and that Elizabeth Riley, Henrietta W. Snead, Littleton T. Elicot, Thomas P. Copes, Teackle Elicot, William Elicot and Catharine Elicot, which last three are infants and under the age of 21 years, and which Elizabeth Riley has intermarried with William M. Riley, would be their heirs at law if they die before arriving to the age of 21 years &c.----- 18 September, 1848 - p. 162

LAND CAUSES 1731-1754

(Northampton County.)

Thomas Goodright, Lessee of Thomas Savage,
vs. - Trespass.
John Notitle.
Jury implaneled and returned the following special verdict:
That John Savage, Sr., Gentleman, late of this County, deceased,
grandfather of the lessor of the plaintiff, was at the time of his death
seized of the lands in question; that the last will and testament of the
said John Savage was proved in this County Court the 11 December,
1678; that Thomas Savage in the said will mentioned sometime since
departed this life, and that the lessor, Thomas Savage, is the eldest
son of the said Thomas Savage; that the land in question is and for
about forty years since has been deemed a part of the land and plantation which Thomas Wilson, deceased, in the said will mentioned lived
on; that Thomas Savage, the father of the lessor, has often in his lifetime declared that all the land from the Roody Branch to the valley
next beyond the Court House in the County on the west side of the
main woods (part of which is the land in question) was entailed on
him, and that if it had not been entailed he would have given it to his
son, George Savage, deceased; that there is a lease from Thomas
Savage of Cherry Stones to Elias Roberts, Innholder, for their lives,
bearing date 14 September, 1726, &c. 8 June, 1731 - p. 1 et seq.

Petition of Isaac Baly and Elisha, his wife:
Sheweth that Elkington Savage, late of this County, Gentleman,
deceased, being in his lifetime possessed of 300 acres of land lying
and being in a place called Savage's Neck, in the County aforesaid,
and also of about 400 acres lying and being near the Court House in
the County aforesaid, in tail, and which said Elkington having a widow
who is now living and married to a certain John Major of the aforesaid
County, who is now in possession of the said lands &c.--- that formerly there having been a division of the said lands among the coheirs
of the said Elkington duly made, amongst which your petitioner and
Alicia is one, for which reason and for that your petitioner cannot get
their portion of their part of the said lands without the assistance of
your worships -- Petition for dower and division. 1 April, 1732 - p. 8
(Dower of Winniford, late widow of Elkington Savage, deceased, laid
out.)

35

Ralph Pigot
vs. - Trespass.
Margaret Waters, widow.

That the said Ralph is seized of one messuage and 500 acres lying in the County aforesaid on Old Plantation Creek, the said 500 acres being granted to a certain George Traveller by patent dated 1 Nov. 1637, and by deed dated 29 Jan. 1676/7 by Peter Reverdy, als Green, late of the County aforesaid, deceased, and Elisheba his wife, grandaughter and heir of the said Traveller, sold unto Francis Pigott, late of the County aforesaid, Gentleman, deceased, and by the said Francis given to his son, Ralph, and from the said Ralph, deceased, to the said Ralph's son Thomas, and from the said Thomas, deceased down to the plaintiff, and being so seized the said Ralph procured Luke Johnson, the surveyor of the County aforesaid, to lay out the bounds of the said 500 acres (surveyed 18 Mar. 1730)--&c. 14 Mar. 1731

And at a later date: Ralph Pigot, Gentleman, vs. Margaret Waters, widow now Margaret Burton by her intermarriage with William Burton &c. 28 July 1731 - p. 16 et seq.

Thomas Marshall, Lessee,
vs. - Trespass.
George Bell.

Jury impaneled and returned the following special verdict:

That George Brickhouse in his lifetime and at the time of his death was seized in fee of the lands in question, and being so thereof seized made his last will and testament, bearing date 19 November, 1688, hereto annexed; that Jonathan Bell was the eldest son and heir at law of Hannah Bell, and was such at the time of the execution of the deed of the said Jonathan Bell to Thomas Marshall, lessor of the plaintiff, bearing date 7 May, 1724; we further find that Hannah Bell, the daughter of the testator, George Brickhouse and mother of the said Jonathan Bell, was dead before the time demise of the lands in question by the lessor of the plaintiff------- we find a copy of a deed from George Bell, late of Northampton County, deceased, and Hannah, his wife, to George Bell, the defendant, and to Jeodiah Bell, their sons, bearing date 20 October, 1719; we further find a copy of a writ of Adquod Damnum directed to the Sheriff of the County aforesaid, dated 1 March, in the 8 year of the present King's Reign, and also the copy of an inquisition thereon taken before John Stratton, Gentleman, late Sheriff of the said County, dated 8 March, 1734; we also find a deed from Hannah Bell to the defendant, Jeodiah Bell, dated 29 March, 1735 &c.------- April, 1736 - p. 28 et seq.

Elenor Welch, widow
vs. - Trespass
Thomas Bagwell.

Jury impaneled and returned the following special verdict.

That a patent was granted by George Wyat to Henry Pendenden, bearing date 12 October, in the 16th year of the reign of King Charles for the land in question; we also find that the said Henry Pendenden had issue Henry Pendenden, Jr., his son and heir and dyed; we also find that the said Henry Pendenden, Jr., died leaving issue a son also called Henry Pendenden his son and heir; we also find that the last mentioned Henry Pendenden, grandson to the Patentee, died leaving issue two daughters, viz: Elenor Welch and Elizabeth Hall, wife of a certain John Hall, daughters and coheirs to the said Henry; we also find the plaintiff to be one of the daughters and coheirs to the aforesaid Henry; we also find a conveyance from the aforesaid John Hall and Elizabeth, his wife, for one moiety of the land in question to the plaintiff, Elenor, duty recorded; we also find that the aforesaid Henry Pendenden, the patentee, and also the aforesaid sons, and also the plaintiff and sister, have been upwards of thirty years out of this Colony; we find that John Smith, late of Northampton, was possessed of the lands in question, and by his deed dated 20 January, 1656, for the term of 99 years from that date (leased?) to William Sterling; we find the deed of Richard Sterling, son and heir of the said William Sterling, to Elizabeth, the widow of the said William, dated 22 May, 1699, and that the said Elizabeth afterwards intermarried with Alexander Bagwell; we find that the said Alexander devised his interest in the lands in question to William Bagwell, son of Henry Bagwell, which William died intestate and was survived by his said father, Henry, who died possessed of the premises in the month of July, 1734; We also find a patent granted by the Honoble William Gooch, Esq., to the defendant for the land in question, dated 7 September, in the 8 year of the Reign of King George the second, and that the said patent hath not hitherto been vacated; we also further find that the lessor of the plaintiff, nor any of the several Henry Pendendens before mentioned were at any time seized of the lands in question within fifty years before the commencement of this suit; we also find an Act of Assembly of this Colony made in the 8 year of the Reign of King George the second, entitled "An Act Amending the Act Intitled An Act for Settling the Titles and Bounds of Lands, and for Preventing Unlawful Shooting and Rangeing Thereon" &c.------- August, 1738 - p. 36 et seq.

Stephen Dunton and Isabell, his wife,
vs. - Partition Suit.
Mary Senior.

That the said Stephen Dunton and Isabell, his wife, and Mary Senior together and undivided hold to them and their heirs three plantations in Savage's Neck, in the Parish of Hungars, in the County of Northampton, containing 300 acres of land--------which said land and premises were devised to Mary Savage, grandmother to the said Mary and Isabell, by the last will and testament of Capt. John Savage, late of this County, deceased, and whereof to them the said Stephen and Isabell, his wife, & their heirs, it belongeth to have one moiety, and to the said Mary it belongeth to have the other moiety &c. -------- 13 January, 1740 - p. 42

Susanna Powell,
vs. - Suit for Dower.
Archibald Godwin.

Came Susanna Powell by George Holden, her Attorney and brought here into Court her certain bill against Archibald Godwin, eldest son and heir of Joseph Godwin, deceased, who was son and heir and devisee of Deverex Godwin, deceased, of a plea of Dower-----which bill followeth in these words: Northampton: S.S. Susanna Powell, widow, late Susanna Godwin and late the wife of Deverex Godwin, deceased, &c. ------- Salathiel Harrison guardian to Archibald Godwin. 14 July, 1741 - p. 45

Henry Goodright,
vs. - Ejectment Proceedings.
Thomas Thrustout.

Jury impaneled and returned the following special verdict:

That Stephen Costen, Sr., late of this County, deceased, was at the time of his death and several years before seized of the land in question as of his own proper estate, and that by his last will and testament, dated 2 June, 1685, devised the said land, with other land, to his son, Francis, and his heirs forever; that the said will was proved 3 June, 1686; that the said Francis Costen immediately from and after the death of the said Stephen Costen, his father, entered upon and was seized of the land in question and died thereof seized, having first made his last will and testament bearing date 13 March, 1721, whereby he devised the land in question to his son Thomas in tail, who immediately after the death of the said Francis Costen entered on the said land and was thereof seized and possessed, and being so seized by his deed of bargain and sale dated ----1739, bargained and sold the said land to the demisor by virtue of a writ of adquod Damnum and an inquisition thereon taken, bearing date 22 October, 1739; that the last will of the said Francis Costen was proved on the 19 April, 1721; that the said deed of bargain and sale was acknowledged in the General Court 17 April, 174_ and recorded; we find a lease from Thomas Coston to Stephen Whitehead dated 4 October, 1733 for the land in question; that the said Stephen Whitehead has been possessed above seven years, and now is of the said land in dispute - 10 March, 1741 - p. 49

Thomas Cable,
vs. - Ejectment Proceedings.
Hillary Stringer.

Jury impaneled and returned the following verdict:

We find that John Savage, Sr., Grandfather of the Demisor, (John Savage, Gentleman) was at the time of his death seized in fee of 9000 acres of land, being in and about a place called Savage's Neck, in the County of Northampton, and that being so seized made his last will and testament dated 26 August, 1678, which said will was proved 11 December, 1678, whereby he devised all or the greatest part of said land; we find a patent for the said land to the said Savage bearing date 8 November, 1673; that the demisor is son and heir of John Savage, the son of the said John Savage, Sr., to whom the eight plantations which are part of the said 9000 acres of land are by the said will devised; that the said John Savage, the father of the demisor, died on or about the 20 day of March, 1720, and that his said son and heir was born the 6 day of August, 1706; that the defendant was on the 21 July, 1737, served by George Kendall, Gentleman, with a copy of a declaration in ejectment wherein Henry Goodright was plaintiff against Thomas Stiles, defendant, and the present demisor was then demisor in order to recover the possession of the same 50 acres of land and which this ejectment is brought for; we also find a patent to Daniel Cugley for 400 acres of land dated 27 June, 1635, which land is now held by the defendant and Alicia Stringer, widow of Jacob Stringer, deceased, or one of the daughters of the said Jacob, and was bounded on the eight plantations aforesaid devised by the said will of the said John Savage, Sr. to his son John before the 50 acres in question was sold by John Savage, the father of the demisor and Thomas Savage, the brother of the said John, to Hillary Stringer, father of the defendant; we find that Thomas and John Savage, father of the lessor, conveyed the said 50 acres by their joint deed to Hillary Stringer, father of the defendant, by deed dated 28 September, 1702; that Thomas Savage in the above deed mentioned, was eldest son and heir at law to John Savage, Sr., the devisor; we also find that the defendant is eldest son and heir at law of the above Hillary Stringer, the vendee, &c. 11 May, 1742 - p. 58

John Wilkins Watts,
vs. - Trespass.
Jonathan Wilkins.
    Jury impaneled and returned the following verdict.
    That a patent was granted to John Wilkins for 100 acres in Northampton County, dated 11 July, 1719; we find a deed of gift from John Wilkins to his daughter, Frances Watts and Thomas Watts, his son in law, for 100 acres in the County of Northampton bearing date 12 September, 1719, in which deed he gave the said land to his daughter and son in law during their lives, with remainder over to his grandson, John Wilkins Watts in fee tail &c. ------- 8 June, 1742 - p. 63

Luke Smaw & Abbigall, his wife, in right of said Abbigall, Comfort
        Waterson & Sarah Waterson,
vs. - Partition Suit.
Tamer Waterson & Mary Waterson.
    Tamer Waterson and Mary Waterson, two of the daughters and coheirs of John Waterson, late of the County aforesaid, Planter, deceased, were summoned to answer unto Luke Smaw & Abbigall, his wife, in right of said Abbigall, Comfort Waterson and Sarah Waterson, the other daughters and coheirs of the said John Waterson --------

who together and undivided hold to them and their heirs 444 acres of land----lying and being at a place called Stubbins, in the County aforesaid &c. ---- 11 January, 1742 - p. 70

Fisher's Lessee,
vs. - Suit for Dower.
Fisher.
That Philip Fisher, late of Northampton County, Gentleman, deceased, was among other lands and at the time of his death seized in fee of the 100 acres of land in question, and that by his last will and testament dated 9 December, 1701, he gave the said land to his son John, grandfather of the Lessor (Thomas Fisher) & the heirs of his body-------that the Devisee, John Fisher, at the time of his death left a son named Thomas Fisher, who was his eldest son and heir, and that the lessor of the plaintiff is the eldest son and heir of the said grandfather of the lessor has been dead many years; that Thomas Fisher, the plaintiff's lessor, at the time of serving the declaration in ejectment, and now, is an infant under the years of 21, to-wit: of the age of 18 years and upwards; that Sarah, the late widow and relict of Thomas Fisher, deceased, and mother of the said Thomas Fisher, the plaintiff's lessor, and now wife of Thomas Edmunds, is in full life, and that her dower has not as yet been set apart &c. -- 8 November, 1743 - p. 75

Luke Smaw & Abigail, his wife, Levi Moor and Sarah, his wife and Comfort Waterson
vs. - Suit for division of 250 acres late belonging to William Waterson. Tamor Waterson and Mary Waterson, infants under the age of 21 years.
Land situate at a place called Nasswadox - Abigail, Sarah, Comfort, Tamor and Mary daughters of John Waterson - 9 April, 1745 - p. 79

Matthew Warren
vs. - Trespass.
Henry Warren.
Jury impaneled and returned the following special verdict:
That Richard Patrick, the elder, late of Northampton County, deceased, was at the time of his death seized of the premises on which the trespass is supposed to be committed; that the said Richard by his last will and testament dated 16 February, 1674/5 devised the said premises to his son Richard Patrick, to him and his heirs forever, by the name of the Homeset Plantation, and soon after died; that the said Richard, the elder, had four children living at the time of his death, viz: Richard, Agnes, Elizabeth and Ursula; that the said Richard and Agnes departed this life in the lifetime of the said Elizabeth and Ursula without issue; that the said Ursula intermarried with Argol Warren, who after the death of the said Richard entered into the said

premises as appears by a verdict heretofore found in a cause between the now defendant plaintiff, and George Monk, defendant, and that they had issue Henry, their eldest son who survived the said Argol and Ursula, which said verdict is in these words, to-wit: At a Court held for Northampton County on Tuesday, the 9 day of May, 1739, in the ejectment brought by Thomas Goodright on the demise of Henry Warren, Plaintiff, against George Monk, defendant, for 200 acres of land and the appurtenances, which being at issue, a jury was impaneled and sworn to try the same------and returned the following verdict: We of the Jury find that Richard Patrick the elder was possessed of the premises in fee; that by the last will and testament of the said Richard Patrick, dated 16 February, 1674, he devised to his son Richard Patrick, Jr., a certain plantation called his Homeset plantation on Governor Hawly's Creek; that after the death of the said Richard, Sr., his son, Richard, was possessed of the premises; that afterwards the said Richard Patrick, Jr., by deed dated 17 November, 1683, conveyed the premises to John Warren, Sr. & Elizabeth, his wife; that the said John Warren survived the said Elizabeth and that he was in possession of the land on Governor's Hawly's Creek, above 49 acres; that the said John Warren was possessed of part of the promises given by the will of Richard Patrick, Sr., to his son Richard as aforesaid, and was thereof possessed until the year 1725; we also find the last will and testatment of the said John Warren, dated 18 November, 1725; that the lessor is the same person in the aforesaid will called by the name of his son Henry: We also find that the plantation in question is the same devised by Richard Patrick, Sr., to his son Richard Patrick, Jr., and the same land conveyed by the said Richard Patrick, Jr., to John Warren and Elizabeth, his wife, also the same with the plantation mentioned in the last will of John Warren, Sr., to his son Henry the lessor. That Richard Patrick, Sr., had four children living at the time of his death, viz: Richard, Elizabeth, Agnes and Ursula; that Richard died first without issue, Agnes next, Ursula after Agnes and that the said Elizabeth survived them all; that John Warren, Sr., late of the aforesaid County, intermarried with the said Elizabeth by whom he had three sons, Richard, John and Henry, the lessor; that Richard died in the lifetime of his father and after the death of his mother, and left a son living named Jacob, who about 11 years since died under age and without issue, and that soon after the decease of the said Jacob John, the second son, entered on the land in question and died thereof seized, and after his death the defendant intermarried with the widow of the second son John, who is now living; that the said Elizabeth died on or about the year 1709, and that the said John Warren, Sr., died in or about the year 1724; and Argoll Warren, who intermarried with the said Ursula, and the said Ursula immediately after the death of the said Richard Patrick, Jr., and in her right, entered upon the part of the said Homeset Planation, and both of them so died thereof possessed; that the said Argol during the life of the said Ursula and their said possession, had issue now living and in possession of part of the said Homeset Plantation; that there was a division between the said Argol & John the elder of the said Homeset Plantation, and that the part whereof the said Argol was possessed, he possessed the same peaceably without any disturbance from the said John Warren &c. -

That the said Ursula died in or about the year 1709, and that the said Argol survived her about 18 years and then died, and after the death of the said Argol the said Henry, his son, entered into the premises and was thereof seized, and being so seized the said Henry departed this life in or about the year 1732, having first made his last will and testament, dated 9 December, 1732, whereby he devised the said premises to his brother Matthew Warren, the plaintiff, by the description of 200 acres; that the plaintiff by virtue of the said devise entered upon the premises and held possession until the time in the declaration mentioned when the defendant entered in and upon the possession of the premises; that the plaintiff and those under whom he claims, have had the quiet and peaceable possession of the premises from the year 1674 till the entry made by the defendant as aforesaid; we also find a deed from the said Richard Patrick, Jr., the devisee of the said Richard Patrick, Sr., to a certain John Warren and his wife, dated 7 November, 1683, in which he devised his whole estate of land and which was left him by the last will of his father, Richard Patrick, deceased. We also find John Warren's will, dated 18 November, 1725, in which he devised his interest in the tract called Homeset plantation to his son Henry Warren and his heirs; we also find that the Henry Warren in the said will mentioned is the defendant, and also that the place where the supposed trespass aforesaid was supposed to be committed was on the land the said Richard Patrick granted and made over to the defendant's father and mother, and that the plaintiff has two brothers older than himself now living who have each of them several children also now living &c. ------- 8 October, 1745 - p. 85 et seq.

Hodges and wife,
vs. - Partition Suit.
Garrison & wife, &c.

Cantwell Garrison & Margaret, his wife, Anne Clarke and Sarah Clarke, coheirs of George Clarke, late of the County aforesaid, deceased, were summoned to answer Edward Hodges and Adah, his wife, of a plea wherefore & whereas the said Edward and Adah, his wife, in right of the said Adah, Cantwell and Margaret, his wife, in right of the said Margaret, Anne and Sarah together and undivided hold 200 acres of land in Old Plantation Neck in the County aforesaid, and also 133 acres on Hog Island, in the aforesaid County &c. ------ 8 October, 1745 - p. 97

Thomas Warren, Infant, by Bartholomew Pettitt, his guardian,
vs. - Trespass
Henry Warren.

Jury Impaneled and returned the following special verdict.

That Richard Patrick, the elder, late of Northampton County, deceased, was seized at the time of his death of the premises on which the trespass is supposed to be committed; that the said Richard by his last will and testament dated 16 February, 1674/5, devised the said premises to his son, Richard Patrick, in the name of the Homeset Plantation; that the said Richard Patrick had four children living at the time of his death, viz: Richard, Agnes, Elizabeth and Ursula; that the said Richard and Agnes departed this life in the lifetime of the said Elizabeth and Ursula without issue; That the said Elizabeth intermarried with John Warren, the elder, late of the said County by whom the said Elizabeth had three sons, viz: Richard, John and Henry, the defendant; that the said Richard died in the lifetime of his father and after the death of his mother, and left a son named Jacob who died about 17 years ago without issue and under age, and possessed of the premises; that the said Elizabeth died in or about the year 1709 and the said John Warren, the elder, in or about year 1724; that soon after the death of the said Jacob the said John, the second son, entered into the premises and so being possessed by his last will and testament, dated 20 April, 1729, devised the said premises to his son Thomas, the plaintiff by the description of the plantation he then lived on after the death of his wife Elizabeth, and that the said Elizabeth died in or about the first of March last past, and after her death the said plaintiff planted some apple trees on the premises in the lifetime of George Monk, and that the said Monk survived his said wife until the month of July next following, and that the plaintiff after the death of the said George Monk came to the house and premises and turned out his horse in the pasture, and that the defendant about the time in the declaration mentioned entered into the premises; that the defendant some time in or about the year 1739 brought an ejectment in the Court of the said County of Northampton for the premises aforesaid, and the George Monk, who intermarried with the widow of the said John, son of John the elder, defended the same, and that upon the trial thereof, at a Court held for the County of Northampton on Tuesday, the 12 day of June, MDCCXXXIX, upon a special verdict found in the said cause, judgment was entered by the Court that the law was for the defendant, as by the record of the said verdict and judgment hereto annexed in these words, to-wit: At a Court held for Northampton County on Tuesday, the 9 day of May, 1739, in the ejectment brought by Thomas Goodright on the demise of Henry Warren, plaintiff, against George Monk, defendant, for two hundred acres of land and the appurtenances, which being at issue a jury was impaneled and sworn to try the same-------who having heard the evidence and received their charge returned the following verdict: We of the jury find that Richard Patrick, the elder, was seized of the premises in fee; we also find the last will and testament of the said Richard Patrick, bearing date the 16th day of February, 1674, duly recorded; we also find that the said will devised to Richard Patrick, Jr., a certain plantation called his Homeset Plantation, on Governor Hawley's Creek; we also find that after the death of the said Richard Patrick, Sr., that his son Richard Patrick was possessed of the premises; we also find that afterwards the said Richard Patrick, Jr., by his deed bearing date the 17 day of November, 1683, duly recorded conveyed the premises to John Warren,

Sr., and Elizabeth, his wife; we also find that the said John Warren survived the said Elizabeth and that he was in possession of the land on Governor Hawley's Creek above 49 years. We also find that the said John Warren was possessed of part of the premises given by the will of Richard Patrick, Sr., to his son Richard Patrick aforesaid, and was thereof possessed until the year 1725; we also find the last will testament of the said John Warren bearing date the 18 November, 1725; we also find the lessor is the same person in the aforesaid will called by the name of his son Henry; we also find the plantation in question is the same in the last will and testament of Richard Patrick, Sr., devised to his son Richard Patrick, and the same land in the deed of Richard Patrick, Jr., to John Warren and Elizabeth, his wife, also the same with the plantation mentioned in the last will and testament of John Warren, Sr., deceased, to his son Henry, the lessor------ we also find the said Richard Patrick, Sr. had four children living at the time of his decease, viz: Richard, Elizabeth, Agnes and Ursula, and that Richard died first without issue, Agnes next and Ursula after Agnes, and that the said Elizabeth survived them all; we also find that John Warren, Sr., late of the County aforesaid, intermarried with the said Elizabeth, by whom he had three sons, viz: Richard, John and Henry, the lessor, and that Richard died in the lifetime of his father, and after the death of his mother, and leaving a son living named Jacob, who about eleven years since died under age and without issue, and that soon after the decease of the said Jacob John, the second son, entered on the Land in question and died thereof seized; after his death the defendant intermarried with the widow of the said second son John, who is now living; we also find that the said Elizabeth died on or about the year 1709, and that the said John Warren, Sr., died on or about the year 1724; we also find that Argoll Warren, who intermarried with the said Ursula, and the said Ursula, immediately after the death of the said Richard Patrick, Jr., and in her right, entered upon the part of the said Homeset Plantation and both of them so died thereof possessed; that the said Argol during the life of the said Ursula, and their said possession, had issue now living and in possession of part of the said Homeset Plantation; we also find that there was a division between the said Argol and John, the elder, of the said Homeset Plantation, and that the part whereof the said Argol was possessed he possessed the same peaceably without any disturbance from the said John Warren------We find that John Warren, the son of John Warren and Elizabeth, his wife, at the time of his death left his widow named Elizabeth in possession of the House and Land, on which the supposed trespass aforesaid was supposed to be committed, and that she a short time after the death of the said John Warren, her husband, intermarried with the said George Monk who survived the said Elizabeth, his wife some months, and from the time of the said intermarriage to the time of his, the said George's, death, the said George was possessed of the said house and land ---- 8 Apr. 1746 - p. 103

44

Thomas Goodright, Lessee of John Savage,
vs. - Ejectment Proceedings.
William Roberts.

Jury impaneled and returned the following verdict:

That John Savage, Sr., late of Northampton County, Gentleman, was at the time of his death seized in fee of a large quantity of land lying and being in a place called Savage's Neck in the County aforesaid, and that he by his last will and testatment gave to his son John Savage, amongst other bequests therein contained, eight plantations therein particularly mentioned, viz: John Webster's, Thomas Bankes, Robert Harrison's, Stephen Lecatt's, Hendrick Abell's, Thomas Duparks', William Lawrence and the widow Webley's, part of the above quantity of land; we find the said will bearing date the 26th August, Anno Domini 1678, in these words (abstract) To son John Savage, whom I do appoint my heir, and his heirs for life, these eight plantations following, viz: John Webster's, &c., containing in the whole, by estimation, 700 acres, also 500 acres being part of 1000 acres which Col. Stringer now holdeth from me by lease, and for want of heirs to my son Thomas Savage, and for want of heirs to my son Elkington Savage, and for want of heirs to the next surviving heir of my family, and for want of heirs to the Crown of England. To my son Thomas the plantation which Lt. Thomas Wilson, Samuel Powell and John Beury now live upon, containing, by estimation 400 acres, and for want of heirs to my son John Savage. To son Elkington Savage three plantations belonging to Edward Coble, John Davis and Samuel Church, containing, by estimation, 350 acres, also 400 acres in the County aforesaid by a branch called Roody Branch. To daughter Mary Savage the plantations whereon Philip Mongom, Edward Perkinson and Peter Duparks live on, the three plantations containing, by estimation, 300 acres. To daughter Susanna Kendall and John Kendall, her husband, all my right, title and interest in 800 acres in the County aforesaid, bounded easterly on the main ocean and adjoining the 400 acres given my son Elkington, and 200 acres I have given to my two grandsons Thomas and John Kendall. To daughter Grace Corbin and to her husband, George Corbin, three planations, viz: Samuel Younge's, John Abbot's and Thomas Churches, containing, by estimation, 250 acres. To grandchildren John and Thomas Kendall, children of the said John and Susanna Kendall, 200 acres adjoining the 400 acres given my son Elkington ---- To grandaughter Susanna Kendall plantation containing 100 acres where William Cowdry, my son in law, now lives, which I have given him during his natural life. To my good friend and relation John Davis 1000 L of tobacco and caske. To Jacob Bishop, John Harmanson, Hannah Webb, Anne Hudson, Mary Baker, each of them a yearling heifer. To my youngest daughter now lately born 500 acres, being one half of 1000 acres by me leased to Col. Stringer. Three children, John, Elkington and Mary to be put to school to remain for the space of five years, and that two or three of the boy servants be put with them towards bearing their necessary charges, and after the five years have expired to work for them. Should my wife Mary marry again my children to be of age at that time. After the payment of my debts there shall be ten hogsheads of good tobacco sent to England to be disposed of according to a letter that shall be written either by me or at my direction. Son John Executor. Friends Lt. Col. William Waters, Col. William Kendall, Mr. John Michael, Sr. and Mr. Thomas Harmanson and my two sons in law, John Kendall and George Corbin overseers. Probated 11 Dec. 1678.

We also find that the devisee, John Savage, after the death of the testator, entered on the said eight plantations and died thereof seized about 24 years since, and left only one son and heir, namely John, who after the death of his father entered on the said eight plantations and died thereof seized about the month of December, Anno Domini 1746, and left an only son and heir also named John, who is the demisor of the plaintiff; we find that John Savage, the grandson, by his indenture bearing date 25 December, 1745, demised the premises whereon the trespass was supposed to be committed, unto the defendant in consideration of 23 L current money during the term of 10 years from the said 25 December, under the yearly rent of one shilling and the quit rents &c., ----- we find that the land is part of the eight plantations demised to the said John Savage, the son, &c. -------- 11 Aug. 1747 – p. 131

William Tazewell,
vs. - Ejectment proceedings.
Elishe Stringer.

Jury impaneled and returned the following verdict.

That John Savage, Sr., late of Savage's Neck, in the County of Northampton, Gentleman, deceased, father of John and Thomas Savage, Gentlemen, deceased, was at the time of his death seized in fee of a very large tract of land lying and being in the said Neck, and that out of that tract of land he leased to one Thomas Dimmer, deceased, and his assigns, a thousand acres for a long term of years; we find that the said lease bears date 31 October, Anno Domini, 1664, in these words --------we find the said Dimmer by an endorsement on the said lease, bearing date the 6 day of April, Anno Domini, 1665, assigned the said lease to John Stringer, late of the said County, Gentleman, deceased-------we find the last will and testament of the said John Savage, Sr., deceased, bearing date the 26 August, Anno Domini 1678, in these words, to-wit: In the name of God, Amen, &c. We find the said John Savage by his last will devised to his son John the reversion of one moiety of the said 1000 acres in tail, and the other moiety of the said 1000 acres of land he devised to his daughter Frances in tail; We find that John Savage, the eldest son and heir of the said John Savage, the devisee, by virtue of an Act of Assembly of this Colony docked the entail of the first mentioned moiety of the said land, and that for the consideration therein mentioned to be paid by Gertrude Harmanson, late of the aforesaid County, widow, deceased, for the uses and purposes in the said Act mentioned, the reversion of that said land was vested in the said Gertrude Harmanson, her heirs and assigns; We find that the said Gertrude Harmanson by her last will and testament devised the said land unto her son Henry in manner following, that is to say, that her said son Henry might give the aforesaid land to any one child of his body lawfully begotten, but if he should not be inclined to give it to one child, then he might give it between more of his children as he should think fit, but if he should die without heirs of his body lawfully begotten, then she gave the said land to her daughter, Sophia, the plaintiff's wife, & her heirs &c. We find the said will bearing date the 11 day of September, Anno Domini 1732, in these words, to-wit: -------- we find that the said Frances, the daughter of the said John Savage, Sr., intermarried with Samuel Powell, late of the said County, Planter, deceased, by whom she had issue a son named John, and that after the said Powell's death she intermarried with one John Jones, late of the said County aforesaid, Planter, deceased, by whom she had two daughters only and no son, one named Sarah and the other Anne Mary, and soon after died; we find that John Powell, the son of the said Frances, at the time of the death of the said Frances, was her son and heir; we find that the said John Powell about ____ years since died without issue. We find that the said Sarah, one of the daughters of the said Frances, intermarried with one Thomas Spady of the county aforesaid, planter, and that Anne Mary, the other daughter of the said Frances intermarried with one Absolum Hall; we find that after the death of the said John Powell the said Thomas Spady and Sarah, his wife, in right of the said Sarah, and the said Absolum Hall and Anne Mary, his wife, in right of the said Anne Mary were seized in reversion of the said 500 acres of land given by their grandfather's will to their mother aforesaid; we find that the said Thomas Spady and Sarah, his wife, by virtue of a writ of Ad quod Damnum, and an Inquistion thereon taken, by a deed of bargain and sale bearing date the 18 day of July, Anno Domini 1743, for the consideration therein mentioned, sold their moiety or half part of the last mentioned 500 acres of land unto the plaintiff and his heirs and assigns, forever, and that the said Absolum Hall and Anne Mary, his wife, likewise by virtue of another writ of Ad Quod Damnum and an Inquisition thereon taken, by deed of bargain and sale bearing date the 16 day of July, Anno Domini 1743, for the consideration therein mentioned, sold their moiety or half part of the said 500 acres of land unto the plaintiff and his heirs and assigns forever, which said two deeds followeth in those words, (to-wit): ----- we find that before the execution of the said two deeds of bargain and sale, the said Thomas and Sarah and the said Absalom and Anne Mary, and the plaintiff and his wife, Sophia, divided the said leased land between them by consent, and that the said Thomas and Sarah and the said Absalom and Anne Mary made choice of the lower western moiety of the said 1000 acres-----and that the plaintiff and his wife chose the upper eastern moiety of the said 1000 acres-----we find a deed bearing date the 8 day of September, Anno Domini 1702, from Thomas and John Savage to Hillary Stringer, by which the said Thomas and John Savage sold to the said Hillary Stringer 50 acres of land upon a condition therein mentioned, under which the said defendant claims title to the land whereon the trespass in the declaration mentioned is supposed to be committed, which deed followeth in those words (to-wit:) -------We find that the defendant, or some persons under her, planted and tended that 50 acres of land, or a great part thereof, which the said Thomas

47

and John Savage sold to the said Stringer----after the expiration of the term granted by the aforesaid lease, & before this suit commenced, we find that Matthew Harmanson, Gentleman, surveyor of this County, by virtue of an order of this Court, bearing date the 11 day of November, Anno Domini 1747, surveyed and laid out the plaintiff's plantations to the land leased as aforesaid, the defendant's plantations to the land sold as aforesaid by the said Thomas and John Savage to the said Hillary Stringer; we find a platt of the said survey made according to the said order of Court as before is recited---- 8 September, 1747 - p. 141

Robert Fletcher,
vs. - Ejectment Proceedings.
William Scott.
    Jury impaneled and returned the following verdict:
    We find the last will and testament of John Savage, late of Northampton County, Gentleman, dated the 26 August, Anno Domini 1678, hereto annexed ---- we also find that the devisee, John Savage, died on or about the year ____ and left an only son also named John, who died on or about the ___ day of ___ Anno Domini, 174_, and left too an only son named John who is now living. We find that the last mentioned John Savage, the great grandson, is an infant under the age of 21 years, and that before the above supposed trespass was supposed to be committed he chose the Defendant in the Court of the aforesaid County as his guardian, who so continues to be; We find that John Savage, the grandson, by his indenture bearing date the 25 day of December, MDCCXLV in consideration of 30 L current money demised the premises on which the supposed trespass was committed, from the 25 Day of December, to the plaintiff for the term of 10 years then next following, under the yearly rent of one shilling & quit rents as by the said indenture hereto annexed (not filed among the papers); we find that the land so demised to the plaintiff is part of the land devised by John Savage, the elder, to his daughter, Grace Corbin and her husband George, and that after her said husband, George's, death she intermarried with one ____ Bloxom, and left issue Savage Bloxom, who after her death entered into the premises and died without issue, and after the death of the said Savage Bloxom the said John Savage the grandson entered - --- 9 June, 1747 - p. 176

William Thrustout, Lessee of John Blackwell,
vs. - Ejectment Proceedings.
Thomas Marshall and Andrew Turner.
    Jury impaneled and returned the following verdict:
    We find that John Read, late of Northampton, deceased, was possessed of the land in question in fee simple; on the 3 day of March, 1695, we find that the said John Read on the day and year aforesaid made his last will in writing, which was duly proved in the Court of Northampton the 30 day of November, 1696, and hereto annexed, in these words, to-wit: (abstract) To son John and son Major my land in

Gilford Creek containing 115 acres, and should either die in their minority the survivor to enjoy the whole plantation, but should both live to be equally divided between them. To sons Thomas and Ishmael plantation where I now live, and should either die the survivor to enjoy the whole, but should both live to be equally divided between them. To wife Hannah Read the balance of my estate during her natural life or widowhood, but should she marry to be divided between my wife and two daughters, Mary and Hannah. Wife Executrix. Probated 30 Nov. 1696. In which said will he devised the land in question in these words, to-wit: "I have given unto my sons Thomas and Ishmael this plantation I now live upon, to them and to their heirs, forever, but should it please God that either Thomas or Ishmael should dye in their minority, then my will is that the survivor shall enjoy, but if both my sons live then this plantation to be equally divided between them". We find that Ishmael survived Thomas and died without issue; we find that John Read, eldest son and heir at law to John Read, the testator, by his deed of bargain and sale bearing date the 29 day of January, 1730, and duly acknowledged with livery & seizen on the 9 day of February, 1730, in the Court of Northampton County, and hereto annexed, did convey the lands in question to one Joseph Blackwell, father of the plaintiff's lessor, which deed is as followeth, to-wit: Articles of agreement made and concluded on this 29 of January, in the year of our Lord 1730 between the parties following, to-wit: John Read of Somerset County, in the Province of Maryland, of the one part and Joseph Blackwell, of Dosset County in the same Province, of the other part---------all my right to the reversion of a certain parcel of land, by estimation 150 acres, situate, lying and being in Northampton County in Virginia, in Nasswadox Neck------- we find that John Blackwell, the plaintiff's lessor, is the surviving heir of Joseph Blackwell, vendee or purchaser of the land in question; we find that John Blackwell, the plaintiff's lessor, is about 21 years and seven months of age; we find that John Read, the vendor of the lands in question to Joseph Blackwell, lived out of the government from the time of his father's death, or soon after, til the 29 day of January, 1730, at which time he sold the lands in question to the aforesaid Joseph Blackwell, and soon after returned to Maryland, and that Ishmael died in his minority; that he survived his brother Thomas who died after he arrived to the age of 21 years, and that Thomas left issue-------- 12 April, 1748 - p. 216

Belleshazer Seekright, Lessee of Jonah Widgeon,
vs. - Ejectment proceedings.
Tabitha Batson.
   Jury impaneled and returned the following verdict.
   We find that William Batson, late of Northampton County, Planter, deceased, was at the time of his death seized in fee of 130 acres of land in the County aforesaid, being the land in question, and being so seized by his last will and testament, bearing date the 24 September, Anno Domini 1720, he gave the said land to his wife, Elizabeth, during her life; we find the said will in these words, to-wit: (abstract) To

wife Elizabeth my land and moveables as long as she liveth, then the land where I now live to my son Francis Batson, my will is that my son Francis should build, but not to molest his mother. Wife Elizabeth Executrix. Probated 16 October, 1720. We find that the said William Batson at the time of his death left several children living, who all died in their minority without issue except his daughter Mary, who intermarried with the demisor, Jonah Widgeon, by whom she had issue only a son during the coverture; we find the said Mary about 16 years since died in the lifetime of her said son; we also find that the son of the said Jonah and Mary about 9 years since died underage and without issue; we also find that Elizabeth, the said testator's widow, survived all her children and soon after died in possession of the said land in question; we also find that John Batson, late of this county, planter, deceased, was the said William's the testator's, eldest brother, and that he died since the said William and before the death of the son of the said Jonah and Mary, his wife. We also find that Jonah Batson late of the said County, Planter, deceased, was the eldest son and heir of the said John Batson, who after the death of the said Jonah and Mary entered on the land in question and died seized thereof. We find the last will and testament of the said Jonas bearing date the 12 August, Anno Domini 1744 in these words, to-wit: (abstract) To son Thomas Batson 130 acres of land where my father, John Batson, did live, 30 of the acres is the land I bought of Abraham Smith. To son John Batson 130 acres of land lying in the Old Town. Should either of my sons die without lawful heirs the survivor to have all the land. To wife Tabitha Batson 1/4 of my personal estate during her natural life, then to be divided between my six children, and the other three parts of my personal estate to be equally divided between my six children, viz: Thomas, John, Leah, Rachel, Bridget & Anne Batson. Wife and son Thomas Executors. Probated 13 December, 1748. We find that Elizabeth Batson, the widow of the said William never disposed of or granted her right of the land in question by deed to the said Jonah and his wife or any other person-------- 14 March, 1748/9 - p. 222

John Wise and Elizabeth, his wife.
vs. - Partition suit.
Sarah Cable.

Mr. John Wise, Gentleman, and Elizabeth, his wife, one of the daughters and coheirs of Thomas Cable, late of the said County, Gentleman, deceased, by George Holden, their Attorney, and Sarah Cable, another of the daughters and coheirs of the said decedent, came by Sorrowful Margaret Cable, her guardian, &c. --------12 Sept. 1749 - p. 225

Goodright, Lessee of Smaw, et ux, et als,
vs. - Ejectment proceedings.
Benjamin Johnson.

Jury impaneled and returned the following special verdict:
We find that John Waterson, late of the County of Northampton,

deceased, was in his lifetime and at the time of his death seized in fee of two hundred and fifty acres of land, the premises in question being part thereof; that the said John by his last will and testament in writing, bearing date the first day of December, 1679, and hereto annexed, duly proved and recorded in the Court of Northampton County, devised the said land to his son Richard, in these words: "Item: I give and bequeath to my son Richard Waterson, two hundred and fifty acres adjoining to my brother Hunt's whereon Dennis Amule you liveth", which will is in these words, to-wit: In the name of God Amen (Abstract) Wife to be my whole Executrix. Household goods, horses, mares & cattle that doth belong wholly to me (excepting my childrens) to be equally divided between my wife and three children, the stock of hogs to be wholly my wife's; wife and son John to have two shares, and she to have her first choice. To son William Waterson the tract of land where I now live. to son Richard Waterson 250 acres of land adjoining my brother Hunt's whereon Dennis Amull you liveth. To son John Waterson 500 acres of land adjoining upon Stubbens. Sons Richard and John to be at age at 18 years, and son William to be at age as soon as I am departed. My little son John to have three years schooling, and my son William to live with his mother so long as he is dutiful and obedient. Son Richard to have my whole part of the Shallop and all belonging to it. The mare which I purchased of Peter Whaples shall be my son William's. Witt: William Nicholls, Nathaniel Capell. Note: before the signing hereof my will and pleasure is that my godson, William Somers, shall have one cow and calfe paid out of my estate. dated 1 December, 1679 - Probated 28 January, 1679/80.

That William Waterson, son and heir at law to the said John, by his deed in writing, bearing date the 15 day of February, 1688, hereto annexed, duly proved and recorded in the Court of Northampton County--------conveyed to his brother, the said Richard and to his heirs &c. forever, the said 250 acres of land so devised to him, the said Richard, which deed is as followeth, to-wit: To all Christian People &c. That the said Richard is since dead possessed of 150 acres of the said land without making any disposition thereof. That the said Richard left his eldest son named Ezekiel and one daughter named Fanny, of the whole blood to the said Ezekiel. That the said Ezekiel after the death of the said Richard lived with one John Hunt till the time of his death, and that the said Ezekiel was at the time of his death under the age of twenty one years and died without issue, and that his sister, Fanny, survived him and is since dead without issue. That the said John Hunt after the death of the said Richard, and during the life of the said Ezekiel, rented out the said 150 acres of land and received the rents thereof to the use and behoof of the said Ezekiel. That John Waterson, son and heir of William Waterson, brother and heir at law of the said Richard, the father of the said Ezekiel, who survived the said Ezekiel and Fanny, by his last will and testament in writing, bearing date the 18 day of November, Anno Domini MDCCXXXlll devised all the rest of his estate in the following words: "Item: I give and bequeath all the rest of my estate after my just debts are paid, to be equally divided between my five daughters, viz:

Abigail, Comfort, Sarah, Tamar and Mary Waterson, to them and their heirs forever" as by the said will duly proved and recorded in Northampton County Court and hereto annexed appeareth, in these words, to-wit: In the Name of God Amen (abstract) To son William Waterson the plantation where I now live, containing 440 acres, and for want of heirs to my son Richard Waterson and his heirs. To son William negro man Paul Carter, personalty. To son Richard Waterson the plantation that Thomas Bullock now lives on, containing 255 acres. My will is that my sister Sarah Bullock shall stay and remain on the plantation they now live on till my son Richard Waterson comes of age for the same rent as they now pay. I give the rents of my plantation between my loving wife Elizabeth Waterson and my son Richard Waterson. To son Richard my negro Edward Carter. To daughter Abigail Waterson, daughter Comfort Waterson, daughter Sarah Waterson, daughter Tamar Waterson daughter Mary Waterson personalty. To wife Elizabeth 1/3 of my estate. Five daughters above named resid. legatees. Wife Elizabeth Executrix. Witt: Ralph Pigot, Mariot Parsons, Lazarus Jacob, John Smith.

Codicil: My son William Waterson to make over his rights of the land I sold to Maj. Peter Bowdoin, and should he refuse to have 1 shilling of my estate, and my will is that my son should have the 35 L - 18 November, 1735 - Probated 12 February, 1733/4.

That the said Abigail, Comfort, Sarah, Tamar and Mary are the female lessors of the plaintiff. We find that Richard Waterson, late of the County of Northampton, Planter, deceased, was at the time of his death seized in fee of the land in question, and that he had several wives, and that by his third wife, Elizabeth, he had issue a son named Ezekiel, and by his fourth wife of the same name he had another son named Richard, and that Ezekiel survived his father but died an infant under the age of 12 years, thirty years before the ejectment brought; We also find that the said Richard survived the said Ezekiel but also died in his minority under the age of nine years. We also find that the said Richard Waterson by his said wives, or some of them, had several daughters who survived both his said sons, &c. -------- 13 March, 1749 - p. 230

Goodright, Lessee of Smaw, et ux, et als,
vs. - Ejectment Proceedings.
Charles Tomson.

That Luke Smaw and Abigail, his wife, Thomas Michael and Comfort his wife, Ralph Batson and Sarah, his wife, Tamar and Mary Waterson, by indenture bearing date 14 February, MDCCXLIX demised and to farm lett to the said Thomas Goodright for the term of seven years, to commence from the feast of the nativity of our Lord Christ then last past, --------112 1/2 acres of land situate, lying and being at Old Plantation Creek in Northampton County--------by virtue of which demise the said Thomas into the lands and tenements aforesaid entered and was thereof possessed, and being so thereof possessed the said Charles afterwards, to-wit, on the said 14 February, in the year aforesaid, into the premises aforesaid, in and upon the possession of him, the said Thomas, his term aforesaid therein not expires, with force and arms entered -------- Jury impaneled and returned the following verdict:

That John Waterson late of the County of Northampton, deceased, was in his lifetime and at the time of his death, seized in fee of 250 acres of land, the premises in question being part thereof, and that the said John by his last will and testament in writing, bearing date first day of December, 1679, hereto annexed, duly proved and recorded in the Court of Northampton County, devised the said land to his son Richard in these words: "Item: I give and bequeath to my son Richard Waterson 250 acres adjoining to my brother Hunt's, whereon Dennis Amule you liveth," which will is in these words, to-wit: (abstract) Wife to be sole executrix. Whole estate of household goods, horses, mares and cattle that doth belong wholly to me (excepting my children's) to be equally divided between my wife and three children. The stock of hogs to be wholly my wife's, and my wife and son John to have two shares, and she to have her first choice. To son William land whereon I live. To son Richard 250 acres adjoining my brother Hunt's, whereon Dennis Amule you liveth. To son John Waterson 500 acres adjoining Stubbins heirs ---- sons Richard and John to be at age at 18 and my son William to be at age at my decease. My little son John to have three years schooling and my son William to live with his mother as long as he is dutiful and obedient. Son Richard to have my whole part of the Shallop and all belonging to it. The mare I lately purchased of Peter Whaples to be my son William's, she and all her increase. Witt: William Nicholls, Nathaniel Capell. Note: That before signing hereof my will is that my godson, William Somers, shall have one cow and calfe out of my estate. Dated 1 December, 1679 - Probated 28 Jan. 1679.

That William Waterson, son and heir at law to the said John, by his deed in writing dated 15 February, 1688, duly recorded in the said Court of Northampton, conveyed to his brother, the said Richard, and to his heirs, &c., the said 250 acres of land so devised to him the said Richard--------that the said Richard since died possessed of 150 acres of the said land without making any disposition of the said land. That the said Richard left his eldest son named Ezekiel and one daughter named Fanny, of the whole blood to the said Ezekiel; that the said Ezekiel after the death of the said Richard lived with one John Hunt till the time of his death. That the said Ezekiel was at the time of his death under the age of 21 years and died without issue. That the said John Hunt after the death of the said Richard, and during the life of the said Ezekiel, rented out the said 150 acres and received the rents thereof to the use and behoof of the said Ezekiel. That John Waterson, son and heir of William Waterson, Brother and heir at law of the said Richard, the father of the said Ezekiel who survived the said Ezekiel and Fanny, by his last will and testament in writing bearing date the 18 day of November, MDCCXXXIII devised all the rest of his estate in these words following: "Item: I give and bequeath all the rest of my estate after my just debts is paid, to be equally divided between my five daughters, viz: Abigail, Comfort, Sarah, Tamar and Mary Waterson, to them and their heirs forever, as by the said will duly proved and recorded in Northampton County Court and hereto annexed appeareth in these words, to-wit: (abstract) To my son William Waterson the plantation I now live on containing 440 acres, and should he die without heirs I give it to my son Richard Waterson and his heirs. To son William my negro Paul Carter - Personalty. To son Richard the plantation that Thomas Bullock now lives on containing 255 acres, and my will is that my sister Sarah Bullock shall stay and remain on the plantation they now live on until my son Richard Waterson comes of age, for the same rent as they now pay. I give the rents of my plantation between my loving wife Elizabeth Waterson and my son Richard Waterson to be equally divided between them. To son Richard negro Edward Carter. To daughters Abigail, Comfort, Sarah, Tamar and Mary personalty. To wife Elizabeth 1/3 of my estate. Five daughters above named resid. legatees. Wife Executrix. Witt: Ralph Pigot, Mariot Parsons, Lazarus Jacob. Dated 18 November, 1733 - Probated 12 Feb. 1733/4.

That the said Abigail, Comfort, Sarah, Tamar and Mary are the female lessors of the plaintiff. We find that Richard Waterson, late of the County of Northampton, deceased, was at the time of his death seized in fee of the land in question, and that he had several wives, and that by the third wife Elizabeth he had issue a son named Ezekiel, and by his fourth wife of the same name he had another son named Richard, and that Ezekiel survived his father but died an infant under the age of 12 years, thirty years before the ejectment brought; We also find that the said Richard survived the said Ezekiel but also died in his minority under the age of 9 years. We also find that the said Richard Waterson by his said wives, or some of them, had several daughters we survived both his said sons, &c. --------13 March, 1749 - p. 237

Goodright, Lessee of Tazewell, et ux,
vs. - Ejectment Proceedings.
Savage.

Jury impaneled and returned the following verdict:

We find that John Savage, Sr., late of Savage's Neck, in the County of Northampton, Gentleman, deceased, father of John and Thomas Savage, Gentlemen, deceased, was at the time of his death seized in fee of a very large tract of land lying and being in the said Neck, and that out of that tract of land he leased to one Thomas Dimmer, deceased, and his assigns, a thousand acres for a long term of years, said lease bearing date 31 October, MDCLXiv. We find that the said Dimmer by an endorsement on the said lease bearing date the vi day of April, Anno Domini MDCLXV assigned the said lease to John Stringer, late of the said County, Gentleman, deceased. We find the last will and testament of the said John Savage, Sr., deceased, bearing date the xxvi day of August, MDCLXXVIII by which he devised to his said son John the reversion of the moiety of the said 1000 acres of land, and the other moiety of the said 1000 acres of land he devised to his daughter Frances, in these words, viz: "Item: I give and bequeath to my well beloved son John Savage (who I do hereby appoint my heir)

and to his heirs for life, these eight Plantations following, viz: John
Webster's, Thomas Banks, Robert Harrison's, Steven Scott's, Hendrick Abel's, Thomas Duparks' William Lawrence and the widow
Webley's, the said plantations containing in the whole, by estimation,
seven hundred acres of land (be the same more or less) and also five
hundred acres of land, part of 1000 acres which Col. John Stringer now
holdeth from me by lease, and if it shall happen my said son dye
without lawful heirs then the same to be and remain to my son
Thomas Savage & heirs during their natural lives, and for want of such
heirs to my son Elkington Savage and his heirs during their natural
lives, and for want of such heirs to the next surviving heir of my
family, and for want of such heirs to the Crown of England.   Item: I
give and bequeath to my youngest daughter now lately born, five
hundred acres of land, begin the one moiety of one thousand acres by
me leased to Col. Stringer, to have and to hold the said five hundred
acres of land, with the appurtenances, to her my said youngest daughter and the heirs of her body lawfully begotten, for and during their
natural lives, and for want of such heirs then to my said son, John
Savage and his heirs, and for want of such heirs then in remainder as
aforesaid:
     We find that John Savage, the eldest son and heir of the said John
Savage, the devisee, by virtue of an Act of Assembly of this Colony
dock't the entail of the said first mentioned moiety of the said land,
and that for the consideration therein mentioned to be paid by Gertrude
Harmanson, late of the said County, widow, deceased, for the uses and
purposes in the said act mentioned, the reversion of the said moiety
was vested in the said Gertrude Harmanson, her heirs and assigns.
We find that Gertrude Harmanson by her last will and testament
devised the said land to her son Henry in these words, viz: "I also
give, devise and bequeath unto my aforesaid son Henry Harmanson
five hundred acres of land, lying and being in Savage's Neck on the
Bayside, in this County, which I lately bought of John Savage, and is
invested in me by an Act of Assembly past the last Session, which
said land I give to him my said son and his heirs in manner and form
following, that is to say, my said son may give the aforesaid land to
any one child of his body lawfully begotten, but if he should not be
inclined to give it to one child then he may give it between more of
his children as he shall think fit, and if he should die without issue of
his body lawfully begotten, then I give the aforesaid five hundred acres
of land to my daughter Sophia Tazewell and her heirs in manner and
form as it is before given to my son", which will we find bearing date
the xi day of September, Anno Domini MDCCXXX11 in these words,
to-wit: (abstract) To son Henry my plantation on the Bayside containing 350 acres which I bought of John West, that is my said son may
give the aforesaid land to some child of his body lawfully begotten
&c., and if he die without heirs to my grandson Littleton Eyre, and for
want of issue to my daughter Sophia Tazewell, and for want of heirs to
my son in law (stepson-S.N.) Capt. Matthew Harmanson.   To son
Henry 500 acres of land in Savage's Neck on the Bayside in Northampton County, which I lately bought of John Savage &c., and for want of
heirs to my daughter Sophia Tazewell. I also give to my said son one

large silver tankard and six silver spoons which I have delivered him, the tankard and spoons marked "GH" - personalty &c. To daughter Sophia Tazewell the plantation I bought of John Bagwell and William Hawkins, situate in Magotty Bay in this County, containing 294 acres, and to the future issue of her body male, and for want of such male issue to my grandson Littleton Tazewell. To my son in law William Tazewell and daughter Sophia Tazewell the use of eight negroes and their increase which they now have in possession, and at their death to be divided between all my grandchildren lawfully begotten of their bodies. To son in law John Stratton negro woman Ann and her increase, to him and to any of his children he shall se fit to give them, but if my said son in law or his heirs should make claim to any part of my deceased husband's estate by right of his marriage with my former daughter, Esther, deceased, I revoke the above gift. To grandson Littleton Eyre my tract of land on Hog Island containing 237 acres, and should he die before lawful age or marriage to descend to my son Henry Harmanson. To grandson Littleton Eyre 380 acres in Somerset County, Maryland, near Swansgut, which land was given me by my deceased father Southy Littleton, and should he die before lawful age and without issue to my daughter Sophia Tazewell. To my grandchildren William Tazewell, Littleton Tazewell, Anne Tazewell and Gertrude Tazewell, 100 L current money of Virginia to be paid them at day of marriage or when they attain the age of 21 years. To son in law Matthew Harmanson one guinea and to each of his children 10 shillings. To kinsman Neech Eyre and to my sister Elizabeth Waters one guinea. To my brother in law Col. George Harmanson and Thomas Cable each 20 shillings to buy them a ring. Balance of estate to be divided in three parts, one third to my son Henry Harmanson, 1/6 to my daughter Sophia Tazewell the other 1/6 to Sophia for life then to be divided between her children, and the other one third part to my grandson Littleton Eyre. Sons Henry Harmanson and William Tazewell Executors. Friends Col. George Harmanson and Thomas Cable to assist my executors. Witt: John Robins, Elias Roberts, Katharine Robins, S. Margaret Cable, Thomas Cable. Dated 11 September, 1732 - Probated 9 January, 1738.

We find that the said Frances, daughter of the said John, Sr., intermarried with Samuel Powell, late of the said County, Planter, by whom she had issue a son John, and that after the said Samuel's death she intermarried with one John Jones, planter, deceased, by whom she had two daughters and no son, one named Sarah and the other Ann Mary, and soon after died. We also find that John Powell, the son of the aforesaid Frances, at the time of the death of the said Frances was her son and heir. We find that the said John died 15 years since, or thereabouts, and that the said Sarah, one of the daughters of the said Frances, intermarried with one Thomas Spady, of the County aforesaid, planter, and that Ann Mary, the other daughter of the said Frances, intermarried with one Abraham Hall. We find that after the death of the said John Powell the said Thomas Spady and Sarah, his wife, in right of the said Sarah, and the said Abraham Hall and Ann Mary, his wife, in right of the said Ann Mary, were seized in reversion of the said 500 acres of land given by their grandfather's will to their mother aforesaid. We find that the said Thomas Spady and Sarah, his wife, by virtue of a writ of Adquod Damnum and an Inquistion thereon taken, by a deed of bargain and sale bearing date the xviii day of July, Anno Domini MDCCXLlll, for the consideration therein mentioned, sold their moiety or half of the last mentioned 500 acres of land unto the male lessor of the plaintiff and his heirs and assigns forever, and that the said Abraham Hall and Ann Mary, his wife, likewise by virtue of another writ of Ad Quod Damnum and an Inquisition thereon taken, by deed of bargain and sale bearing date the xvi day of July, Anno Domini MDCCXLlll for the consideration therein mentioned, sold their moiety or one half part of the said 500 acres of land unto the male lessor of the plaintiff--------we find that before the execution of the said two deeds of bargain and sale the said Thomas and Sarah and the said Abraham and Ann Mary and the plaintiff and his wife, Sophia, divided the said lease lands between them by consent, and that the said Thomas and Sarah and the said Abraham and Ann Mary made choice of the lower western moiety of the said 1000 acres, and that the said plaintiff and his wife chose the upper eastern moiety of the said 1000 acres &c. -----12 January, 1747 - p. 247

LAND CAUSES – 1754–1771

Goodright, Lessee of Moor,
vs. – Ejectment Proceedings.
Thomas.

Jury impaneled and returned the following verdict.

We find that John Tilney, late of the County of Northampton, deceased, grandfather of the lessor of the plaintiff, was seized in fee of 200 acres of land in Northampton County, of which the land in question is a part. That the said John Tilney by his deed in writing bearing date the xxvi day of September, MDCXCIX hereto annexed in these words (abstract) John Tiley, Sr., of Northampton, Gentleman, for and in consideration of the love and affection I bear to my son in law John Moor of the same place, and Margaret, his wife, my daughter – Gift – 100 acres of woodland ground situate, lying and being in the County aforesaid, being the full moiety or half of two hundred acres of land by me taken up between the lands at the heads of some of the branches of Nasswadox Creek and the lands of the seaboard side, and is next adjoining to the lands of Philip Jacob and John Wattes, during their natural lives, and at their decease to the heir of their bodies – Recorded 7 Oct. 1699 – gave to his son in law John Moore and Margaret, his wife, his daughter, during their natural lives, and at their death to the heirs or heirs of their bodies, male or female, as they or the survivor or survivors of them shall think fit forever, the lands in question, as by said deed will appear: That the said John Moore and Margaret are both since dead without making any will or disposition of the said land; that the same after their decease descended to and became vested in Jonathan Moor, their then eldest son and heir at law; that the said Jonathan is since dead without issue, and that the lessor of the plaintiff is his eldest brother and heir at law, both of the body of the said Margaret by the said John begotten. We also find that the said Jonathan Moor being of lawful age, entered into the lands and premises in the declaration mentioned, and became thereof seized, and being so thereof seized by his indenture bearing date to 10 February, in the year of our Lord 1731, conveyed to George Thomas the land and premises herein mentioned--------11 September, 1753 – p. 1

58

Goodright, Lessee of Parker,
vs. - Ejectment Proceedings.
Johnson.

Jury impaneled and returned the following verdict:

That Jacob Dewey, late of the County of Northampton, deceased, was in his lifetime seized in fee of a certain tract of land lying and being in Occohannock Neck, in the County aforesaid, containing 100 acres (which is the land in question); that the said Jacob Dewey by his testament and last will in writing, bearing date the 26 September, 1732, among other things therein contained, devised as follows, to-wit: "Item: I give unto my loving wife, Matilda, the plantation whereon I now dwell, with all the houses, orchards, lands and tenements I am possessed of, during her natural life, to act and do as she thinks proper during her life aforesaid, and after my wife's death then I give the above mentioned lands and tenements to my daughter Tabitha Parker during her natural life, and after her death I give and bequeath all my lands, houses, orchards and tenements unto my grandson Jacob Dewey Parker, and the heirs of his body lawfully begotten, and for want of such heirs then I give the said land to my daughter Tabitha's heirs of her body, but if my said daughter Tabitha should have no heirs of her body, then the said land to go to my daughter Beautifila and her heirs" as by the said will (reference being thereto had) duly acknowledged and recorded among the records of the said County Court of Northampton may more fully and at large appear.

That Matilda, the testator's widow, refused to accept of the estate so as aforesaid devised to her, and that Philip Parker, in right of his wife, the said Tabitha, entered into the said lands and tenements and was thereof seized as tenant for his said wife's life; That Jacob Dewey Parker, the testator's grandson, died in the lifetime of his mother, the said Tabitha, and without any issue of his body; That Philip Parker, the said Tabitha's husband, died also and that she afterwards intermarried with a certain Richard Johnson, who in right of his said wife sued out of the Secretary's Office of this Colony a writ in the nature of an ad quod damnum in order to dock the entail of the said land. That the entail thereof was dock't pursuant to the Act of Assembly, and by a deed of bargain and sale made by the said Richard and Tabitha they conveyed the said land to a certain Benjamin Dingly Gray, by deed duly recorded in the General Court, bearing date 18 October, 1750, hereto annexed, which deed is as follows: This indenture made this 18 day of October, 1750, between Richard Johnson and Tabitha Johnson, his wife, of the County of Northampton, in the Colony of Virginia, of the one part, and Benjamin Dingly Gray of the other part, in the County and Colony aforesaid, planter: that whereas the said Richard Johnson and Tabitha, his wife, stand seized in right of the said Tabitha Johnson of 185 acres of land with the appurtenances, in the County of Northampton, on Occohannock Creek, in fee tail general, and whereas by a writ of ad quod damnum and Inquisition thereon had, dated 2 July, in the 24th year of the reign of our Sovereign Lord, King George the second, before Edward Holbrooke, Deputy Sheriff of the County of Northampton the day and year aforesaid, the said land aforesaid was found to be a separate parcel and not contiguous to

other entailed lands in the seized and possession of the said Richard
Johnson and Tabitha, his wife, and that the said lands are of the value
of 136 L 10 shillings and no more &c.-------that no valuable consideration was by the said Benjamin Dingly Gray bonafide paid to the
said Richard and Tabitha either before, at the time of making over the
said lands, or since; this appears by the oath of Benjamin Dingly
Gray--------that the said Benjamin Dingly Gray afterwards by a deed
of bargain and sale, bearing date the 14 day of May, 1751, duly recorded and hereto annexed, reconveyed the said land to the said Richard
Johnson, father to the defendant, in fee. We further find that Joshua
Johnson, the defendant, is heir at law to Richard Johnson; we further
find that sometime after the said Tabitha died, leaving issue of her
body by her former husband, Caleb Parker, who is also since dead
leaving issue of his body lawfully begotten, Thomas Hall Parker, the
lessor of the plaintiff--------12 Aug. 1755 - p. 8

Thrustout, Lessee of Savage,
vs. - Trespass and Ejectment Proceedings.
Holdfast.
    Thomas Holdfast was attached unto John Thrustout of a plea where-
of with force and arms one dwelling house and one hundred acres of
land, with the appurtenances, in the Parish of Hungars, in the County
aforesaid, which Nathaniel Savage, Infant, under the age of 21 years by
Esther Savage, of the Parish and County aforesaid, his next friend, to
the said John Thrustout had demised for a term which is not yet past,
hath entered and him from his farm aforesaid hath ejected, and other
harms to him hath done, to the great damage of the said John, and
against the peace, &c.--------13 January, 1756 - p. 20

Thrustout, Lessee of Kendall &c.,
vs. - Trespass.
Justice and others.
    Jury impaneled and returned the following verdict:
    We agree that William Andrews, deceased, in his lifetime, being
seized in fee of 1000 acres of land, granted to Philip Taylor by letters
patent, bearing date the 19 December, 1643, did make and in due form
of law execute a deed poll in the following words, to-wit: To all
Christian people unto whom this present writing shall come, &c. I
William Andrews, of Northampton in Virginia, Gentleman, for divers
good causes me hereunto moving------do by these presents demise,
lett, lease and to farm let, unto Thomas Harmanson, Sr., of the same
place, one parcel or quantity of land containing 1000 acres, it being
situate on the seaboard side, adjoining northerly on the Indian Town
named Gingaskin, and Southerly on the land of Col. Obedience Robins,
deceased, which said 1000 acres was lately in the possession of
Thomas Taylor, son and heir to Capt. Philip Taylor, also
deceased--------for and during the natural lives of Thomas Harmanson, Sr., and Joane, his wife, the said Thomas and Joane paying
yearly at the feast of the Blessed Nativity of our Lord and Saviour

Christ, one good ear of sound Indian corn, or within ten days after the said Feast upon lawful demand to pay the same, as also the King's Rent,&c.--------and after the deccease of the said Thomas Harmanson and Joane, his wife, I, the said William Andrews, do grant and confirm the said 1000 acres of land as follows, that is to say: I freely give, grant, enfeoff and confirm unto Thomas Harmanson, Jr., 300 acres of the said land whereon the dwelling house of Thomas Harmanson, Sr., is situate, running directly southeasterly to the full extent of the said 300 acres--------to William Harmanson, second son unto the said Thomas Harmanson, Sr., 250 acres of the said land--------unto John Harmanson 250 acres --------to Henry Harmanson, the fourth son of Thomas Harmanson, Sr., 200 acres of land, being part of the said 1000 acres, and in case the said Thomas Harmanson, Sr., and Joane, his wife, shall die before the said Thomas Harmanson, Jr., William, John, and Henry Harmanson shall arrive to full age according to law, or any of them, then it shall and may be lawful at the age of 20 years for him, the said Thomas Harmanson, Jr., William, John and Henry Harmanson to enter in and upon their several parts and parcels of land according to this deed of fooffment, as they shall arrive to their said full age of one and twenty years, provided that the said Thomas Harmanson, Jr., William Harmanson, John Harmanson and Henry Harmanson, before livery of seizen and entry into the said parcels of land so enfeoffed by me, the said William Andrews, Gentleman, that they shall subscribe and seal such bond as shall be presented unto them severally and respectively, to all intents and purposes, as also shall be therein mentioned and inserted, and in case either of them refuse so to do, then their part or parts shall remain and devolve to me, the said William Andrews, Donor, to no other end and purpose but to be disposed of unto such of those bretheren as shall willingly subscribe and seal the same--------in case any of the said bretheren shall decease in their minority, before they attain to their said lawful age, then the decedent's part to be equally divided between the survivors, and in case all the said bretheren, Thomas, William, John and Henry Harmanson die without issue of their bodies lawfully begotten, then all the said land I do by these presents freely give, grant, enfeoff and confirm to my loving niece, Susan Harmanson, to her and her heirs forever - Given under my hand and seal this 31 January, 1664.   (signed) William Andrews (L.S.)

That the 1000 acres of land in the said deed poll mentioned in the same granted to the said Philip Taylor by the patent before mentioned. That Thomas Harmanson, the father in the said deed poll mentioned, sometime after the execution of the said deed, entered into the said 1000 acres of land and was thereof seized, and being so thereof seized obtained letters patent bearing date the 17 April, 1667, or 800 acres of land as surplus land within the bounds of the said Patent for 1000 acres; to hold to him, his heirs and assigns forever as by the last mentioned letters patent more at large may appear; that in the life of the said Thomas Harmanson, the father, a division was made of the said 1000 acres of land among his four sons, to-wit: Thomas, William, John and Henry Harmanson, according to the respective rights and interests which they claimed under the aforesaid deed poll from

the aforesaid William Andrews, which said division has been acqui-
esced to ever since. That the said Thomas Harmanson, the father,
being seized of the said 1000 acres and 800 acres, made his last will
and testament, bearing date the 26 March, 1696, and thereby, among
other things, devised as followeth: "Item: I do confirm unto my four
eldest sons afore named, Thomas, William, John and Henry Harmanson, the several dividents of land by me given them and their heirs
forever, as the same was divided by Mr. Daniel Eyre, which they have
passed bonds to each other, to be content according to the penalties
and according to the conditions they inherited-------Item: I give,
devise and bequeath unto my four oldest sons afore herein named, viz:
Thomas, William, John and Henry Harmanson, and their heirs, forever, all the remaining part of my divident which lieth at the head of the
land given them, and was not divided with the rest by Mr. Daniel Eyre,
to contain their several divisional lines as they now run, to the head
line of my divident, and was since so divided by Mr. William
Waters--------"

That the premises mentioned in the last devise are the 800 acres of
land granted to the said Thomas Harmanson, the father, by the letters
patent hereinbefore mentioned. That after the death of the said
Thomas Harmanson, the father, Thomas Harmanson, the son, entered
into 300 acres, parcel of the said 1000 acres allotted to him by the
division hereinbefore mentioned, and also the into 358 acres of land,
parcel of the said 800 acres adjoining to it, and contiguous to the said
300 acres before mentioned, and was thereof seized; that Thomas
Harmason, the son, had issue William, Katharine, Esther, Elishe and
Elizabeth, and that William, son of Thomas Harmanson, Sr., the
donee of Andrews, arrived to the age of 21 years and upwards and had
issue a son and died seized of his divident to him allotted by the will
of his father, or by the deed from Andrews aforesaid; soon after his
death his son also died seized of the said last mentioned divident of
land under age, intestate and without issue. That after the death of
the issue of William Harmanson, the elder, without issue, Thomas
Harmanson, son to Thomas Harmanson, Sr., entered into the divident
of the issue of the last named William Harmanson as heir at law to
the said issue, amounting to 250 acres of land, parcel of the said 1000
acres before mentioned, and died so thereof seized, after whose death
his son, William hereinbefore mentioned entered into the said 300
acres, parcel of the said 1000 acres, and into the said 250 acres,
parcel of the said 1000 acres, and also into the said 358 acres, parcel
of the said 800 acres herein before mentioned, and was thereof seized
as the law requires, 1/4 part of which said 908 acres of land are the
tenements in question--------that the last named William Harmanson being so seized and possessed of the said 908 acres aforementioned, by his last will in writing, bearing date the 28 March, 1733,
devised to his sisters, Katharine, Esther and Elishe, all the said tract
of 300 acres and 250 acres of land parcel of the aforesaid 1000 acres,
and the 358 acres, parcel of the said 800 acres of land, to them and
their heirs forever. That soon after the making of the said will the
said last named William Harmanson died seized of the said 908 acres
without issue. That John Kendall, lessor of the plaintiff, intermarried

with the aforesaid Elizabeth Harmanson, one of the sisters of the said last named William Harmanson, who is yet in full life. We also find that Thomas Respess intermarried with Esther, one of the devisees of the latter William Harmanson, by whom he has issue now alive, and that George Kendall intermarried with Elishe, since dead, and the said Elishe is now discovert, and that Catharine intermarried with Ralph Justice, who have conveyed to the said defendant Justice, and that the said Elishe Kendall is the same Elishe in the last named William Harmanson's will mentioned -------- 13 December, 1757 - p. 28

Kendall, et ux,
vs. - Suit for division of land.
Justice and others.

That on the 9 May, 1758, came John Kendall and Elizabeth, his wife, by James Henry, their Attorney, and brought into the Court their certain bill against William Justice, Thomas Respess, Patrick Harmanson and Elishe, his wife, and John Burton, infant, of a plea which bill followeth in these words, to-wit:

Northampton, S.S: William Justice, Thomas Respess, Patrick Harmanson and Elishe, his wife and John Burton, were summoned to answer unto John Kendall and Elizabeth, his wife, of a plea wherefore, that whereas the said John Kendall and Elizabeth, his wife, in right of the said Elizabeth, William Justice, Thomas Respess, in right of Esther, late his wife, deceased, Patrick Harmanson and Elishe, his wife in right of the said Esther, and John Burton, together and undivided do hold 908 acres of land with the appurtenances in the County aforesaid, and the said William Justice, Thomas Respess, Patrick Harmanson and Elishe, his wife, and John Burton among them according to the form of the statute in such case be made, very unjustly will not permit, according to the form of the statute aforesaid, partition to be made, &c.--------and whereupon the said John and Elizabeth, by James Henry, their Attorney, say that whereas the said John Kendall and Elizabeth, in right of the said Elizabeth, William Justice, Thomas Respess, in right of Esther, late his wife, deceased, Patrick Harmanson and Elishe, his wife, in right of the said Elishe, and John Burton together and undivided do hold to them and to their heirs the aforesaid tract or parcel of land and tenements, with the appurtenances, one part (1/4) of 606 acres whereof belong to the said John Kendall and Elizabeth, in right of the said Elizabeth, and the heirs of the body of the said Elizabeth; 300 acres belong to the said Thomas Respess and the heirs of Esther, late his wife, to Patrick Harmanson & Elishe, in right of the said Elishe, and to the heirs of her body do belong 1/3 part of the residue; to the said William Justice doth belong one other one third of the residue, and to the heirs of the body of Catherine, the wife of Ralph Justice, and the residue of the premises doth belong to John Burton and to his heirs, or to the heirs of his body to be held by them in severalty, so that the said John Kendall and Elizabeth of their fourth part aforesaid do take of the premises aforesaid coming separately themselves may appear, nevertheless the said

William Justice, Thomas Respess, Patrick Harmanson and Elishe, his wife, and John Burton, do make partition thereof between them according to the form of the statute in such cases made and provided, do gainsay and the same unjustly will not permit to be done in accordance with the form of the statute aforesaid, whereupon they say they are damaged twenty pounds and thereof they bring suit &c. 9 May, 1758 - p. 36

Warren &c.
vs. - Trespass and Ejectment.
Warren &c.

Came William Thrustout, by Mitchel Scarburgh, his Attorney, and brought into the Court of our said Lord the King, his certain bill against Henry Warren and Esau Jacob, of a plea of trespass and ejectment, which bill followeth in these words, to-wit:

Northampton County, to-wit: William Thrustout complains of Henry Warren & Esau Jacob, in custody, &c., that whereas Elizabeth Warren the first day of August in the year of our Lord 1758, in the Parish of Hungars, and County aforesaid, had demised, granted and to farm let to the said William, one plantation and tenement and 200 acres of land, lying and being in the Parish and county aforesaid--------to have and to hold from the said 1st day of August, now last past, unto the full end and term of seven years from thence next following fully to be complete and ended, by virtue of which demise the said William into the tenement aforesaid, with the appurtenances, entered and was thereof seized until the aforesaid Henry and Esau afterwards, to-wit: the second day of August, in the year aforesaid, with firce and arms into the tenement aforesaid, with the appurtenances, in and upon the possession of him, the said William Thrustout, entered, and the said Thrustout from his farm aforesaid, his term aforesaid not then nor yet ended, ejected, expelled and amoved the said William &c. -------- 10 Oct. 1758 - p. 41

Thrustout & Gibson, &c.,
vs. - Trespass and Ejectment.
Preeson.

Jury impaneled and returned the following verdict:

We find that Elizabeth, the wife of Thomas Preeson, late of Northampton County, deceased, was seized in fee of the tenement in which the trespass in the declaration mentioned is supposed to be committed, and being so thereof seized the said Thomas Preeson and Elizabeth, his wife, by their deed bearing date the xxviii day of August, in the year of our Lord 1706, granted, made over, conveyed and delivered unto a certian Zerobabel Preeson and his heirs, the tenement in which the said trespass is supposed to be committed, which deed we find in these words: (abstract) We, Thomas Preeson and Elizabeth Preeson, lawful wife of the said Thomas Preeson, for divers causes and considerations us thereunto moveing, but more especially for the natural love and affection we bear to our well beloved son, Zerobabel Preeson, do give, grant and convey unto the said Zerobabel Preeson, his heirs and assigns, forever, that tract or parcel of land whereon our father, Thomas Brown, formerly lived, and by his last will gave the same to me, Elizabeth Preeson, containing, by estimation, 600 acres--------that the said deed was duly acknowledged by John Custis, Esq., by virtue of a letter of attorney from the said Thomas & Elizabeth--------that the said Zerubabel Preeson, by permission of his parents, the said Thomas and Elizabeth, entered into the said lands and appurtenances, and was thereof possessed until his death, and his widow after him, during the whole lifetime of the said Thomas and Elizabeth; that the said Elizabeth survived the said Thomas, her husband, who died on the 5 day of April, 1723, and the said Elizabeth on the 1st day of April, 1733; That the said Zerobabel, grantee in the said deed, was heir at law to the said Elizabeth and died in the lifetime of his said mother, the aforesaid Elizabeth, leaving issue Thomas Preeson his only son and heir at law, and that the said Elizabeth by her last will and testament, bearing date the 8 September, 1732, devised the said lands and appurtenances to the said Thomas Preeson, her grandson and heir at law as aforesaid in manner following, to-wit: (Abstract of will) dated 8 September, 1732 - Probated 12 June, 1733 - I give and bequeath to my grandson, Thomas Preeson, my plantation whereon his mother now lives, containing 600 acres, to him and his heirs lawfully begotten, provided my said grandson when he attains to age shall convey or make over 600 acres of land that my late husband, Thomas Preeson, sold to Hill Drummond to them that the said Hill Drummond gave it, and if he refuse I give the aforesaid plantation to my son Brown Preeson and his heirs, and the said Brown to pay the bond his father gave. To my grandson John Gibson two negroes that I bought of Thomas Blair in Accomack, and one negro man more called Jacko, provided his mother pays Matthew Harmanson the sum of 16 L 19 shillings and 2 pence by the first of May next, and if not the said negro to be sold to pay the money. I leave my daughter Hannah under the care of my daughter Susanna, and I leave one negro girl named Kesiah to my daughter Hannah, only Susanna to have the use of her, and if she survive the said Hannah to have the said negro forever. To daughter Susanna Preeson personalty and one half the fourth part of the cattle here and at Assawoman. To son Brown Preeson the 1/8 part of all the cattle here and at Assawoman, and the 1/4 part of all the hogs, sheep &c. Son and daughter Brown and Susanna Executors - Friends Jonathan Stott and Matt: Harmanson overseers. Witt: Matt: Harmanson, Jane Hill, Sarah Gibbons - In order of probate: Presented by Brown Preeson, her Executor, and Susanna Preeson, (now Susanna Bowdoin by her intermarriage with Peter Bowdoin) Executrix, and the said Brown made oath thereto and the said Susanna her solemn affirmation (she being a Quaker) &c.

After that the said grandson entered into the lands and tenements aforesaid, after the death of the said Elizabeth, and was thereof seized. That the said Thomas, the grandson, by his deed duly recorded, bearing date 2 June, 1736, conveyed in fee simple to the heirs of Hill Drummond the 600 acres of land in the said Elizabeth's, the grandmother's, will mentioned according to the purport of the said grandmother's will, which deed is in these words following, to-wit: (abstract) This indenture made the 2 day of June, Anno Domini 1736, between Thomas Preeson, of the County of Northampton, Gentlemen, grandson and heir at law to Thomas Preeson, late of the County aforesaid, deceased, to Thomas Stayton, who intermarried with Elizabeth, the second daughter of Hill Drummond, late of Accomack County, deceased, witnesseth: That whereas the said Hill Drummond in his lifetime did pay to the said Thomas Preeson, the elder, the quantity of 10,000 L of tobacco in consideration that the said Thomas would afterwards convey to the said Hill, his heirs and assigns, a certain 600 acres of land called Wests Ridge, formerly conveyed to the said Thomas, the elder, by the three sons of Col. John West, and the said Preeson dying before he conveyed the said land to the said Hill Drummond; and whereas the said Hill Drummond afterwards by his last will and testament did appoint the same to be conveyed to his three eldest daughters, Barbary, Elizabeth and Tabitha by the heir of the said Thomas the elder, and whereas Daniel Welburn and the said Barbara, daughter of the aforesaid Hill and George Douglas and the said Tabitha, another daughter of the said Hill Drummond, have by their deeds duly executed, conveyed to the said Thomas Stayton, who intermarried with the said Elizabeth, the other daughter of the said Hill Drummond, all their interest in the premises, now this indenture witnesseth: That the said Thomas Preeson, the younger, heir at law of the said Thomas Preeson the elder, conveys to the said Thomas Stayton the said 600 acres called Wests Ridge &c. We also find that the aforesaid Thomas Preeson, the grandfather, and the said Elizabeth, his wife, had issue also besides the aforesaid Zerobabel two daughters, Sarah and Susanna; Sarah intermarried with a certain James Gibson, who had issue John Gibson, one of the lessors of the plaintiff, her eldest son and heir at law; Susanna intermarried with a certain Peter Bowdoin, and had issue the said Preeson Bowdoin, the other lessor of the plaintiff, her eldest son and heir at law, and that the said lessors of the plaintiff are now the only surviving heirs in reversion of Elizabeth Preeson, the grandmother. That Thomas Preeson, the grandson, was seized and possessed of the tenement in which the trespass aforesaid is supposed to be committed, during his life, and by his last will and testament duly proved and recorded in Northampton County Court, bearing date 8 April, Anno Domini MDCCLVl, devised the said lands and appurtenances to the defendant, his wife, in fee simple, and after having so made and duly published his said will afterwards, to-wit: the 20 day of November, Anno Domini MDCCLVlll died of the premises seized without issue, which will we find in these words following: (abstract) Dated 8 April, MDCCLVl - Probated 9 January 1759 - I give and bequeath to my wife Esther, provided she have a child born which shall be living at the time of my decease, or the said Esther be then encient, the plantation and lands whereon I now live, lying and being in Nasswadox Creek in the County of Northampton, for and during the term of her natural life in full satisfaction of her dower or thirds of all my lands, and after her decease to such child and the heirs of such child, and in case I have no child, or said child should die under the age of 21 and without issue, I give the said lands and plantation to my said wife and her heirs forever. Whereas I have conveyed to me by the Church Wardens of the Parish of Hungars, in the said County of Northampton, by the consent and direction of the Vestry (on consideration of my having conveyed to the said Church Wardens and their successors for the use of the said Parish forever one acre of land whereon the new church now stands, upon Hungars Creek, in the said County) one pew in the said church marked TP 1751, and to my heirs and assigns forever, I give and devise to my said wife Esther one moiety of the said pew, and to her heirs and assigns forever, and if any such child shall be born and living at my decease, or my wife be then encient, and when such child shall be born, I give to such child when born and until it arriveth to the age of 21 years, the moiety of the said pew if it so long live, and when it arriveth to the age of 21 years then to such child and the heirs and assigns of such child forever, and if no such child be born then to my said wife and her heirs. Should such child be born and my wife should die in the lifetime of such child before it shall arrive to the age of 21 years and unmarried and without issue, and such child should afterwards die under age and unmarried without issue, then I give and devise all the estate, both real and personal herein given by me to such child, unto Peggy Custis, daughter of Col John Custis, of the County of Northampton, late deceased, and Ann, his wife. Wife Executrix. Witt: Elias Dunton, Sr., Jonathan Teague, Thomas Dolby, William Haggoman, Daniel Dunton, Isaac Dunton, John Matthews-------- 13 Feb. 1759 - p. 43

Savage,
vs. - Suit for Division.
Costin, et al.
    Came Nathaniel Savage by James Henry, his attorney, and brought into the Court here his certain bill against Margaret Costin, Lucretia Respess and Esther Respess, of a plea &c. which bill followeth in these words, to-wit: Northampton SS: Margaret Costin, Lucretia Respess and Esther Respess were summoned to answer unto Nathaniel Savage of a plea for that whereas the said Margaret, Lucretia and Esther together and undivided do hold with the said Nathaniel one hundred acres of land, with the appurtenances, situate in the County aforesaid, and called and known by the name of Harman's Field-------- 1/3 part whereof belongs to the said Nathaniel and to his heirs, one other third part thereof also belongs to the said Nathaniel and to the heirs of his body, and the other one third part thereof doth belong one moiety thereof to the said Nathaniel and his heirs, or to the heirs of his body, and the other moiety of the said last third part doth belong to the said Margaret Costin, Lucretia Respess and Esther Respess, and to the heirs of their bodies -------- 10 April, 1759 - p. 57

Seekright & Warren,
vs. - Trespass and Ejectment.
Warren.

Jury impaneled and returned the following verdict:

We find that Richard Patrick being seized in fee simple of the lands and premises in question by his last will and testament in writing, bearing date the 16 day of February, in the year 1674/5, devised the same to his daughter Agnes in these words (abstract - Probated 3 Mar. 1675) - I bequeath to my children my whole estate as follows: Children Richard, Elizabeth, Ursly and Anges Patrick to live together at the now dwelling house upon my Homeset Plantation to the age of 16 years or marriage, then to enjoy their estates as hereafter mentioned. I will that if my daughter Anges' Godfather is pleased to take her he may have her. To son Richard Patrick the Homeset Plantation beginning at the mouth of Governor Hawlie's Creek. To daughter Elizabeth and her heirs the parcel of land lying on the North side of the line of marked trees beginning at the marsh to the outward line of trees that parts my brother Joseph Godwin and me, and so westerly to the head of the Branch before mentioned. To daughter Ursly that parcel of land from the first branch to the second that runs northerly the full breadth of all my land. To daughter Agnes all that parcel of land that begins upon the Branch at the head of my daughter Ursly's, to the full extent of all my divident. To daughter Elizabeth her mother's wedding ring and a round painted box that was her mother's. To daughter Ursly a silver buckle that was her mother's. To daughter Agnes her mother's silver bodkin. To son Richard and three daughters personal property, cattle, &c. Son Richard Executor; friends Thomas Teackle and Richard Nottingham, Jr., overseers. Witt: John Kendall, Hendrick Abel, John Burroughs. Codicil: Whereas I have ordained that my childred should all live together at my now dwelling house upon my Homeset Plantation, havng since considered over it and find several inconveniencies which may happen by it, I have thought fit and do by these presents will and ordain that my eldest daughter, Elizabeth who is (in April the 20th day) next ensueing the date hereof 13 years of age, shall remain with her uncle Joseph Godwin till she comes to the age of 16 years or be married, and then to have her share of the goods and chattels I have given her. Daughter Ursly to remain with her Godmother, Elizabeth Harman until she comes to the age of 16 or marries, then to have her share of the goods and chattels given her. Ursly was 11 years old on the 28 February last past. Daughter Agnes, who was on the 28 of February last past, 9 years old to remain with her Godfather, Mr. John Teackle until she comes to the age of 16 or marries, then to have her share of the goods and chattels given her. Son Richard Executor. 13 Mar. 1674/5 - Witt: Hendrick Abel, William Abbott, John Burroughs.

That the said Richard Patrick died so seized leaving issue Richard, Ursly, Elizabeth and Agnes Patrick, his children named in the said will. That after the death of the testator the said Agnes entered into the said lands and premises and died seized thereof, having attained the age of 21 years, and that she left issue at her death Timothy Steer (?) her only child and heir, who attained his age of 21 years and died seized of the said land intestate and without issue. We find that Richard Patrick, the son, died in the lifetime of the said Timothy Steer and without issue.

We find that the said Ursly and Elizabeth survived the said Timothy and Richard; that the said Ursly died in the lifetime of the said Elizabeth leaving issue Henry Warren, her eldest son and heir at law with other children. That the said Elizabeth also died leaving issue Richard Warren her eldest son and John Warren her second son, brother of the whole blood to the said Richard Warren. That after the death of the said Timothy and Elizabeth the said Richard Warren entered into the lands and promised aforesaid and died seized thereof, leaving issue Jacob Warren, his only child and heir at law. That the said Jacob soon after departed this life under age and without issue, and after his death the said John Warren, his uncle and heir at law, entered into the said lands and premises and died seized thereof, leaving issue Moses Warren, his oldest son and heir at law, who entered into the same and by his certain indenture dated 10 July, 1738, conveyed the said lands and premises, among other things, to the said Henry Warren in fee simple (Bridget Warren wife of Moses). That the said Henry Warren died seized thereof without issue sometime in the year 1740, and that the lessor of the plaintiff is his eldest brother of the whole blood and heir at law. We find that the said Henry Warren before the said conveyance made his last will and testament in writing, dated the 29 December, 1732, to which we refer. We find that the defendant is the daughter and heir of the said Moses Warren who is deceased.-------- 10 July, 1759 - p. 61

Thrustout & Warren,
vs. Ejectment.
Warren.
  William Thrustout complains of John Warren in custody.
  Jury impaneled and returned the following special verdict:
  We find that a certain Robert Warren had granted him by patent dated in the year 1657, which is hereto annexed, 150 acres of land in the County of Northampton, bounding easterly on the Seaboard side, northerly upon John Wilkins' land, Southerly on John ____ and Westerly into the woods, and by his will duly executed and dated the 12 day of November, 1673, devised the same to his children in these words: (abstract) I bequeath all my estate as well personal as real, after my debts are paid, unto my four children, my wife having as good an interest as either of them until she marry. Children to live together in unity and peace and make use of what estate I have given them, but to have no power to divide or imbezell their estate. Friends Lt. Col. William Waters & Mr. Francis Pigot, that they be pleased, to have a care of my wife and children. Son James?(John-S.N.) Executor. Probated 27 March, 1679. Witt: John Willott, ____ Adolfe.
  That the said Robert Warren at the time of his death left two or three children among whom was one Henry. That the said Henry Warren after the death of his father entered upon 50 acres of the said land which is the lands in the declaration mentioned, and was thereof

seized in severalty, and died years afterwards leaving issue Joseph Warren, his eldest son and heir at law, with several other children. That the said Joseph, son of the said Henry, entered upon the said 50 acres of land with the appurtenances after the death of his father, and was thereof seized, and by his will, bearing date the 8 day of November, MDCCXX111, devised the same unto his son Hillary Warren, who was also his eldest son and heir at law, in fee simple, which will is in these words: (abstract) To son Hillary Warren all my plantation whereon I now live containing 50 acres, more or less: To son Hillary Warren my little gun, my riding mare, saddle and bridle, pistols and holsters - Personality. To son Joseph Warren my musket - Personality. To daughter Susanna Warren personalty. Personality to be divided between my three children Hillary, Joseph and Susanna Warren. John Coffin to take care of my children and their estates until they come to age to receive the same. Sons to be at age at 18 and daughter to have her part at the time of her going off from the plantation. John Coffin to live with my children until my son Hillary comes to the age of 18, he, the said Coffin, to give each of my sons a years schooling and to be schooled the 17th year of their age, the eldest being 14 and the youngest being 12 years of age. Robert Warren and William Ware to be overseers of this my will. Son Hillary Executor. Witt: Chas: Guilding, Robert Warren, William Ware - Probated 12 February, 1725/4 -

That the said Joseph soon afterwards died possessed of the said land. That the said Hillary at the time of his father's death was only 14 years of age, and that John Coffin, guardian of the said Hillary after the said Joseph Warren's death, entered upon the said lands in question and was thereof possessed for some small time, but that long before the said Hillary came to the age of 21 years the said Coffin left the premises vacant, and a certain James Warren, father to the defendant, entered upon the premises and was thereof seized about the year 1729. That the said Hillary Warren died about the year 1737, leaving issue the lessor of the plaintiff, his eldest son and heir at law, then under the age of one year. That the said James Warren is since dead and the defendant is his eldest son and heir at law. We find that John Warren, the defendant, is son and heir of James Warren, and that he and they under them he claims title hath been in possession of the land in question--------13 May, 1760 - p. 78 et seq

Henry Pettitt, an infant under the age of 21 years, by Sarah Pettitt, his
    next friend,

vs. -
John Pettitt.

That a certain John Pettitt, of the County of Northampton, being seized in fee of land on one side of a run or gut of water in the aforesaid County, convenient for building a water grist mill, was applied unto by a certain Jonathan, being father of the complainant and brother of the said John, to know whether he would build a mill on that property and allow the said Jonathan to build with him in partnership, but the said John declined, -------- but told the said Jonathan that if he inclined to build alone he had his leave to proceed in his name to get an acre condemned on the opposite side of the stream of water according to law, &c.--------that the said Jonathan built the said mill about the year 1756-------- that the said Jonathan, your orator's father afterwards, in the year of our Lord MDCCLX was suddenly and by misfortune drowned--------leaving your orator his only son and heir at law an infant of very tender years--------

Thomas Dolby - Deposition - Age 42 - Taken 5 Feb. 1763.

Laban Stott -	"	"	42	" " "
Reubin Dennis -	"	"	22	" " "
George Bell -	"	"	72	" " "
John Brickhouse -	"	"	40	" " "
Solomon Scott -	"	"	26	" " "
William Pettitt -	"	"	33	" " "
Thomas Downs -	"	"	67	" " "
Edward Belote -	"	"	35	" " "
Peter Pettitt -	"	"	32	" " "

11 May, 1762 - p. 86 et seq.

Major Wilkins,
vs. - Ejectment.
John Wilkins, Sr., and Judith, his wife.

That a certain Stockly Wilkins, the complainant's father, being seized in fee tail of a certain tract of land in the said County, containing, by estimation, 117 acres, was several times applied to by the defendant, John Wilkins, for the purchase of the said lands. After sundry solicitations and several offers made by the said defendant, the said Stockly Wilkins agreed to and with the defendant, for and in consideration of the sum of 60 L to convey the said lands in fee simple unto the said defendant, after reserving to himself, the said Stockly Wilkins, his own life and that of his wife, and the complainants life, and that the said defendant, John, agreed with the said Stockly Wilkins -------- that on the 14th April, 1752, the said Stockly Wilkins made and executed a certain deed for the conveyance of the said lands agreeable to the express terms of the said contract, as the said Stockly Wilkins imagined, but inasmuch as the said Stockly Wilkins was illiterate, and one who could neither read nor write, the said defendant fraudulently got a deed executed by him, for the absolute conveyance of the said lands--------that soon after the death of the said Stockly Wilkins the said defendant took possession of the said lands, and would not suffer the complainant's mother to enjoy any part of the same save what she claimed by right of dower--------

Deposition of Edward Robins - Age 48 - Taken ____1765.

"	" Thomas Speakman-	"	46 -	"	"
"	" Custis Kendall-	"	57 -	"	"
"	" William Wilkins-	"	29 -	"	"
"	" William Holland	"	45 -	"	"
"	" John Floyd	"	40 -	"	"

14 June, 1763 - p. 95 et seq.

George Jourdan & Susanna, his wife,
bs. - Suit for Dower.
Elizabeth Caul.

That the said Elizabeth and the said George and Susanna, in right of
the said Susanna, together and undivided do hold one plantation,
messuage and 84 acres of land, with the appurtenances, in Northampton County, and the said Elizabeth, partition between them according
to the form of the statute in such case made and provided gainsays,
and the same she unjustly will not permit &c. -------- that the said
Elizabeth and George Jourdan and Susanna, his wife, in right of the
said Susanna, together and undivided hold to them and their heirs
-------- one plantation, messuage and 84 acres, with the appurtenances in the County of Northampton, coheirs, and daughters of a
certain Daniel Caul &c. -------- 8 October, 1765 - p. 106 et seq.

John Parsons,
vs. - In Chancery.
Bishop and others.

John Parsons complains that a certain Littleton Smith of the
County aforesaid, being seized in his demesne, as of fee, of and in a
certain tract of land situate, lying and being in the said County of
Northampton, containing, by estimation, 80 acres, for the consideration of 66 L 2 shillings and 11 pence, bargained and sold the premises
unto your orator and his heirs, with a clause, nevertheless, of redemp-
tion upon the repayment of the said sum, with lawful interest from
date, on or before the 30 March then next ensueing, which the said
Littleton had borrowed of your orator before that time (deed dated 14
August, 1764)-------- that the said Littleton failed to pay the princi-
pal and interest; that the said Littleton is since dead intestate, to-wit:
about the month of May, Anno Domini MDCCLXV, and the said Grace,
wife of the respondent, John Bishop, one of the sisters and coheirs of
the said Littleton, and the said George Green, an infant under the age
of 21 years, son and heir of Thomas Green and Sarah, his wife, who
was the other sister and coheir of the said Littleton, who departed this
life before her brother, Littleton Smith, are the heirs at law of the said
Littleton-------- 12 Nov. 1765 - p. 112, et seq.

James Trititle,
vs. - Trespass.
Archibald Godwin.

Jury impaneled and returned the following cerdict:

That Richard Patrick, the elder, being seized in fee simple of the
premises and sundry other lands in the said County of Northampton, in
the year of our Lord 1674/5 devised the lands and appurtenances in
question unto his son, Richard Patrick, who was also his heir at law,
in these words: "I do will and bequeath to my son Richard Patrick, to
him and his heirs lawfully begotten, to them forever, the homeset
plantation, with all the Housing, fencing, orchards, with all privileges

72

whatsoever belonging to the said plantation, beginning at the mouth of Governor Hawley's Creek, and extending along the said Creek to the first little branch that runs northerly into the woods &c."

That the said Richard, the son and devisee aforesaid, by virtue of that devise, entered upon the premises aforesaid to him devised, and was thereof seized as the law requires--------that the said Richard afterwards, to-wit: on the ___ in the year 1683, by his deed which we find in these words, Know all men &c. (see the preceeding book p. 113) granted the same unto John Warren and Elizabeth, his wife, who was the said Richard's sister, with the appurtenances--------that the said Richard afterwards died intestate and without issue, leaving the said Elizabeth Warren and Ursula Patrick, who intermarried with Argol Warren, his sisters of the whole blood and coheirs; that the said John Warren, husband of the said Elizabeth, and the said Argol, husband of the said Ursula, entered upon the premises after the death of the said Richard in right of their wives, and continued possessed thereof during their lives, having made a division between them of the premises; that Elizabeth Warren died before her husband, leaving issue by the said John Warren, Richard Warren, her eldest son and heir at law lawfully begotten, who died before his father leaving issue Jacob Warren, his eldest son and heir at law; that the said Jacob, after the death of the said John, his grandfather, in the year MDCCXXV, entered into one moiety of the said lands devised to Richard Patrick, the younger, which is the lands now in question, as heir to his grandmother, Elizabeth Warren, and was thereof seized as the law requires, and in a short time died intestate and without issue. We find that John Warren, the elder, who intermarried with Elizabeth Patrick by his will dated in the year 1725, devised the lands in question to his younger son Henry, which will we find in these words, viz: In the name of God Ames &c. (see the preceeding book of Land Causes page 115). That after the death of the said Jacob, John Warren, uncle of the whole blood to the said Jacob and next eldest brother of the said Richard, entered upon the premises and was thereof possessed until the month of May, Anno MDCCXX1X, and departed this life so as aforesaid of the premises seized, leaving Moses Warren his eldest son and heir at law, and Thomas, a younger son by a second wife, to whom he devised the premises during his lifetime, which will is in these words, to-wit: (see the said book of Land Causes page 109). That the said Thomas, being an infant under age, by his guardian entered upon the premises with the appurtenances, and was thereof seized, and continued seized thereof until the 10 August, 1745, when Henry Warren, youngest son of Elizabeth Patrick by John Warren the elder, entered upon the premises. That the said Thomas soon after commenced an action of trespass against the said Henry for the entry aforesaid, and recovered judgment by trail, but the said Thomas dying in May, MDCCXLV1, the said Henry continued from that time in possession thereof until his death, which happened in the year MDCCLX1, leaving Esther Warren, his grandaughter and heir at law, who still is, by her guardian, in possession. That the said John Warren, who was uncle of Jacob as aforesaid, dying in the year MDCCXX1X, as aforesaid, left Moses Warren his oldest son and heir at law who died about the month of

January, Anno Domini 1753, leaving his wife pregnant of a daughter, who was afterwards born on the 2 day of March, Anno Domini MDCCL111, who is now the fame Lessor of the plaintiff--------12 August, 1766 - p. 118, et seq.

Goodright p: Dunton,
vs. - Trespass.
Dunton.

Came the parties by their attorneys, and in lieu of a special verdict agreed as follows:

That Michael Dunton, father of the lessor of the plaintiff, and also of the defendant, was seized in fee of the lands in question, and by his last will and testament in writing, bearing date the 12 March, 1754, which was duly exhibited and proved in Northampton County, which will we agree was in these words, to-wit: (abstract) To son Elias Dunton my house and plantation where I now live. To son Southy Dunton that part of my plantation which I bought of my brother Elias Dunton, and if either of my aforesaid sons die without issue my son William Dunton to enjoy their part of the land. To son William Dunton negro man Pete. To my two daughters Elizabeth Andrews and Leah Dunton negroes to be equally divided between them when my youngest daughter comes to the age of 20 years. To my wife cattle. Three sons and two daughters resid. legatees. Son Elias Dunton and son in law John Andrews Executors. Witt: Laban Stott, Lovin Dunton, Elias Dunton, Jr., Addison Nottingham - Probated 12 March, 1754.

We do also agree that Southy Dunton, being the second after the death of the testator, by virtue of the said devise entered into the lands and was thereof legally possessed, and so thereof being possessed on the ___ day of __ was of the age of 21 years and upwards, and soon afterwards died leaving a wife then pregnant and now living, and having made his will in these words: (abstract) To wife Rose Dunton my land dueing her life, being 100 acres, more or less, and if my wife have a child I give my land to the child and its heirs after the death of my said wive. Wife Executrix. Witt: Laban Stott, William Satchell, Hancock Jacob - Dated 18 June, 1759 - Probated 10 July, 1759.

And that the wife of the said Southy so being pregnant at the time of his death was soon after the said Southy's death delivered of the said child, which child lived about the space of 26 or 28 days and then died. We also agree that Elias Dunton, the lessor of the plaintiff, is son and heir of the testator and also uncle and heir at law of the aforesaid infant, the son of the said Southy, deceased. We also agree that the aforesaid William Dunton, by virtue of the devise to him in remainder, after the death of the said child entered into the aforesaid lands and was seized and possessed thereof at the time of the commencement of this suit, and also the said William, the defendant, is the same person mentioned in the will of the testator-------- 14 August, 1766 - p. 123, et seq.

74

Holdfast p: Eliason,
vs. - Trespass and Ejectment.
James.

Jury impaneled and returned the following verdict:

We find that John Birt, formerly of the County of Northampton, now deceased, being seized of the premises in question in fee, by his deed in writing bearing date the 27 October, 1687, conveyed the same in fee simple to John Hugbin, who entered by virtue of the said conveyance into the land in question and was thereof seized, and being so thereof seized afterwards, to-wit: the 19 day of December, 1687, made his last will and testament in writing duly published, whereby he devised the promises in question unto Susanna Carpenter in fee, which will we find in these words: (abstract) I give to Susanna Carpenter 100 acres of land known by the name of Forked Neck, to her and her heirs forever, to be deliver to her when she comes to the age of 16 years, and my desire is that it may be kept in the custody of Mrs Frances Birt until she comes to age. To Frances Birt one black horse running at the plantation she lives on. Unto John Birt, Jr., my gun &c. Balance of estate to John Birt and his wife to pay my debts and make a funeral for me as they shall see fit. Witt: Thomas Bell, John Scammell. Probated 28 May, 1688.

That the said John Hugbin soon after departed this life and his will was afterwards duly proved and recorded. That the said Susanna Carpenter was then an infant of about the age of three years and lived under a certain Obedience Oben, who was her father in law, and in a short time after removed from off the lands in question and went up to the head of Chesapeake Bay, out of this Colony, during her lifetime. That the said Susanna while out of this Colony intermarried with a certain Cornelius Eliason, to whom she bore issue Elias Eliason, heir at law, who is now the lessor of the plaintiff. That a grant was made unto a certain John Custis, Jr. dated in the year 1701, which we find in these words: (abstract) Whereas a certain tract of land lying in Northampton County and containing 100 acres, late in the possession of John Culpeper, deceased, lately found to escheat to his sacred Majesty from the said John Culpeper--------for which said land John Custis, Jr. of the said County of Northampton hath made composition according to the said letters pattent--------do grant to the said John Custis, Jr. the said 100 acres &c. - Dated 24 October, 1701.

That the said John Custis afterwards by his last will and testament in writing, duly published, dated _____ devised the lands so last granted unto his son Henry Custis in fee, whose will was afterwards duly proved and recorded after the said John Custis' death. That the said Henry Custis afterwards by his deed dated 4th September, 1729, conveyed the lands thus last granted, unto Thomas Savage in fee simple, which said deed is in these words: (abstract) Col. Henry Custis, and Anne, his wife, of the County of Accomack and Thomas Savage of the County of Northampton on the other part - Sale - 100 acres, more or less, now in our possession, beginning at a gut or marsh running out of Nasswadox Creek, &c. To have and to hold &c., and that the said Thomas Savage afterwards by his deed bearing date the 14th November, 1749, conveyed the premises unto the defendant, which deed is in these words: (abstract) Thomas Savage of the County of Northampton of the one part and Thomas James of the same place, planter, of the other part - Sale - 100 acres of land beginning at a gut or marsh running out of Nasswadox Creek &c. Elizabeth Savage, wife of Thomas, release of dower. That the said defendant into the premises by virtue of his said deed entered, and was and still is possessed thereof -------- 14 January, 1768 - p. 128, et seq.

Goodright p: Johnson,
vs. - Trespass and Ejectment.
Milby.

Jury impaneled and returned the following verdict:

That a certain Obedience Johnson being seized in fee of land on one side of the branch in question, and a certain John Benson being seized in right of his wife of an estate for life on the other side of the said branch, on the 8th day of July, 1735, set forth a petition to the Northampton County Court (petition for a water mill); that the said Johnson and Benson by virtue of the said judgment entered into the premises and erected a water grist mill thereon at their joint expense, and continued to occupy the said mill jointly during their lives. That the said John afterwards, in the year 1739, made his last will and testament in writing, duly published, and devised the said mill to his wife during her lifetime and soon afterwards died, whose will was duly proved in Northampton County Court. That the said widow and devisee of the said John Benson entered into a moiety of the said mill and was thereof possessed until the year 1736, jointly with the said Obedience, and those claiming under him, and then departed this life, after whose death a certain Thomas Fisher, who was the heir in reversion of the widow, and after her death became entitled to the lands formerly in possession of John Benson, entered into the moiety of the premises now in question; That the lessor of the plaintiff, Edmund Johnson, is heir at law to the aforesaid Obedience Johnson, who is now in possession of the other moiety of the premises, and those under whom he claims have always been in possession thereof. That Samuel Benson, heir at law to the aforesaid John Benson, by a deed duly executed and proved conveyed all his right of the said moiety of the premises unto the defendant; at the time of such conveyance the aforesaid Thomas Fisher was in possession thereof, in these words (abstract) Dated 10 January, 1764, between Samuel Benson, of Accomack County in Virginia, of the one part, and Gilbert Milby of Northampton County of the other part - Sale - "the undivided equal moiety and full half of a certain water grist mill in the county of Northampton on a branch or stream called Hickerson Branch, together with the privileges, &c.---- and the undivided right to a moiety of one acre on each side of the said mill which was heretofore petitioned for and obtained by Obedience Johnson and John Benson, late of the said County of Northampton, deceased, ancestor of the said Samuel Benson, as by the records of Northampton County Court plainly may appear----"

That soon after the coveyance aforesaid the defendant by an ejectment recovered the moiety aforesaid so conveyed from the aforesaid

Fisher, and is still in possession thereof-------- 12 May, 1768 - p. 136

Simon Seekright, by James Henry, his Attorney,
vs. - Trespass and Ejectment.
Pleas at the Court House of Northampton, before his Majestie's Justices of the said County on Tuesday, the 25 June, 1770.
Came Simon Seekright, by James Henry, his Attorney, and brought into the Court of our said Lord the King, a certain bill against John Thomas of a plea of trespass and ejectment--------
That whereas William Moore, of the Parish of Hungars, in the County aforesaid, on the first day of May, in the year of our Lord MDCCLX1X had demised, granted and to farm let unto the said Simon, and his assigns, one messuage, plantation and 150 acres of land, situate in the County aforesaid--------to have and to hold unto the said Simon Seekright and his assigns from the said first day of May in the year of our Lord aforesaid, unto the full determination of 10 years thence next following--------by virtue of which demise the said Simon afterwards the same day and year aforesaid entered the tenements aforesaid and was thereof possessed until the said John, afterwards, to-wit: the 2 day of May in the year aforesaid, in the Parish and County aforesaid, with force and arms into the tenements aforesaid, in and upon the possession of the said Simon entered, his said term not then nor yet begin ended, and the said Simon for his said term objected, expelled and amoved, and the said Simon so ejected &c.-------- in lieu of a special verdict it was agreed that John Tilney, formerly of Northampton County, ancestor of the said William Moore, was seized in fee of land in question--------that the said John by his deed in writing duly executed, dated September 26, Anno Domini, DCXC1X gave unto his son in law. John Moore and Margaret, his wife, the said Tilney's daughter, the premises during their natural lives, and after their death to the heir or heirs of their bodies, male or female, as they or their survivor or survivors of them should think fit, forever, which deed is in these words, to-wit: (see this book p. 3). That the said John Moore and Margaret, his wife, are both dead, leaving several children, without making any appointment to whom of their children the same should descend, whereby the same descended unto Jonathan, their eldest son and heir at law, who entered into the premises and was thereof seized as the law required, and being so thereof seized afterwards by his deed duly executed on the 10 February, Anno Domini MDCCXXX1 -------- conveyed the same unto the defendant in these words following, to-wit: (see this book page 5); that the said defendant by virtue of the said deed entered into the premises and was thereof seized and is still possessed thereof. That the said Jonathan Moor afterwards, to-wit: about seventeen years now last past departed this life "Detesable" and without issue, leaving Thomas Moor his next eldest brother and heir at law, who is lately dead leaving the lessor of the plaintiff his eldest son and heir at law -------- 7 October, 1769 - p. 146

77

Tom Toby, by Nathaniel Ramsey, his Attorney,
vs. - Trespass.
Azariah Tankard.

Pleas at the Court House of the County Court of Northampton, before has Majestie's Justices of the said County, on Tuesday, the 11th day of September, in the year 1770.

Came Tom Toby, by Nathaniel Ramsey, his Attorney, and brought his action of trespass against Azariah Tankard--------that whereas John Wilkins, Guardian to William Pettitt, an infant under the age of 21, to-wit: of the age of 12 years, and son and heir to William Pettitt, deceased, on the second day of January, Anno Domini, MDCCLXX, in the Parish of Hungars, in the County aforesaid, had demised, granted and to farm let to the aforesaid Toby three messuages, one hundred and twenty five acres of land, with the appurtenances--------to have and to hold the tenements aforesaid for the full term of seven years from thence next following--------That the said Azariah on the 3rd day of January, in the year aforesaid, with force and arms into the tenements of the said Toby entered, and the said Toby ejected, and that the said Azariah hitherto hath withheld and still doth withold from him the possession thereof.------- 13 February, 1770 - p. 149

Jacob Goodright, by Robert Pitt, his attorney,
vs. - Trespass and ejectment.
Esau Jacob.

Pleas in the Court House of the County of Northampton, before his Majestie's Justices of the said County, on Tuesday, the 14 day of May, 1771 - Came Jacob Goodright by Robert Pitt, his attorney, and brought into the Court his bill against Esau Jacob of a plea of trespass and ejectment &c.

Jury impaneled and returned the following verdict:

We, the Jury, find that Richard Patrick the elder was seized in fee of the lands in question, and having four children, viz: Richard, Elizabeth, Ursula and Agnes, by his last will and testament in writing, bearing date the 16 day of February, Anno Domini 1674/5, duly proved and recorded in Northampton Court, hereto annexed, devised the said land to the daughter Agnes, which will we find in these words and figures, to-wit: (see this book page 63) and that the said Agnes, who intermarried and survived 21 years, and Richard Patrick departed this life in the lifetime of the said Elizabeth and Ursula, without issue. That the said Elizabeth intermarried with John Warren the elder, late of the said County, by whom he had three sons, Richard, John and Henry, and that the said Richard Warren died in the lifetime of his father, John Warren, leaving a son named Jacob Warren who died an infant without issue. That Ursula intermarried with Argol Warren by whom she had issue four sons, Henry, Robert, Benjamin and Matthew, and that the said John Warren, Sr. and Argol Warren in right of their wives entered into the premises in question, and were thereof seized and died seized thereof, and that John Warren, the second son and heir to Elizabeth, and Henry Warren as heir to Ursula, entered into the premises in question and was thereof possessed, and being so possessed made partition thereof by mutual deeds of bargain and sale, bearing date the 14 day of August, 1728-------- and after the said partition the said John Warren became sole seized of the premises in question, and having three children, Moses, his heir at law, and Thomas and Sarah by a second wife, made his last will and testament in writing, bearing date the 20 day of April, 1729, in which said will the said John Warren devised the premises in question to his daughter Sarah, who intermarried with Luke Batson, who entered and was thereof possessed and died seized thereof without issue, which will we find in these words following, to-wit: (see in preceeding book of Land Causes page 109); and that Moses Warren, son and heir of the last mentioned John Warren died in the lifetime of the said Sarah Warren leaving issue Elizabeth, the plaintiff in this case. We also find that the said Moses in his lifetime by his deed bearing date the 10 July, A.D. 1738, conveyed the premises in question to Henry Warren, son and heir to Ursula, and that the said Henry on the 29 day of December, 1732, made his last will and testament in writing, to-wit: (see in book of Wills from 1735 to 1740 - page 376), and that the said Henry living and the aforesaid Sarah died without issue, and that Robert Warren, brother and heir of Henry Warren, by his deed of bargain and sale dated 19 November, A.D. 1759, conveyed the premises in question to the defendant, which deed will be found in book of Deeds &c. from 1750 to 1763, page 430, and that the said Luke Batson, with the aforesaid Sarah, his wife, by their deed of bargain and sale dated 10 September, A.D. 1751, conveyed the lands in question to the defendant, which deed will be found in book of Deeds &c. from 1750 to 1763, page 53 -------- 11 September, 1770 - p. 151

Dick Fenn, Lessee of John Griffith, Moses Griffith, Thomas Griffith, William Griffith and Nathan Griffith,

vs. - Ejectment.

Nathaniel Hickman and Louisa, his wife, Anne Griffith and Rachel Griffith.

Jury impaneled and returned the following verdict:

We, the Jury, find that Moses Griffith was seized in fee or and in the lands in the declaration mentioned, and being so seized upon the 2 day of March, 1800, duly made and published his last will and testament in these words, to-wit: (abstract) To my son Jeremiah Griffith the plantation called Dogwood Neck, and for want of issue to go to my grandaughter, Louisa Griffith. The plantation whereon I now live I lend the use of it to my son Benjamin Griffith for his life, and after his death, if not a male heir, to go to my son Jeremiah Griffith. I lend to my son Nathan Griffith the plantation he now lives on for his life, and at his death to go to his son Thomas Griffith if he should be living, if not to go to his next son, if any, but if no son living to go to his lawful heirs. To my son Moses Griffith 53 acres of that land I bought of Daniel R. Hall on the westward end of the land, also my part of the windmill with it. To my son John Griffith the balance of the land purchased of Daniel R. Hall joining the marsh. After the payment of my debts the balance of my estate to be divided equally between all my children. If my son Benjamin Griffith should die without male heirs so that Jeremiah Griffith or his heirs gets possession of the plantation that I lend to my son Benjamin Griffith, the plantation called Dogwood Neck to go immediately to my grandaughter Louisa Griffith - Dated 2 May, 1800 - Witt: Azariah Williams, Sarah Spady, Martha Pratt -- and shortly after departed this life.

That the said will was duly proved and admitted to record in the County Court of Northampton on the 14 day of April, 1800. We also find that Benjamin Griffith entered into the lands in the declaration mentioned upon the death of the said Moses Griffith, the testator, and continued to hold the said land until the time of his death on the 2 day of January, 1817; that the said Benjamin Griffith died intestate, and at the time of his death left no male issue nor the descendant of any male issue; that upon the death of the said Benjamin Griffith his two daughters, Louisa and Anne, and his widow, Rachel Griffith, the

female descendants, entered upon the lands aforesaid and still hold possession of the same. We also find that Jeremiah Griffith in the will aforesaid named departed this life on the __day of __, in the year 1806, intestate and without issue, leaving as his next of kin the lessors of the plaintiff, to-wit: John and Moses Griffith, his only brothers; William, Major, Nathan and Thomas, the children of Nathan Griffith, another brother of the aforesaid Jeremiah, all of the whole blood, and Benjamin Griffith, a brother of the whole blood and father of the female defendants, Louisa and Anne, and that the mother of the said Jeremiah departed this life prior to his death. We also find that after the death of the said Jeremiah Griffith, and in the lifetime of the said Benjamin Griffith, the said Benjamin had a son born, who was named Hiram, who lived about ten months, and then died in the lifetime of the said Benjamin Griffith. We also find that the defendant, Louisa, is the same person mentioned in the will of the said Moses Griffith by the name of Louisa Griffith, and that the said Benjamin Griffith at the time of his death left no children except the aforesaid Louisa and Anne, and that he left no descendants of any deceased child--------
18 May, 1818 - p. 1

John Goodright, Lessee of John M. Harmanson,
vs. - Ejectment.
William Lyon and Margaret Lyon.
    Jury impaneled and returned the following verdict:
    That Margaret M. Harmanson was seized in fee of and in a tract of land situate in the County of Northampton, containing 150 acres, more or less; that the said Margaret intermarried with a certain Benjamin Stratton, late of the said County, on the 6 of June, 1794. That the said Margaret being so as aforesaid seized departed this life on the 6 of April, 1795, leaving her said husband and an only child, to-wit: William H. Stratton. We also find that the said William H. Stratton depared this life on the 10 day of September, 1796, an infant, leaving as his next of kin his father, the said Benjamin, a maternal grandfather, viz: William Harmanson and two uncles on the part of the mother, viz: William P. Harmanson and John H. Harmanson (the lessor of the plaintiff) brother of the said Margaret and the only brothers or sisters, or descendants of brothers or sisters of the said Margaret. We also find that the said Benjamin Stratton on the 19 day of December, 1797, by deed conveyed the said land to a certain James Lyon, late of this county, who entered on the same and continued seized thereof until the time of his death upon the___ day of December, 1811. We also find that after the death of the said James Lyon, who died intestate, William E. Lyon and Margaret Lyon, his only issue, entered upon the lands in question and still hold the same. We also find that the said William Harmanson, the grandfather, departed this life on the 22 day of November, 1811, having first duly made and publiched his last will and testament. That William P. Harmanson, one of the brothers of the said Margaret, departed this life on the 2 of February, 1809, without issue, leaving as his next of kin an only brother, to-wit: John H. Harmanson, the lessor of the plaintiff; that

81

Sally Harmanson, the widow of the said William P. Harmanson, departed this life in the year 1811. We also find that the said Benjamin Stratton departed this life on the ___day of April, 1817 --------18 May, 1818 – p. 4

LAND CAUSES
1815-1834

Upshur, et al,
vs. - Suit for Division of Land.
Upshur, et al.
    Your orators and oratrix, Caleb B. Upshur, John T. Elliott and Juliet, his wife, Arther B. Upshur, Abel P. Upshur and John Upshur, show that your orators and oratrix' father, Littleton Upshur, was in his lifetime and at the time of his death, seized in fee simple of a tract of land containing 1200 acres, situate in the County of Northampton aforesaid, and also was seized of 12 acres for the life of a certain Sally Fisher, who is now alive and in being; and your orators and oratrix further show unto your worships that your orators and oratrix' said father being so seized and possessed of and in such real estate as aforesaid, on or about the 27 day of August, 1812, died intestate leaving Nancy Upshur, his widow and relice, and your orators Caleb B. Upshur, Arthur B. Upshur, Abel P. Upshur and John Upshur and your oratrix, Juliet, who on the 22 of February, A. D. 1814, intermarried with your orator John T. Elliott, and also Leah C. Upshur, George P. Upshur and Elizabeth P. Upshur his children and coheirs, all of whom are now alive and in being, &c.--------19 July, 1814 - p. 1

Nottingham, et al,
vs. - Suit for division of Land and Slaves.
Wilson, et al.
    That a certain Bishop Wilson, late of this county, was in his lifetime seized was possessed in his own right of a certain piece of land containing about three acres, more or less, adjoining the lands of William E. Nottingham and Thomas Wilson and also of two negro slaves, viz: George and Daniel; That being so seized and possessed the said Bishop Wilson in the year 1800 departed this life intestate, leaving as his only children and heirs your oratrix, Letitia, Nancy and Peggy Wilson, to all of whom the said land and slaves descended equally to be divided; that the said land and slaves remaining undivided one of the aforesaid slaves, to-wit: George, departed this life; That Peggy, one of the aforesaid daughters, departed this life in December, 1813, leaving as her only heir a child, to-wit: William Wilson, to whom her undivided part of said land and slaves descended. That your oratrix, Letitia, upon the ___ day of November, 1814, sold and conveyed by deed her undivided one third part of said land to your orator, William E. Nottingham &c. -------- 21 February, 1815 - p. 4

Williams,

vs. - Suit for division of Land.

Williams.

That a certain John Williams, Sr., late of this County, father of your orators Samuel, William and Thomas Williams, and of your oratrices Sally, wife of Smith Nottingham and Margaret, wife of William Jarvis, being in his lifetime seized and possessed of a large estate, real and personal, upon the ___ day of ___ duly made and published his last will and testament, and shortly after departed this life having in no wise altered or revoked his said will, which was upon the ___day of ___duly proven in this Court and admitted to record; that by his said will the said John Williams devised a tract of land situate in the lower part of this county, adjoining the lands of John Nelson, James Goffigon, Ann Wilson and William E. Nottingham, and containing 370 acres, more or less, with a mill thereon, to three of his sons, to-wit: Benjamin, James and your orator, Thomas, subject, however, to the dower of your oratrix, Margaret, his widow. That said land remaining thus undivided Benjamin, one of the said devisees, departed this life on the ___day of ___, an infant, intestate and without issue, leaving as his next of kin and heirs your orators and oratrices, Thomas and Sally, a brother and sister of the whole blood, and Samuel, John, William, James, Margaret and Betsy, brothers and sisters of the half blood on the side of the father, to all of whom his undivided one third of said land descended to be divided in the following manner, to-wit: To each of the whole blood one fifth, and to each of the half blood one tenth thereof; That sometime after this, to-wit: on the ___day of ___, James, one other of the said devisees, departed this life an infant, intestate and without issue, leaving as his next of kin and heirs a mother, to-wit: Margaret, the widow of John the elder, and two sisters of the whole blood, viz: Margaret and Betsy, and Samuel, John, William and Thomas and Sally, brothers and sister of the half blood on the part of the father, to all of whom his undivided one third of said land derived from the father, and one tenth of one third derived by descent from Benjamin, descended to be divided in the following manner, viz: to each of the whole blood two ninths of one third and two elevenths of one tenth of one third; to each of the half blood one ninth of one ninth and one eleventh of one tenth of one third, and to Margaret, the mother, two elevenths of one tenth of one third, subject, however, to the dower of Sukey, the widow of James therein.

That sometime after this viz: on the 25 November, 1815, John Williams, Jr., one of the aforesaid brothers, departed this life having first duly made and published his last will and testament, and thereof appointing Southy Goffigon and William S. Williams the executors; that the said will was duly proved in this Court and admitted to record; that by said will the said John Williams directed his undivided part of the aforesaid land to be sold by his executors, all of which will more fully appear by reference to said will---- thus situated your orators and oratrices desire that partition be made &c.--------21 February 1816 - p. 7

84

John Widgeon and Nathaniel Collins and Molly, his wife,
vs. - Partition Suit.
Anne, Patsey, Walter, George and Adah Widgeon, orphans of
Westerhouse Widgeon, deceased.

That a certain Westerhouse Widgeon, father of your orator, John
Widgeon, and of your oratrix Molly Collins, was in his lifetime and at
the time of his death seized in his demesne as of fee,of and in a
plantation and tract of land, with the appurtenances, situate in this
County, containing 140 acres, more or less, and adjoining the lands of
Jacob Nottingham, John Eyre and William Nottingham, and ten acres
adjoining John Eyre and John Wilkins; that being so seized the said
Westerhouse Widgeon departed this life on the 5 day of October, 1815,
leaving a widow, viz: Nancy Widgeon and the following children, to-
wit: Your orator John, your oratrix Molly, wife of your orator Nathaniel
Collins, and the present defendants, to-wit: Anne, Patsey, Walter,
George and Adah Widgeon, to which said children the aforesaid lands
and appurtenances descended equally to be divided, subject, however,
to the dower of Nancy Widgeon, the widow aforesaid &c. -------- 21
February, 1816 - p. 13

Thomas S. Brickhouse and Smith Brickhouse,
vs. - Suit for Division of Slaves.
John N. Brickhouse, Mahala Brickhouse and Elem Brickhouse.

That a certain John Brickhouse, late of this County, and father of
your orators, was in his lifetime and at the time of his death possessed of the following negro claves in his own right, to-wit: Old
James, Comfort, George the elder, Leah and child Sarah, Mark, Stephen, Mary, Dolly, Eliza, Jacob, little George, Edath, Fanny, Siller,
Nancy, Tony, Nat and little James, and being so thereof possessed
and seized upon the ___day of November, 1815, departed this life
intestate.   That the said John Brickhouse left five children, to-wit:
Your orators Thomas and Smith, and the present defendants, John N.
Brickhouse, Mahala Brickhouse and Elem L. Brickhouse, to all of
whom the said negro slaves and lands descended to be equally divided; That the said John Brickhouse did in his lifetime, viz: in the year
1805, give to your orator, Thomas S. Brickhouse upon his marriage,
the following negro slaves, to-wit: Agnes, an old woman and her child
Sam, then at the breast, and a girl comfort, then about seven or eight
years old; that he also gave to your orator Smith Brickhouse in the
year 1808 two negroes, to-wit: Nanny, then about nine years old and
Abel, about eleven.   Your orators are advised that in the division of
the aforesaid slaves those as aforesaid given to your orators are to be
brought into hotchpot or accounted for by your orators at their respective values &c. -------- 11 December, 1815 - p. 16

Margaret Williams,
vs. - Suit for division of Land.
Pamela Powell.

That a certain Betsy Williams, deceased, late of this County was in her lifetime and at the time of her death, seized in fee simple of and in a certain tract of land with the appurtenances, situate in this County, containing about 130 acres, more or less, adjoining the lands of Abel Powell, William Satchell and others. That being so seized the said Betsey Williams upon the said ___ day of ___1815, departed this life intestate and without issue, leaving as her nearest of kin and only heirs your oratrix, a sister, and the infant respondent, Pamela Powell, the only issue of Abel Powell, deceased, who was a brother of the said Betsey. to both of whom the said land with the appurtenances descended equally to be divided, &c. -------- 12 March, 1816 - p. 20

John Goffigon, William Nottingham, Sr., and Polly, his wife,
      Jacob Nottingham, Sr., and Sally, his wife, and Severn
      E. Nottingham and Betsey, his wife.
vs. - Suit for division of Land and Slaves.
Polly, Sally, Thomas, Robert and Anne Dunton, children and heirs of
      Thomas Dunton, deceased, and _____, his wife.

That a certain Robert Bell, late of this County, was in his lifetime possessed in his own right of a considerable estate in lands and slaves; that the said Robert Bell departed this life about the year ___ intestate, leaving a widow and five daughters, viz: Nancy, who intermarried with your orator John Goffigon, your oratrixes Polly, Sally and Betsey and Sukey, who intermarried with a certain Thomas Dunton, late of this County, to whom the said lands descended, together with the slaves, equally to be divided subject, however, to the dower of the widow therein --------that Nancy, one of the said Daughters departed this life on or about the year ___ intestate, and without issue, whereupon the 51 acres allotted to her in the division descended to her surviving four sisters, subject to the dower as aforesaid of the widow, and the right of your orator, John Goffigon, as tenant by the courtesy. That Sukey, who intermarried with Thomas Dunton as aforesaid, departed this life in or about the year 1813, intestate, leaving the following children, viz: Polly, Sally, Thomas, Robert and Ann Dunton, to whom her interest in the said land and slaves descended. That the aforesaid widow _____ departed this life on the 17 March, 1816, upon which the aforesaid slaves devolved upon your orators and oratrixes to be divided in the following manner, viz: To your orator John Goffigon one fifth; to your orator and oratrix William Nottingham, Sr. and Polly, his wife, one fifth; to Jacob Nottingham, Sr. and Sally, his wife, one fifth; To Severn Nottingham and Betsey, his wife, one fifth and to the aforesaid children of Sukey Dunton the remaining one fifth -------- 11 November, 1816 - p. 22

Shepherd B. Floyd, et ux, et als,
vs. - Suit for division of land.
Sally Clay, et als.

That a certain Christopher Freshwater, late of this County, departed this life on the ___ day of ___, 18__, intestate and without issue, being seized of a tract of land in fee simple, containing, by estimation, 100 acres, which upon his death descended to your orators and oratrixes and the said defendants in the following proportions, to-wit: To your orator and oratrix Shepherd B. Floyd and Susan, his wife, in right of the said Susan, she being a sister of the whole blood to the said Christopher Freshwater, two sevenths thereof; to your orator and oratrix Peter Jefferson and Polly, his wife, in right of the said Polly, two sevenths thereof, she being also a sister of the whole blood. To your orator Nathaniel Freshwater, his brother of the half blood, one seventh thereof. To your oratrix Nancy Williams, wife of Peter Williams, and to the said Sally, Susan, Benjamin, Thomas, John and Elizabeth Clay, who are the children of his deceased sister Sally Clay, of the half blood, the one seventh thereof to be equally divided between them, and to the said Sally, William, Nathaniel, George and Sylvester Bishop, who are the children of his deceased sister of the half blood, Nancy Bishop, the remaining one seventh thereof, equally between them ------- 10 September, 1816 - p. 26

Peter Williams and Nancy, his wife, William Clay, James Clay, Matthew Floyd and Sally, his wife,
vs. - Suit for division of Land.
Sukey, Benjamin, Eliza, Thomas and John Clay.
That a certain Thomas Clay, late of this County, being in his lifetime and at the time of his death, seized in fee of and in one tract of land situate on Old Planation Creek, and adjoining a tract of land called Arlington and others, containing 131 acres, also of one other tract of land containing 80 acres, more or less adjoining the lands of Nathaniel Burris and others. That the said Thomas Clay departed this life on the 4 day of July, 1816, intestate, having nine children, to-wit: Your orators William and James Clay, children by a first marriage, and your oratrixes Nancy Williams and Sally Floyd, and the defendants, infants, Sukey, Benjamin, Eliza, Thomas and John Clay children by the marriage by Sally Clay, the last wife of the said Thomas Clay, deceased, to all of whom the aforesaid two tracts of land descended equally to be divided. That Sally Clay, the last wife of the said Thomas Clay, was in her lifetime and at the time of her death seized in fee of and in two pieces or parcels of land in this County, the one containing 10 acres, more or less, on Old Plantation Creek, adjoining the lands of Thomas Fitchett and others, the other containing 70 acres, more or less, and adjoining the lands of Nathaniel Burris and others; that the said Sally departed this life on the ___ day of December, 1815, intestate, leaving seven children, to-wit: Your oratrixes Nancy Williams and Sally Floyd, and the infant defendants Sukey, Benjamin, Thomas, Eliza and John Clay, to all of whom the lands descended, equally to be divided between them, &c. -------- 8 September, 1817 - p. 30

Thomas Nottingham and Sukey, his wife,
vs. - Suit for division of Land and Slaves,
John, Nancy and Molly Biggs.

That a certain Thomas Biggs, late of this County, being in his lifetime and at the time of his death, seized and possessed of and in one
messuage and plantation, with all the appurtenances, in fee simple,
containing 200 acres, more or less, and adjoining the lands of Nathaniel Widgeon and others, and the following negro slaves, to-wit: Lity,
Jim, Sarah, old Rachel, young Rachel and Bridget, and being so thereof seized and possessed upon the __day of ___ 1805, departed this
life intestate, leaving a widow, viz: Nancy Biggs, and four children,
to-wit: your oratrix Sukey, who has since intermarried with your orator, and the infant defendants John, Nancy and Molly Biggs, to whom
all of the aforesaid lands and slaves descended, equally to be divided,
&c. -------- 9 December, 1816 - p. 34

Margaret Powell,
cs. - Suit for Division of Land.
George Savage.

That a certain Littleton Savage, late of this County, was in his
lifetime and at the time of his death, seized in fee of and in a certain
messuage and plantation, situate in this County, adjoining the lands of
George Parker and others, containing 578 1/2 acres, more or less, and
being so thereof seized upon the __day of ___ 1815, departed this life
intestate, leaving your oratrix and George Savage his only children, to
whom the said lands descended by virtue of the statute of descents, to
be equally divided between them. Rickards Dunton appointed Guardian
to George Savage, infant defendant. ------ 10 September, 1816 - p. 37

Dennard Travis and William Travis,
vs. - Suit for Partition of Land.
Peggy Travis, Molly Travis, Shadrack Travis and Meshack Travis.

That a certain Shadrack Travis, late of this County, father of your
orators, being in his lifetime and at the time of his death seized in fee
of a certain tract of land situate, lying and being in the County aforesaid, containing 81 acres, more or less, adjoining the lands of the
heirs of Thomas Parsons, deceased, and those of the heirs of I.
Evans, deceased, did on or about the 4 of January, 1815, duly make
and publish his last will and testament in writing, by which he devised
the aforesaid tract of land to be equally divided between his children,
viz: your orators and Peggy, Molly, Shadrack and Meshack Travis, as
by the said will will appear. That after the making of the said will
aforesaid, on the ___ day of ____ the said Shadrack Travis departed
this life. That the said will was duly proved and admitted to record on
the 12 day of February, 1816, in the Court of the County of Northampton as will more fully appear by the records thereof. That after the
death of the said Travis, the testator, all the devisees entered upon
the premises and so there in parcenary held the same subject, however, to the dower of Rachel Travis, the widow of the said Shadrack

William Fitchett and Sally, his wife,
vs. - Suit for Division of Land.
John G. and Thomas O. Hunt.

That a certain Obediah Hunt, late of this County, being in his life-time and at the time of his death seized and possessed of a tract of land situate in the lower part of this County, containing 230 acres, more or less, and adjoining the lands of Joshua Fitchett and others, and of a number of negro slaves, and being so thereof seized and possessed upon the 15 of February, 1806, duly made and published his last will and testament in writing, and afterwards departed this life, having in no wise altered or revoked his said will, which was proved on the 13 October, 1806. That among certain other directions &c., the said testator devised that after the payment of his debts his whole estate to be equally divided between his three children, viz: your ora-trix Sally, John G. Hunt and Thomas O. Hunt. That the said testator left a widow, viz: Nancy Hunt, who has since intermarried with a certain John G. Ames of this County, and being entitled to dower in the said lands and slaves the same has been laid off and assigned to the said John G. Ames and Nancy, his wife.

Richard Dunton appointed guardian to John G. and Thomas O. Hunt, infant defendants -------- 10 September, 1816 - p. 43

John Taylor and Princessa, his wife, and William Groten,
vs. - Suit for division of Land.
Eliza L. Groten.

That a certain Edmund Groten, late of this County, being seized in fee simple of a small piece of land situate in this County on the waters of Occohannock Creek, containing 18 acres, more or less. That being so seized the said Edmund Groten left this Commonwealth in the early part of the year 1808, and went to sea. That about two years after the departure of the said Edmund Groten a letter was received from him in which he stated that he was then in the State of New Hampshire on board a leaky ship, since which time the said Edmund Groten has not been heard from or of, so that your orators and oratrix presume that he is dead. Your orators and oratrix are also advised that by an Act of the General Assembly of this Commonwealth, it is enacted that when any person shall have been absent and unheard of for the space of seven years together, that such person shall be presumed to be dead; this being the ease of the said Edmund Groten, he is embraced by that law. That the said Edmund Groten left as of his next of kin and heirs your oratrix, a sister, your orator, William Groten, a brother, and Eliza L. Groten, another sister, who is an in-fant, to all of whom the said lands, descended equally to be divided &c. -------- 9 November, 1818 - p. 46

John Widgeon and Maria, his wife,
vs. - Suit for Division of Land.
William J. Nottingham.

That a certain Joseph Nottingham, late of this county, departed this life intestate on the ___ day of ___in the year___, being at the time of his death seized in his demesne, as of fee, of and in a certain plantation and tract of land situate in the County aforesaid, containing, by estimation, 188 acres, adjoining the lands of William L. Eyre, John C. Wilson, & al. That at the time of the death of the said Joseph Nottingham he left two children, viz: Your oratrix, Maria Widgeon, formerly Maria Nottingham, and William Nottingham, to whom the said land descended, &c.-------- 14 June, 1819 - p. 49

Robert Haley and Peggy, his wife, Frances Grear, Molly Evans, John
  Costin, Abram Costin, Thomas, John, William H., Peggy
  and Polly Williams, Sally Spady, Sally Elliott, William
  Widgeon, Sr., William Widgeon by Sally Elliott, his next
  friend, Nathaniel, Ralph P., Francis and Bowdoin Costin,
  Edmund Lilliston and Sukey, his wife, Coventon and
  Charlotte Costin, by Polly Costin, their next friend, William
  H. Shaw, William Goffigon and Polly, his wife, and
  Richard Jones,
vs. - Suit for Division of Slaves.
Amelia Spady and Evelina Jones.

That a certain William Griffith, formerly of this County, being possessed in his lifetime in his own right, among other things, of a negro girl by name Rose, and being so thereof possessed upon the ___ day of ___, duly made and published his last will and testament, which was upon the ___ day of ___ duly proved in this Court and admitted to record. That by the said will he gave to Elizabeth Costin, during her life, the aforesaid negro girl Rose, and after her death the said Rose and her increase to be divided between her children, as by reference to said will which is hereto annexed and prayed to be taken as part of this bill will appear more fully and at large. That the said Elizabeth Costin departed this life on the ___ day of October, 1818, leaving the following children, viz: Peggy Haley, Abram Costin, John Costin, Frances Grear and Nelly Evans, and the following grandchildren, viz: Thomas, John, William G(?), Peggy and Polly Williams and Sally Spady, the children of Anne Williams, deceased, who was a daughter of the said Elizabeth; and Sally Elliott and William Widgeon, Sr., children of Susan Widgeon, another daughter; Nathaniel, Ralph P., Bowdoin, Coventon, Francis and Charlotte Costin and _____ Lilliston and Sukey, his wife, children of Samuel Costin, a son; William H. Shaw, the only child of Elizabeth, another daughter, and Polly Goffigon, wife of William Goffigon, the only child of Lucretia, another daughter, and Amelia Spady, a child of Sally, another daughter, and the following great grandchildren, viz: William Widgeon, Jr., the only child of Levin, who was a child of Susan aforesaid, and Evelina Jones, the only child of Peggy, who was the daughter of Sally aforesaid; to all of whom the said Rose and her increase belong

John F. Stringer and Walter Luker,
vs. - Suit for division of Land.
Thomas Lytt: Savage, by Severn E. Parker, his guardian, and Samuel
Saunders.

Be it remembered that heretofore, to-wit: at a Court held for Northampton County the 9 day of November, 1819, came the complainants
by Thomas R. Joynes, their Attorney, and filed their bill of complaint
against the defendants in these words, viz:

To the worshipful Justices of Northampton County Court, in Chancery - Humbly complaining, shew unto your worships your orators,
Walter Luker and John F. Stringer. That sometime in the year 1805
your orator, and George Powell, Stewart Saunders and James Floyd, of
this County, contracted with a certain George Washington Park Custis,
of Arlington, for the purchase of an Island on the sea coast of this
County, commonly called and known by the name of Mockon, and
containing, by estimation, 1600 acres, more or less. That pursuant to
the said contract your orator, Walter Luker, and the said Powell,
Saunders and Floyd entered upon and became seized of the said Island. That the said George Powell in his will duly executed on the 20
April, 1809, and recorded after his death on the 9 October, 1809,
devised his one fourth part of Mockon Island to his two sons, George
and Thomas Powell; That the said George Powell the younger, by
deed duly executed on the 1st of January, 1817, sold and conveyed his
interest in Mockon Island, being one eighth part thereof, to a certain
William E. Nottingham, who on the ___day of ___ 1819, sold the same
to your orator John F. Stringer. That on the 26 July, 1819, the said
Thomas Powell sold his one eighth part of said Island to your orator
John F. Stringer; that on the ___day of ___ 18__, the said James Floyd
sold his one fourth part of said island to a certain Thomas Littleton
Savage, who in his last will dated the 1 August, 1812, and proved after
his decease on the 12 July, 1813, devised his one fourth part of said
Island to his son Thomas Littleton Savage. That Stewart Saunders
departed this life intestate on the ___day of ___ 18__, leaving three
children, viz: Sarah, James and Samuel, to whom the said Stewart's
one fourth of said Island descended. That the said James Saunders on
the 7 day of September, 1819, sold and conveyed his one twelvth part
of said Island to your orator John F. Stringer. That on the ___day of ___,
1819, Thomas Copes and Sarah, his wife, who is the said Sarah Saunders, sold his interest in the said Island to your orator Walter Luker.
That pursuant to the several contracts, conveyances and devises
aforesaid, the said Mockon Island is held now as follows, viz: By
your orator John F. Stringer the one third part thereof; by your orator
Walter Luker the one third part thereof; by the said Thomas Littleton
Savage the one fourth part thereof; by the said Samuel Saunders the
one twelvth part thereof, &c. -------- p. 59

91

Jesse Bell and Ann, his wife, and Custis Kellum and Margaret,
    his wife,
vs. - Suit for Division of Land.
Levin Richardson, George Richardson, Polly Richardson and
    Cassey Richardson.

That a certain Abel Richardson, late of this county, being seized in
fee of and in 27 2/3 acres of land derived by devise from Kendall
Richardson, his father, subject to the dower of Susy (Susanna) his
mother; that the said Abel Richardson departed this life in September,
1818, intestate, an infant without issue, leaving the following brothers
and sisters on the part of his father, viz: Levin and George Richardson, Polly and Cassey Richardson, your oratrixes, to all of whom the
said land descended equally to be divided, subject to the dower of
Susy as aforesaid---- 8 March, 1819 - p. 62

Elijah Costin and Charlotte, his wife, and William Wilkins and
    Nancy, his wife,
vs. - Suit for division of Land and Slaves.
Thomas Young and Elizabeth, his wife and Rosey Trower.

That a certain John Trower, late of this County, being in his lifetime and at the time of his death seized and possessed in fee simple
of a large estate, both real and personal, and amongst other things of a
tract of land lying to the eastward of the County road, containing, by
estimation, 140 acres, more or less, and adjoining the land of William
Jarvis, John Trower and others, and the following slaves; Jack,
James, &c. and being so seized and possessed on the 22 March,
1811, duly made and published his last will and testament in writing,
and shortly after departed this life--------that the said testator gave
the use of his land and negroes to his wife Sally Trower to bring up her
small children until his son Robert should arrive at the age of 16, and
when her said son should arrive at that age he gave the land lying to
the westward of the County road, together with all his negroes, to his
daughters, to-wit: your oratrixes and Betsy, the wife of Thomas
Young, and Rosey Trower, equally to be divided--------that the said
Sally Trower departed this life in _____181_, upon which event your
orators conceive and are advised that they were entitled to divide the
said lands and negroes under the will of the said testator--------your
oratrixes show further that all the daughters of the said testator are
married except one, which is now ___ years of age and has ample
means for her support; that Robert Trower is aged ___ years and has
also ample means of support, &c. -------- 13 December, 1819 - p. 64

Nathaniel W. Rodgers and Ann, his wife, Hezekiah P. Wescoat &
    Susanna, his wife, Margaret Savage and Michael R. Savage,
vs. - Suit for division of land and slaves.
John and George Savage, children and heirs of George S. Savage,
deceased.

That a certain Nathaniel Savage, late of this County, being in his
lifetime and at the time of his death, seized and possessed in fee

simple of a plantation and tract of land in this County containing 150 acres, more or less, and being so thereof seized duly made and published his last will and testament in writing, and shortly after departed this life----which said will was proved in this Court at December, 1818, and admitted to record; That after sundry bequests he devised one third of the remainder of his estate to his wife, who is your oratrix Margaret, and the balance to be divided equally between his brothers and sisters, then living and his brother, George Savage's, heirs--------that of the estate so devised to be divided consisted of the aforesaid tract of land, and also five negro slaves, &c.--------John C. Mapp appointed Guardian of John and George Savage, infant defendants to this suit-------- 9 August, 1819 - p. 67

John Griffith and Moses Griffith and Thomas, William, Major and Nathan Griffith, by Moses Griffith, their next friend, vs. - Suit for Division of Land.
Nathaniel Hickman and Louisa, his wife, and Ann Griffith.
    That a certain Moses Griffith, Sr., late of this County, being seized in fee of and in a certain tract of land in this County, containing 80 acres, more or less, and adjoining the land of Moses Griffith, et al, upon the ___day of March, 1800, duly made and published his last will and testament in writing, and shortly after departed this life--------that by the said will he devised the said tract of land to his son Benjamin during his life, and if no male heir living at the time of his death he devised his said land to his son Jeremiah, in fee----that the said Jeremiah Griffith departed this life about the year 1807 or 8 , intestate and without issue, leaving as his next of kin and heirs your orators John and Moses Griffith and the said Benjamin Griffith, his brother, and your orators Thomas, William, Major and Nathan Griffith, the descendants of Nathan Griffith, who was also a brother, to all of whom the said Jeremiah's interest in said land descended. That the said Benjamin Griffith departed this life in the year 1817, leaving no male issue, but leaving two daughters, viz: Louisa, now the wife of Nathaniel Hickman, and Ann Griffith, both of whom entered upon the said tract of land and became seized thereof. That sometime after your orators instituted an ejectment in the Superior Court of Law for this County against the said Louisa and Ann for the recovery of three undivided fourths of said land, and at November term, 1819, of said Court, obtained a judgment for the recovery of the same--------so that your orators and the said Nathaniel Hickman and Louisa, his wife, and the said Ann Griffith together and undivided hold the said land, which belongs to them to be held in severalty in the following manner, to-wit: To your orators John and Moses Griffith each one fourth; to your orators Thomas, William, Major and Nathan, the children of Nathan, one fourth to be divided between them, and to the said Nathaniel and Louisa, his wife, in right of said wife, one eighth, and to the said Ann Griffith the remaining one eighth, &c. -------- 13 December, 1819 - p. 70

James Saunders and Thomas Copes, et ux,
vs. - Suit for division of Land.
Samuel Saunders.

That a certain Stewart Saunders, late of this County, being in his lifetime and at the time of his death, seized in fee simple of and in two tracts or parcels of land, situate in this County, one containing 115 acres adjoining the lands of Walter Luker and others, the other 45 acres adjoining the lands of William and others, and being so seized the said Stewart Saunders departed this life on the ___ day of August, 1813, intestate, leaving three children, viz: Your orator James Saunders, your oratrix Sally, and Samuel Saunders, an infant, to all of whom the said land descended to be equally divided, &c. -------- 10 July, 1820 - p. 75

James Waters and Sally, his wife, John Waters, George D. Waters, and Mary, his wife, Richard J. Waters, William W. Waters, Dolly, George, Harriet, Joseph, Margaret and Thomas U. Waters, by Thomas Waters, their next friend,
vs. - Suit for Division of Land.
Ismey Johnson.

That a certain James Johnson, late of this County, was in his lifetime and at the time of his death, seized in fee of a certain plantation and tract of land with the appurtenances, containing, by estimation 52 1/2 acres, in the County aforesaid, and adjoining the lands of John R. Waddey, James Carter and others, and being so seized thereof upon the ___ day of August, 1815, duly made and published his last will and testament in writing, by which he devised the aforesaid lands, with the appurtenances, to his son James, and in case of his death under age and without issue at his death, then the said land to be divided amongst the children of his sister, Peggy Waters, who are your orators and oratrixes, and his brother Isma, the one half to Isma and the other one half to the said children of his sister Peggy Waters-------- 10 June, 1817 - p. 77

Edward A. Joynes, an infant, by Thomas W. Mears, his next friend, Nancy Joynes, Sally Joynes and Tully Joynes, by James Stewart, their next friend.
vs. - Suit for Division of Land.
James Twiford and Livia, his wife, and Melinda Joynes, an infant child of William Joynes, deceased.

That a certain William Joynes the elder, late of the County of Northampton, was in his lifetime and at the time of his death, seized in his demesne, as of fee, of a tract of land in this County adjoining the lands of Edmund W. P. Downing and others, near the head of Matchepungo Creek, containing, by estimation 100 acres, and being so thereof seized the said William Joynes departed this life intestate on the ___ day of December, 1816; that at the time of the death of the said William Joynes, he left four children, viz: your orator Edward Armistead Joynes, your oratrixes Sally and Nancy, and the said Melinda

Joynes, and leaving also one grandson, viz: your orator Tully, who is the only child of his deceased son William Joynes, and leaving also a widow Livia, who is now the wife of a certain James W. Twiford, &c. -------- 8 March, 1819 - p. 79

James Poulson and Elizabeth, his wife, John C. Mapp and Kessey, his wife, Jeptha Johnson and Rosey, his wife, Hancock Jacob and Anne, his wife, Nathaniel Savage and Margaret, his wife and Margaret James, an infant, by Nathaniel Savage, her next friend,
vs. - Suit for division of land.
Robert James.

That a certain Thomas James, late of this County, departed this life intestate on the 16 day of March, 1818, being at the time of his death seized in his demesne, as of fee, of and in a certain plantation and tract of land situate in Occohannock Neck, in the County aforesaid, containing, by estimation, 400 acres, and adjoining the lands of John C. Parramore, William A. Christian and others. That at the time of the death of the said Thomas James he left six children, viz: your oratrixes Elizabeth, Cassey, Rosey, Ann and your oratorix Margaret Savage, and a certain Robert James, and leaving also a grandchild, viz: your oratrix Margaret James, who is the only child of his deceased son William D. James, &c. -------- 9 June, 1818 - p. 82

Hillary Stringer and Kitty, his wife,
vs. - Suit for Division of Land.
John S. Gayle.

That a certain Rachel Cowles, late of this County, being in her lifetime seized in fee of and in a lot of one acre of ground, with the appurtenances, situate in this County at Franktown, and being so seized thereof upon the ___day of ___ 1814, departed this life intestate, leaving your oratrix an only child and John S. Gayle a grandchild, the only issue of another daughter, deceased, to both of whom the said lot with the appurtenances descended equally to be divided --------

Christopher Gayle appointed guardian of John S. Gayle, to defend this suit - 8 June, 1818 - p. 84

James Sanford,
vs. - Suit for sale of land.
Teackle Ames.

That a certain William Ames, late of this County, being in his lifetime and at the time of his death, seized in reversion, in fee, of a certain piece of land in the County aforesaid, which said land was held in dower by a certain Bridget Ames; that the said William Ames being indebted to your orator in the sum of £ 133-15-4, in order to secure the payment of the aforesaid sum, with interest thereon, the 4 May, 1813, executed a mortgage deed conveying the aforesaid land, subject, however, to the dower of the said Bridget Ames--------that shortly after this, to-wit: the 4 May, 1813, the said William Ames departed this life, having in no wise paid or satisfied the aforesaid deed--------that the said William Ames left an only child, to-wit: Teackle Ames, to whom the aforesaid land descended, subject, however, to the dower of the said Bridget Ames as aforesaid, &c. -------- 11 October, 1819 - p. 86

John P. Johnson,
vs. - Suit for sale of land.
William K. Savage and Preson Savage.

That a certain Anne Pitts, late the wife of John Pitts of this County, being in her lifetime seized in fee simple of and in a tract of land situate in Occohannock Neck, in this County, and containing, by estimation, 400 acres, more or less, and being so thereof seized the said Anne, in conjunction with her said Husband John Pitts, by deed bearing date 22 June, 1807, conveyed the said tract of land to their son, John R. Pitts, in fee simple, reserving to themselves a life estate----that the said deed contained a provision to the following effect: That the said John R. Pitts should die under age and without issue, and the said John Pitts and Ann, his wife, should leave no other issue, in that event the said land should revert to the right heirs of the said Ann. That the said Ann departed this life about the year 1811, leaving the said John R. Pitts her only issue, who departed this life in the year 1815, an infant and without leaving issue, leaving as the right heirs of the said Ann your orator, an only brother of the whole blood, and William K. Savage and Preson Savage, brothers of the half blood to the said Ann, in whom the right to the said land vested subject to the life estate of the said John Pitts. That the said John departed this life on the 2 day of March, 1819, after whose death your orator, together with the said William K. Savage and Preson Savage became entitled to the said tract of land to be divided in the following manner, to-wit: To your orator one half thereof, and the remaining one half to be equally divided between them, the said William K. Savage and Preson Savage, &c. -------- 10 Dec. 1821 - p. 88

Edmund Wescoat, John Wescoat, Major Wescoat, George Wescoat, Hezekiah Wescoat and Polly Wescoat, William Underhill and Polly, his wife, and Jemima Mears,
vs. - Suit for Division of Land.
Anne Wescoat and Rosey Wescoat.

That a certain Joshua Wescoat, late of this County, being in his lifetime and at the time of his death, seized in fee of and in a tract of land in this County near Franktown, adjoining the land of William Wescoat and others, and containing 180 acres, more or less, and being so seized the said Joshua Wescoat departed this life in the year 1798, leaving your oratrix, Polly Wescoat, his widow, and nine children, to-wit: Edmund, John, Major, George, Hezekiah, Rosey, who intermarried with John Wescoat, deceased, Vianna, who intermarried with Samuel Matthews, Polly, the wife of William Underhill and Jemima

96

Mears, the widow of Shadrack Mears, to all of whom the said land descended equally to be divided, subject to the dower of the said Polly, the widow; That John, by deed of record in this Court, sold and conveyed his one ninth of said land to your orator Hezekiah Wescoat; that Vianna, who intermarried as aforesaid with Samuel Matthews, departed this life in the year 1817, of full age, intestate and without issue, leaving as her next of kin her mother and the aforesaid brothers and sisters, to all of whom her undivided one ninth of said land descended; that Rosey, one of the aforesaid children, departed this life in the year 1818, intestate, leaving two children, to-wit: Ann and Rosey Wescoat, infants, to whom her interest in said land descended, equally to be divided between them, &c. ------- 13 June, 1820 - p. 90

Major Richardson, Susan Richardson, John Richardson, Thomas
　　　Richardson and William Richardson, by Severn Dalby, their
　　　next friend.
vs. - Suit for division of land.
Smith Richardson.
　　That a certain Kesiah Richardson, late of this county, departed this life intestate on the __ day of __ in the year 1819, being at the time of her death seized in her demesne, as of fee, in a certain plantation and tract of land lying in the County of Northampton, containing 10 1/2 acres, and adjoining the land of Southy Webb, John S. Robertson, et al; That at the time of her death, the said Kesiah Richardson left six children, to-wit: Major, John, Thomas, William, Susan and Smith Richardson, to all of whom the said land descended equally to be divided, &c. ---- 15 June, 1819 - p. 92

Thomas S. Satchell,
vs. - Suit for sale of land.
Shadrack, Juliet, Harriet and Margaret Kellam, infant
　　　children of Walter Kellam, deceased.
　　That the said Walter Kellam was in his lifetime, to-wit: on the 23 January, 1821, indebted to your orator in the sum of $1,520.04, and the said Walter for the purpose of securing to your orator the payment of the aforesaid sum, on the 23 January, 1821, conveyed to your orator the tract of land aforesaid, containing, by estimation, 150 1/2 acres, situate on Hungars Creek, adjoining the lands of Major S. Pitts and others--------that the said Walter Kellam departed this life intestate shortly after the deed aforesaid and without having in any manner paid or discharged the money secured thereby, or any part thereof; That the said Walter Kellam at the time of his death left four children, Shadrack, Juliet, Harriet and Margaret Kellam, to all of whom the said land descended, subject to the mortgage of your orator, &c. ---- 12 June, 1821 - p. 96

Ames, et ux, et als,

vs. - Suit for division of land.

William A. Christian.

That a certain John Christian, late of this County, an idiot, being in his lifetime and at the time of his death, seized in fee simple of a plantation and tract of land situate in this County, in Occohannock Neck, containing 750 acres, more or less, adjoining the lands of William James, Richard Johnson, Teackle White, John Ross and others, and being so seized the said John Christian departed this life on the 7 day of March, 1821, of full age, intestate and without issue, leaving as his next of kin your oratrix, Sally Ames, wife of Thomas Ames, a sister of the whole blood; your orator and oratrix, George E. Christian and Margaret Ames, wife of Richard Ames, and the defendant, William A. Christian, the only issue of William Christian, a brother of the half blood on the part of the father, from whom the said John derived the land aforesaid; Mahala Ames, wife of Jesse Ames, and Watkins Joynes, the only descendants of Betsy Milby, deceased, a paternal sister, and the said Mahala Ames, Shadrack T. Ames and Tabitha Ames, the only descendants of Ann Ames, deceased, who was a maternal sister; Ann Johnson, the only issue of Catherine Johnson, deceased, who was also a maternal sister, and James Fisher, the only issue of Rosey Fisher, deceased, who was a paternal sister, to all of whom your orators and oratrixes are advised the said land descended, to be divided in the following manner and proportions, to-wit: To your orator and oratrix Thomas Ames and wife, in right of said wife, two sevenths; To your orators and oratrix George E. Christian, Richard Ames and Margaret, his wife, in right of said wife, and the defendant William A. Christian, one seventh to be divided between them; to Jesse Ames and Mahala, his wife, in right of said wife, and Watkins Joynes, one seventh by descent form Betsy Milby, their grandmother as aforesaid; to the said Jesse Ames and Mahala, his wife, in right of said wife, Shadrack T. Ames and Tabitha A. Ames one seventh to be divided between them by descent from Ann Ames, deceased, their mother, a sister as aforesaid; to Ann Johnson one seventh and to James Fisher the remaining one seventh, &c. -------- 14 May, 1822 - p. 102

Robert Hadlock,

vs. - Suit for sale of land.

Joanna Stott, widow of Ralph Stott, and Betsey Benson,
      formerly Betsey Stott, Keely Stott and Teackle Stott,
      children and heirs of Ralph Stott, deceased.

That a certain Ralph Stott, late of this County, in his lifetime became indebted to your orator in the sum of $100., and in order to secure the payment of the said debt the said Robert Stott and Joanna, his wife, on the 7 August, 1810, executed a deed of mortgage by which they conveyed to your orator a certain tract of land situate in the County aforesaid, containing, by estimation, 20 acres, more or less, adjoining the lands of John Upshur and Isaac Dalby, deceased--------That the said Robert Stott departed this life intestate on the ___ day of ___, leaving the said Joanna his widow, and Betsey Benson, formerly Betsey Stott, Keely Stott and Teackle Stott his only children and heirs, to which said children the said land descended, subject to the lien of your orator as aforesaid, &c. -------- 4 February, 1822 - p. 106

Copes and Leatherbury, Assignees of John Addison, vs. - Suit for sale of land.
Juliet Smith, widow, and John E. Smith, infant heir of Richard Smith, deceased.

That a certain Richard Smith, late of this County, being indebted to a certain John Addison, in the sum of $791.70, and in order to secure the payment of the same on the 20 September, 1821, duly executed a deed of mortgage, by which he conveyed to the said John Addison a certain tract of land situate near Franktown, in this County, containing 125 acres--------that the said John Addison upon the ___ day of January, 1822, duly assigned the said mortgage to your orators -------that the said Richard Smith departed this life on the ___ day of _, ___ 1821, intestate, leaving a widow, to-wit: Juliet Smith and an only child, to-wit: John Smith, to whom the said land descended, subject to the dower of the said widow, and subject to the mortgage aforesaid.

John R. Fisher appointed guardian to John Smith to defend this suit - 8 July, 1822 - p. 111

John Hyslop and Nancy, his wife, Dennard Travis and Susan, his wife, and Stephen Whitehead and Thomas Whitehead, by Dennard Travis, their next friend, vs. - Suit for Division of Land.
William Whitehead.

That a certain John Whitehead, late of the County of Northampton, departed this life the ___ day of ___ A.D. 18__, being at the time of his death seized in fee simple of a certain tract of land touching the lands of ___, containing ___ acres, more or less; that at the time of his death the said John left five children, viz: your orator and oratrixes, Nancy Hyslop, Susan Travis, Stephen Whitehead, Thomas Whitehead and William Whitehead, and a widow Sukey Whitehead, &c. -------- 10 June, 1822 - p. 117

Levin Copes, vs. - Suit for sale of land.
Eliza Downs and William Downs, infant children of William Downs, deceased.

That a certain William Downs of this county, was in his lifetime and at the time of his death seized in fee of a certain tract or parcel of land containing, by estimation, 12 acres, and being so seized in or about the year 1811, died intestate leaving the following children, to-wit: Daniel Downes, Henry Downs, Eliza Downs and William Downs; that upon the death of the said William Downs, the intestate, father of the aforesaid children, the said 12 acres of land descended to his aforesaid children who became seized thereof, and the said Daniel Downs and Henry Downs being seized each of one undivided one fourth part of said 12 acres of land, sold and conveyed their each one undivided one fourth part to your orator, Levin Copes - 14 October, 1822 - p. 119

William Travis, William Warren and Peggy, his wife,
    Shadrack Travis and Meshack Travis and Molly Travis,
    by said William Travis, their next friend,
vs. - Suit for division of land.
Dennard Travis.

That a certain Shadrack Travis, late of the County of Northampton, departed this life on the __ day of __, 18__, leaving a will, being at the time of his death seized in fee simple of a certain tract of land in the County aforesaid. That at the time of his death the said Shadrack Travis left other children as well as your orators and oratrixes; your orators and oratrixes have the following names, to-wit: William Travis, Shadrack Travis, William Warren and Peggy, his wife, and Meshack Travis and Molly Travis aforesaid, and Dennard Travis is also son of Shadrack Travis deceased. At the death of the said Shadrack Travis. At the death of the said Shadrack Travis his land went according to his will to your orators and oratrixes and Dennard Travis aforesaid, which land has since been divided in equal parts to them as the will aforesaid gave it, leaving to the widow, Rachel Travis, her dower, which was found on survey to be 47 1/2 acres. That the widow, Rachel Travis, departed this life on the __ day of __, A.D. 18__, and your orators and oratrixes are advised that on the death of the said Rachel Travis the 47 1/2 acres of land, her dower, was the property of them, your said orators and oratrixes and the said Dennard Travis, and subject to be equally divided between them &c. -------- 10 June, 1822 - p. 120

James Wilson and Susanna, his wife, &c.,
vs. - Suit for sale and division.
William Spady, James, John, Benjamin, George, Mary, Samuel,
    Ann and William Spady, infant children of John Spady,
    deceased.

That a certain James Spady, late of this County, departed this life on the __ day of __, 1814; that previous to his death, viz: on the 10 March, 1813, the said James Spady duly made and published his last will and testament in writing, in which, among other things, there is the following clause: "I lend my loving wife all my estate after paying my just debts, as long as she lives my widow, and at her death or marriage all the remaining part of my estate to be sold and equally divided between my brother John Spady's children and my sister Adad Spady's daughter Sukey Spady, and my sister Betsey Spady's son William Spady." That your oratrix, Amelia Spady is the widow of the said James Spady, and that your oratrix Sukey Wilson is the same person mentioned in said will as the testator's sister, Adah Spady's, daughter Sukey Spady - Your orator and oratrix have been married since the date of the said James Spady's will, &c. ------- 9 December, 1822 - p. 122

Laban Johnson,
vs. - Suit for recovery of land.
Hezekiah Dalby and James Dalby, administrators of William
      Richardson, deceased, and Edward, Pamela and
      Euphemia Richardson, children and heirs of William
      Richardson, and Margaret Richardson, widow of
      William Richardson.
That a certain William Richardson, late of this County, being in his lifetime seized in fee of a certain tract of land, containing, by estimation, 10 1/3 acres, more or less, adjoining the land of Archibald Dennis and others, and being desir-out to sell the said tract of land, your orator in or about the month of January, 1823, came to an agreement with the said William Richardson for the absolute purchase of the said land--------that the said William Richardson departed this life intestate, leaving his widow, the aforesaid Margaret Richardson, and the following children, to-wit: Edward Richardson, Pamelia Richardson and Euphamia Richardson, all of whom are still alive. That administration on the estate of the said William Richardson was on the __ day of __, 1823, by the County Court of Northampton, granted to Hezekiah Dalby and James Dalby. Your orator further shows that he was always ready and willing to perform his part of the said agreement, &c. -------- 14 July, 1823 - p. 136

Smaw, et ux, et als,
vs. - Suit for division of land.
Rosey Elliott.
That a certain John Elliott, late of the County of Northampton, departed this life on the __ day of __, A. D. __, leaving his last will and testament, being at the time of his death seized in his own right of a certain plantation or tract of land on which he in his lifetime resided, touching the land of Thomas W. Scott's heirs, those of William Wilkins, William Stratton's heirs and those of Major S. Pitts. That at the time of his death John Elliott left four children, to-wit: your oratrix Nancy Smaw, wife of Daniel Smaw, and Polly Elliott, John Elliott and Rosey Elliott --------that since the death of the said John Elliott, his widow, Polly Elliott, has also departed this life on the __ day of __ intestate, being at the time of her death seized in her own right of a lot of land touching the land of John Elliott aforesaid, and a part of the same plantation, containing four acres, more or less---------that she was also seized in her own right of a tract of land or plantation touching the lands of James Saunders, John Spady and William Stratton's heirs, and that she was also seized in her own right of another tract of land or plantation touching the land of Walter Luker's heirs, &c. All of which land, both of John Elliott and his

101

widow Polly, is situate in Northampton County. That at the time of her death the said Polly left four children, viz: your orator and oratrixes, John Elliott, Nancy Smaw, Polly Elliott and Rosey Elliott, they being the same four children that were of the said John Elliott, deceased, &c. ---- 11 August, 1823 - p. 145

Alexander Wales Ward and Jennett, his wife, William White and
       Sally, his wife, Robert Sanford, Jacob Sturgis and Margaret,
       his wife,
vs. - Suit for division.
Edward Turner.

    That a certain James Sanford and Sarah, his wife, late of this County, were on the 4 day of July, 1792, seized and possessed in fee simple, in right of the said Sarah, of a plantation situate near Nasswadox Creek in this County, containing, by estimation, 300 acres, adjoining the lands of Joseph White's heirs, Littleton Major's heirs, Ellison Armistead's heirs and others, and being so thereof seized the said James Sanford and Sarah, his wife, by deed duly executed on the 4 day of July, 1792, conveyed the said plantation in fee simple to their son, James Sanford, from and after the death of the said James Sanford and Sarah, his wife, and the survivor of them.-------- That the said Sarah Sanford departed this life on the __day of __, 179_; that the said James Sanford the younger departed this life under age, intestate and without issue on the __day of __, 1799; that the said James Sanford the elder departed this life on the __day of October, A. D. 1819-------- that at the death of the said James Sanford the younger, he left two brothers and one sister of the whole blood, viz: your oratrix Sally and your orator Robert, and a certain John Sanford; one neice, your oratrix Jennet, who is the only child of his deceased sister of the Whole Blood, Nancy Turner, formerly Nancy Sanford, and one nephew and one neice, viz: your oratrix Margaret and the said Edward, who are the only children of his deceased maternal sister of the half blood, and the said James Sanford, Jr., left no other brothers or sisters, &c. -------- 13 March, 1820 - p. 149

Polly Dunton and Thomas Dunton, by Severn E. Parker, their Attorney, vs. - Suit for division of Land.
Robert Dunton and Ann Dunton, children of Thomas Dunton, deceased.

    That a certain Thomas Dunton, father of your orator and oratrix, was in his lifetime and at the time of his death, seized in fee simple of a small tract or parcel of land, containing five acres, more or less, and being so seized the said Thomas Dunton departed this life on or about ____ day of ____, in the year 1815, intestate, and leaving as his next of kin your oratrix, Polly Dunton, your orator Thomas Dunton, Robert Dunton and Ann Dunton his only children, &c. ---- June, 1822 - p. 170

John Collins and Sally Collins, infants, by George Smith,
    their next friend,
vs. - Suit for sale and division of land.
William Collins and Polly Griffith.

That Gracy Collins, mother of your orator and oratrix, died about the year 18_ seized and possessed of 11 3/4 accres of land, lying in the County of Northampton, she also died intestate leaving your orator and oratrix and Polly and William Collins her only children and heirs. The said Polly married Littleton Griffin, who is since dead --------
12 April, 1824 - p. 173

William Costin, by Thomas R. Joynes, his attorney,
vs. - Suit for recovery of land.
William Thomas, and Fanny, his wife, formerly Fanny Nottingham,
    Jacob Nottingham, Patsey Nottingham and Elizabeth
    Nottingham, children and heirs of Thomas Nottingham,
    deceased.

That on the 10 December, 1810, Abraham Costin and Thomas Nottingham, late of this County, sold and conveyed to your orator a certain tract of land situate in this County, containing, by estimation, 60 acres, being part of a tract of land formerly belonging to Francis Costin, deceased, and the said Abraham Costin and Thomas Nottingham in and by the said deed did warrant and defend the title to the said land to your orator, in fee simple--------that one moiety of the tract so sold and conveyed as aforesaid was held by the said Abraham Costin as tenant by the curtesy, and the remaining moiety was held by the said Thomas Nottingham as tenant by the curtesy with remainder to his two children, Fanny and Jacob, who were children of his deceased wife Patsey Nottingham, formerly Patsey Costin, a daughter of the said Francis Costin--------That the said Thomas Nottingham in order to secure the title to the moiety of the land sold and conveyed as aforesaid, duly executed a deed conveying to your orator in mortgage a certain tract or parcel of land situate in this County on Old Plantation Creek, adjoining the land of Benjamin Stratton, John Nivison and others, and containing, by estimation, 75 acres, with a proviso that same should be void if the said Thomas Nottingham should make or cause to be made to your orator, his heirs or assigns, a good and sufficient title in fee simple to the said 30 acres of land ---------
that the said Thomas Nottingham departed this life intestate in the year 1814, leavving four children, viz: the said Fanny and Jacob by the first marriage, and Patsey and Elizabeth by his second marriage, to all of whom the said 75 acres descended, subject to the aforesaid mortgage------that since the death of the said Thomas Nottingham the said Fanny Nottingham intermarried with a certain William Thomas; that on the _day of _, 1823, the said William Thomas and Fanny, his wife, and the said Jacob Nottingham, sued out of the Clerk's Office of the Superior Court of this County a writ of quod reddat against your orator to recover the 30 acres of land sold and conveyed as aforesaid--------that at the May term of said Superior Court, in the year 1823, a verdict and judgment were rendered in favor

of the said William Thomas and Fanny, his wife, and Jacob Nottingham against your orator for the said 30 acres--------that since the determination of the said suit your orator has frequently applied to the said William Thomas and Fanny, his wife, Jacob, Patsey and Elizabeth Nottingham and requested them to pay him the sum of $275., the purchase price of the said 50 acres, or else to deliver up to your orator the possession of the 75 acres aforesaid, &c.--------- August, 1823 - p. 178

Williams, et ux,
vs. - Suit for division of land.
Clay, et als.

That Benjamin Clay and John Clay, both late of this County, were in their lifetimes seized each of 30 acres of land by descent from their father, Thomas Clay, and also the said Benjamin Clay was in his lifetime and at the time of his death, seized of 8 acres of land descended to him from his mother, and the said John Clay was also in his lifetime and at the time of his death seized of 14 1/2 acres of land descended to him from his mother; That the said Benjamin and John Clay being so seized both departed this life in the year 1823, under the age of 21 years and without issue, leaving as their next of kin your oratrix Nancy, their sister of the whole blood, who intermarried with your orator Peter Williams on the __day of __18__; your oratrix Sukey, their sister of the whole blood, who intermarried with your orator Azariah Williams on the __day of __, 182_; James Clay, a brother of the half blood, and Eliza Clay and Thomas Clay, their brother and sister of the whole blood, all of whom are now alive except James Clay, who departed this life on the __day of __, in the year 182_, having first duly made and published his last will and testament, and by said will he gave and devised the whole of his estate, real and personal, to his wife, Elizabeth Clay, your oratrix--------so that your orators and oratrixes and the said Elizabeth Clay and Thomas Clay are entitled to have division of the said several parcels of land &c. --------- 13 July, 1824 - p. 187

William E. Lyon,
vs. - Suit for division of land.
Margaret Lyon.

That the late Dr. James Lyon departed this life intestate on or about the ___day of December 1811, leaving your orator and Margaret Lyon his only children and heirs. That the said Dr. Lyon at the time of his death was seized and possessed of the following tracts of land, viz: - A tract situate near Eastville, containing 206 acres; a tract containing 100 acres in Northampton County; a tract containing 220 1/2 acres in Northampton; a lot of land with two houses thereon in Eastville; also a small house and lot in Eastville on the main street.

John Eyre appointed guardian of Margaret Lyon, infant, to defend this wuit. 13 Sept. 1824 - p. 191

William P. Johnson,
vs. - Suit for sale of land.
A. B. Johnson's heirs.

That by deed dated 15? July, 1821, a certain Abel B. Johnson mortgaged to your orator, William P. Johnson, twelve acres of land, more or less, lying in Occohannock Neck, being "all that part of the land which fell to the said Abel B. Johnson by the death of his mother", in order to secure to your orator the sum of $400.--------that the said Abel B. Johnson departed this life on or about the __day of __, leaving the said debt wholly due and unpaid. Your orator hath qualified as the administrator of the said Johnson, but no assets have come into his hands wherewith to pay and satisfy the said debt; he is ready, however, to render an account of his administration whenever the Court shall require it. The heirs of the said Abel B. Johnson are your orator, John Young and Susan, his wife, Edmund Ayres and Kessy, his wife, in right of their said wives, Richard Johnson and Rachell Abdell, all of whom refuse the said mortgage, &c. -------- January, 1824 - p. 201

Arthur R. Savage,
vs. - Suit for sale of land.
William Dixon's Ex'r. & heirs.

That the late William Dixon, Sr., of William, of this County, being indebted to your orator in the sum of $1,242. by note, did on the 7th day of March, 1820, execute to your orator a mortgage on a tract of land containing, by estimation, 237 acres, more or less, adjoining the land of William Satchell, which he purchased of Elias Dunton, &c. -------- that the said William Dixon departed this life on the __day of __, leaving Joanna Dixon, Polly Dixon, William Dixon and Elizabeth Dixon his children and only heirs and devisees, and William Satchell his Executor. The said William Satchell hath also departed this life, having first made his will, of which he constituted John H. Harmanson Executor. The said children of the said Dixon are all infants of tender years -------- March, 1824 - p. 204

Edward Turner,
vs. - In debt.
Joynes, et al.

The complaint of Edward Turner sheweth that a certain Kendall Joynes, late of the County of Northampton, but now of the County of Nansemond, was on the 9th August, 1819, indebted to your orator in the sum of 798.83, for which the said Kendall executed a bill obligatory to your orator; that on the 29 September, 1819, your orator instituted an action of debt on said bill obligatory in the Superior Court of this County, and at the May term, in the year 1820, judgment was rendered in favor of your orator for his said debt, &c. -------- October, 1822 - p. 211

105

Savage's Executor

vs. - In Debt.

Harmanson, et al.

The complaint of Severn E. Parker, Executor of the last will and testament of Thomas L. Savage, deceased; that Elizabeth Harmanson being seized in fee of and in a certain plantation or tract of land hereinafter mentioned, and being indebted to the said Thomas L. Savage in his lifetime in the sum of $1,083.33, and in order to secure the payment of same did propose to mortgage to the said Thomas L. Savage in his lifetime the aforesaid tract of land, in which said tract of land a certain Lucretia Kendall (who departed this life on or about the __ day of __, in the year 1823) had a life interest. That the said Thomas L. Savage in his lifetime did accept of the said proposal of the said Elizabeth Harmanson, and that the said Elizabeth Harmanson, together with the said Lucretia Kendall, did on the 28 September, 1812, in order to secure the payment of the said sum, convey to the said Thomas L. Savage a certain tract or parcel of land situate in the County of Northampton, containing, by estimation 128 acres, more or less, adjoining the lands of the late Dr. James Lyon, deceased, the county road, the land of Capt. Parrot and the lands formerly belonging to Matthew Harmanson, deceased--------That the said Thomas L. Savage departed this life on or about the 13 day of June, 181_, having first made his last will and testament, &c. -------- April, 1824 - p. 230

William Warren, Jr.,

vs. - Suit for division of land.

Ira Wingate, Henry Wingate and Sarah Wingate.

Your orator, William Warren, Jr., humbly complains that on the __ day of __ his mother, Amy Wingate, (widow of William Wingate, deceased) departed this life being at the time of her death legally seized in fee simple of a tract of land in the County aforesaid; that your orator, together with Ira Wingate, Henry Wingate and Sarah Wingate are the only surviving children and heirs of the aforesaid Amy Wingate, and as such are legally entitled to the said land, &c.

Daniel Wingate appointed guardian of the infant defendants, Ira, Henry and Sarah Wingate, to defend this suit. 12 September, 1825 - p. 239

William Evans,

vs. - Suit for division of land.

Nancy Evans, widow, and John, Sarah Ann and Caroline Evans,

       infant children of William S. Evans, deceased.

That William S. Evans departed this life leaving your orator and John Evans, Sarah Ann Evans and Caroline Evans his only children and Nancy Evans his widow. That the said William S. Evans at the time of his death was seized of a tract of land in the said County, containing 28 acres, &c. -------- 9 January, 1826 - p. 258

John K. Floyd,
vs. - Suit for sale of land.
Custis Kendall's devisees, et al.

That about the year 1818 Custis Kendall, of Northampton, being or pretending to be, seized in fee of and in a tract of land hereinafter mentioned, and having occasion for money did apply to your orator to lend him the sum of $760.; and in order to secure the payment of the same did propose to mortgage to your orator the said tract of land, and did on the 16 November, 1818, mortgage to your orator a certain tract of land lying in the County of Northampton containing 175 acres, more or less, adjoining the land of Elizabeth Wilkins, George F. Wilkins and Margaret Wilkins, Scott's Branch and King's Creek--------- that the said Custis Kendall duly made and published his last will and testament, bearing date on or about the 21 day of March, 1822, and among other things devised as follows: "All the balance of my estate after paying my just debts, that I have not before given I leave to be equally divided between my loving wife, Elizabeth W. Kendall, my son William H. Kendall and a child not yet born but soon expected, to be equally divided between them and their heirs forever."

That the said Custis Kendall departed this life on or about the __day of __, 1822, after which the said will, on the 10 June, 1822, was duly proved and admitted to record--------that the child spoken of in the above recited clause as "not yet born but soon expected, was born on the __ day of __, 1822, and was christened and called by the name of Elizabeth Custis Kendall. That the said mortgaged premises were included in the balance of the said testator's estate not before given--------June, 1825 - p. 261

John Casey and Ann, his wife,
vs. - Suit for division of land and slaves.
Thomas Rippin and Susan, his wife, John Joynes and Letitia, his wife,
     Frances Willis, also Sarah Ann, Margaret and Emily Win-
gate, infant children of Daniel Wingate, and Daniel Wingate,
     guardian by nature to the said infant defendants.

That one Marriot Willis of the aforesaid County, departed this life on the __ day of __, 1825, seized in fee of __acres of land, situate in the aforesaid County, and possessed of the following slaves; Esther, Sarah and two infant children, Peter, Adah, John and Alfred, together with other personal property--------that your orators, together with Susan, wife of Thomas Rippin, Letitia, wife of John Joynes, Frances Willis and Comfort Willis, now deceased, were the only children of the aforesaid Marriot Willis; That Comfort Willis married Daniel Wingate and died leaving Sarah Ann, Margaret and Emily Wingate her only surviving children and heirs; That your orator qualified as administrator of the estate of the said Marriot Willis and is now ready to deliver the said slaves aforesaid to those who may be entitled to the same, &c. -------- 15 November, 1825 - p. 267

107

William Smith, Sr., and Esther, Elizabeth, Susan, Henry, Sarah,
    John and Ann Smith, infants, by the said William Smith
    their next friend,
vs. - Suit for division of land.
George Smith, Jr.
    That George Smith, Sr., late of the said County, died seized of two
tracts or parcels of land situate in said County, the one containing 96
acres, or thereabouts, and the other 45 acres, or thereabouts, more or
less; That your orators and oratrixes, together with George Smith, Jr.,
are the only surviving children and heirs of the said George Smith, Sr.;
That the said Esther is deaf and dumb, and the aforesaid Elizabeth,
Susan, Henry, Sarah, John and Ann are infants, &c. ------- 10 April,
1826 - p. 271

Elizabeth, Susan, Henry, Sarah and John Smith, by Daniel Fitchett,
    their next friend,
vs. - Suit for sale and division.
Ann Smith.
    That your orators and oratrixes, together with Ann Smith, are infant
children of George Smith, Sr., deceased, by his wife Lucretia, formerly
Lucretia Costin, also deceased; That the aforesaid Lucretia, their
mother, was before and at the time of her marriage seized in fee
simple of a certain piece or parcel of land containing about 12 acres,
more or less, and that she died on the __day of __ without having
conveyed the said land in any manner; that their father, George Smith,
Sr., also died on the __ day of __, whereby the interest in and to said
land in fee simple held by their mother aforesaid, has descended to
your orators and oratrixes and the defendant aforesaid, &c. -------- 8
May, 1826 - p. 274

George Eshon, Jr.,
vs. - Suit for sale and division.
Daniel, William, Samuel and Harriot Eshon & Abel Belote, Jr.,
    & Susan, his wife.
    That George Eshon, Sr., departed this life on the __day of __ seized
of land lying in said county containing ___acres. That the said Daniel
Eshon, Sr. had the following children besides your orator, to-wit:
Daniel Eshon, Jr., William Eshon, Samuel Eshon, Harriet Eshon and
Ann Eshon, now deceased, who married Hezekiah Belote and left Abel
Belote, Jr., his only surviving child, &c. -------- 15 November, 1825
- p. 290

David C. Taylor,
vs. - Suit for land.
William Warrington, et al.
    That a certain Josiah Heath of this county departed this life on or
about the __day of __ seized and possessed of two tracts of land and
houses thereon in the village of Bridgetown. He left a widow and one

child, an infant of very tender years who inherited his property. On the __day of __, the said child departed this life under age and without issue, leaving as his heirs at law John S. Heath and William Warrington, which William is the son of a sister of the half blood to the said Josiah. On the __ day of __ the said John S. Heath executed a deed of mortgage, or deed of trust, on his interest in said lots to A. P. Upshur, Littleton Upshur and John Fox, (who was lately married to the widow of the said Josiah Heath) to secure the payment of sundry sums of money due them respectively--------That the said interest was sold under said deed, at which sale your orator, Daniel C. Taylor, became the purchaser, &c. -------- December, 1825 - p. 292

Read, et ux, et al,
vs. - Suit for sale and division.
N. B. Turner and Nancy, his wife.

That a certain Tabby Wainhouse being seized in fee of and in a certain piece or parcel of land situate in this County on Occohannock Creek, containing 70 acres, more or less, adjoining the lands of Golding Ward's heirs and James Turner; That the said Tabby intermarried with a certain Joshua Turner, late of this county, by whom she had issue, to-wit: Zilla, Comfort, Peggy, Nancy and Nathaniel Turner. That the said Tabby departed this life on or about the __day of __1814, leaving her said husband then living and the following children and grandchildren, to-wit: Nancy, wife of Edmond Read, Peggy and Nathaniel, children; Catharine, wife of William Henderson and only issue of Comfort; George L. E. Tankard, Fanny, Mary and Hannah Tankard and Peggy Wyatt, wife of William Wyatt, children of Zilla and grandchildren of the said Tabby; Ann and George Lewer, only children of Hannah Lewer, deceased, formerly Hannah Tankard, to which said children and grandchildren the aforesaid land descended (subject to the right of the said Joshua Turner as tenant by the curtesy)-------- that the said Joshua Turner, the tenant by the curtesy as aforesaid, departed this life on or about the 4th day of September, 1821, upon which event your orators and oratrixes became entitled to enter and take possession of the said land &c. ------- 9 September, 1822

On the 9 August, 1824, the plaintiffs filed a new bill as follows:
The bill of complaint of Edmund Read and Nancy, his wife, William Henderson and Catharine, his wife, William Wyatt and Peggy, his wife, George L. E. Tankard, Peggy Turner, William Pettit and Fanny, his wife, formerly Fanny Tankard, Mary Tankard, Anne Lewer and George Lewer, infants, by George L. Tankard their next friend, humbly sheweth unto your worships:
That a certain Tabitha Turner departed this life in or about the year 1812, being at that time seized in fee simple of a tract of land containing, by estimation 96 acres, situate on Occohannock Creek in this County, adjoining the lands of James S. Turner and others, and subject to a life estate in a certain Joshua Turner as tenant by the curtesy: That the said Joshua Turner departed this life sometime in the year 1821, and upon his death your orators and oratrixes are advised that

109

the said tract of land became subject to division among the heirs at law of the said Tabitha Turner. That the following persons are the heirs at law of the said Tabitha Turner, viz: Your oratrix Nancy B. Read, her daughter; Margaret Turner, her daughter; your oratrix Catharine Henderson, her grandaughter, being the only child of her deceased daughter, Sally Michael, formerly Sally Turner; also your oratrix Margaret Wyat, the wife of William Wyat, George L. Tankard, Fanny Pettit, formerly Fanny Tankard, Mary Tankard and George and Ann Lewer, the only children of Hannah Lewer, formerly Hannah Tankard, the said Margaret, George L., Fanny, Mary and Hannah Tankard being the only children of Zilla Tankard, formerly Zilla Turner, a daughter of the said Tabitha Turner. The said Tabitha Turner also left one grandaughter, Elizabeth Kellam, the wife of Samuel Kellam, the only child of Comfort Downing, deceased, Comfort Turner, a daughter of the said Tabitha Turner; the said Tabitha Turner also left one son Nathaniel Turner -------- p. 298 et seq.

William P. Johnson,
vs. - Suit for division of land.
Margaret, Harriet, Mary and Kitty Johnson, heirs of Richard
        Johnson, deceased, and Polly Johnson, widow of the said
        Richard Johnson.
    That a certain Abel B. Johnson, late of this County, being seized in fee of one undivided one seventh of a certain tract of land situate, lying and being in the County of Northampton, containing 79 acres, and mortgaged the said undivided one seventh of said land to your orator by deed dated __day of __, 182_, to secure the payment of a certain sum of money in said deed mentioned. That said land was sold under a former decree of this Court, at which sale your orator became the purchaser--------that the remainder of the said tract of land was held by a certain Richard Johnson in fee: That the said Richard Johnson on the __day of __18__, departed this life intestate, leaving a widow, Polly Johnson, and the following children: Margaret Johnson, Harriett Johnson, Mary Johnson and Kitty Johnson, all of whom are now alive and in being, so that your orator is entitled as purchaser under the said decree to one seventh of the said tract containing 79 acres, &c. -------- 15 November, 1825 - p. 305, et seq.

Nancy Travis and William Elliott,
vs. - Suit for sale and division of land.
Thomas, James, John and Polly Elliott and Nathaniel Hickman
        and Sally, his wife.
    That a certain Thomas Elliott, late of this County, was in his lifetime and at the time of his death, seized in fee of a certain parcel or tract of land in said County, containing 70 acres, or thereabouts: That the said Thomas Elliott being so seized of said land on or about the __day of __ 18__, departed this life intestate leaving your oratrix, Nancy Travis, your orator, William Elliott, Thomas Elliott, James Elliott, John Elliott and Polly Elliott his only children, and Sally

Hickman, formerly Sally Elliott, his widow, who on the __day of __ in the year 1818, intermarried with Nathaniel Hickman ------- 14 November, 1826 - p. 308

Benjamin N. Scott and Elizabeth N. Scott,
vs. - Suit for division of land.
John T. P. Scott.
That a certain Benjamin Scott, Sr., late of the said County, was in his lifetime and at the time of his death, seized in fee of and in the following tract of land containing 340 acres, or thereabouts, in the County of Northampton, and that the said Benjamin Scott, Sr., being so seized of the real estate, on the __day of __, in the year 1826, died intestate leaving your orator Benjamin N. Scott and your oratrix Elizabeth N. Scott his only son and daughter, and John T. P. Scott a grandson, the son of John N. Scott, deceased, who was a son of the said Benjamin Scott, Sr., and that the said real estate descended to your orator and oratrix and the said John T. P. Scott, &c.
Peter S. Bowdoin appointed Guardian to the infant defendant. 13 November, 1826 - p. 312

Molly Powell, et al,
vs. - Suit for division of Land.
Sally Powell, et al.
That a certain Sally Harmanson being seized and possessed of a certain tract or parcel of land containing ___ acres, more or less, situate, lying and being in the County of Northampton, duly made and published her last will and testament in writing, bearing date the 31 day of January, A. D. 1811, and thereby gave the said tract of land to Dicky Bunting and Lishea Bunting, to hold for the term of three years, and after the expiration of the said term she gave the said tract or parcel of land to be equally divided between her two cousins, Sally Powell, daughter of Nathaniel and Betsy Powell, the daughter of George. That the said Sally Harmanson departed this life about the __day of __ 181_, without having altered her said will, which on the 8 April, 1811, was duly proved and admitted to record in the County Court of Northampton County -------- that the said Sally Powell, daughter of Nathaniel, and Betsy Powell, daughter of George, the devisees aforesaid, survived the said Sally Harmanson, the testatrix, and upon her death entered into and became possessed of the said tract or parcel of land--------that the said Sally Powell, daughter of Nathaniel, being seized and possessed of her undivided moiety of the said tract of land on the __day of __, 181_, departed this life intestate and of the age of 21, leaving as her next of kin your oratrix, Molly Powell, her mother, your orators George Powell and Thomas Powell, her brothers, and your oratrixes Margaret Fitchett and Hannah Fitchett, and Sally Powell and Nancy Powell her sisters, all of whom are now alive and in being-------- that the aforesaid Sally Powell, daughter of George, one of the devisees aforesaid, is intermarried with a certain William Ridley of this County and is now alive and in being,

so that your orators and oratrixes the said Sally Powell and Nancy Powell, and the said William Ridley and Sally, his wife, are entitled to have division of the said tract of land in manner following, to-wit:

To the said William Ridley and Sally, his wife, in right of his said wife, one half to hold to them as their own proper land; to your oratrix Molly Powell one seventh of the remaining one half; to your orators George and Thomas Powell each one seventh; to your orators and oratrixes Charles Fitchett and Margaret, his wife, in right of said wife, one seventh; to Thomas Fitchett and Hannah, his wife, in right of said wife, one seventh, and to Sally Powell and Nancy Powell each one seventh.

The will of the said Sally Harmanson referred to in the foregoing bill, filed and prayed to be taken as a part thereof, is in these words and figures following, to-wit: "In the Name of God Amen, I Sally W. Harmanson" &c. (abstract) To Thomas K. Dunton silver watch, gold sleeve buttons, $100. To Amy Tankard clothing - The rents of my two plantations lying Occohannock for three years to come to Dicky Bunting and Lishea Bunting to school and support them. I give the plantation my father gave me to my loving niece Rosey Savage after the said three years. I give the plantation that my brother Moses Johnson gave me to my cousin Sally Powell, Sr., daughter of Nathaniel and Betsey Powell, daughter of George, to be equally divided between them after the said three years - Wearing apparel. Money to be divided between my niece Rosey Savage and Sally Powell, Sr., of Nathaniel. Niece Rosey Savage and Sally Powell, Sr., of Nathaniel, resid. legatees. Friend William Dunton and brother in law John H. Harmanson Executors. Witt: Thomas Dowty, Amy Tankard, Matthew H. Dunton. Dated 31 January, 1811 - Probated 8 April, 1811.

Before a final decree was entered in the above case Sally Ridley departed this life leaving Mary Ann Ridley her only child and heir who is hereby made a party to this suit - 21 February, 1814 - p. 320

Sally Bishop and William Bishop,
vs. - Suit for sale and division.
George Bishop, Nathaniel Bishop and Sylvester Bishop, infant children
 of Nathaniel Bishop, deceased.

That your oratrix, Sarah Bishop and your orator William Bishop, of Northampton, together with George, Nathaniel and Sylvester Bishop, the two former brothers and the latter as sister of your orator and oratrix, all of the County and State aforesaid, and the defendants hereinafter named, are now seized in fee simple in possession as tenants in coparcenary in undivided five parts of and in the lands in the bill mentioned, &c., containing 79 acres, more or less, lying and being in the County of Northampton, adjoining the lands of John Goffigon, Levin Dix, Thomas Jefferson, Thomas Fitchett, Sr., &c., which said lands formerly belonged to Nathaniel Bishop, the father of your oratrix and orator, and of the said George, Nathaniel and Sylvester Bishop -------- 11 June, 1827 - p. 330

Thomas Williams, Jr., Samuel S. Williams, William B. Jarvis & Margaret, his wife (formerly Margaret Williams), Thomas S. Spady and Elizabeth, his wife, (formerly Elizabeth Williams), Margaret Williams, devisee of John Williams, Jr., Juliet, Elizabeth, Smith and John Nottingham, infants of Smith Nottingham and Sally, his wife, (formerly Sally Williams) now deceased, by Smith Nottingham their next friend,

vs. - Suit for sale and division of land.
William S. Williams.

That a certain James Williams on the __day of __, died leaving no children or issue, but leaving a widow, Susan, late Susan Pede, who is now dead; That the said James Williams at his death was entitled to an undivided share of the lands of John Williams, Jr. That his share in said land, exception which his widow aforesaid, Susan, late Susan Pede, was entitled to as dower, was equally divided among his collateral heirs after his death. That the dower portion of the said Susan yet remains undivided and is bounded by the lands of William Goffigon's heirs and Southy Nelson's heirs, James Goffigon and William S. Williams, and contains about ___ acres; that the aforesaid Margaret Jarvis, formerly Margaret Williams, and Elizabeth Spady, formerly Elizabeth Williams, are sisters of the said James of the whole blood; that the said Thomas Williams, Jr. and Samuel S. Williams, John Williams, Jr., devisor of Margaret William, and Sally Nottingham, formerly Sally Williams, and mother of Juliet, Elizabeth, Smith and John Nottingham, infants as aforesaid, and a certain William S. Williams are brothers and sisters of the said James of the half blood, that therefore the said William B. Jarvis and Margaret, his wife, and the said Thomas S. Spady and Elizabeth, his wife, are entitled to a whole share each in the lands aforesaid, being all the dower of the aforesaid Susan, and that the aforesaid Thomas Williams, Jr., Margaret Williams, devisee of said John Williams, Jr., Samuel S. Williams, the children of the said Sally Nottingham aforesaid, and the said William S. Williams are entitled to one half share each in the said land, &c. -------- 10 September, 1827 - p. 335

John Addison,
vs. - Suit for sale of land.
William Nottingham and Margaret, his wife, Alexander W. Ward and Jenny, his wife, and William, Thomas, Samuel and Esther Nottingham.

That a certain James S. Turner, late of this county, being seized in fee of and in a certain tract or parcel of land hereinafter mentioned, and being desirous to secure your orator from all loss or injury which your orator might sustain from your orator being bound as the said James S. Turner's security in a bond formerly due to John Eyre, and on the 30 November, 1825, in a suit in the Court of Northampton in the name of William E. Lyon for the use of John C. Wilson, and for the sum of $375.36, dated 1 January, 1824, and being also desirous to secure your orator & a certain John Widgeon from all loss or damage in their securetyship for the said James S. Turner in his admistration on the estate of Michael Savage, deceased, did by deed dated 30 November, 1825, mortgage to your orator and the said John Widgeon a tract or parcel of land situate, lying and being in the County of Northampton, containing, by estimation, 420 acres, more or less, adjoining the lands of Thomas E. Addison's heirs, Edward R. Turner, et al, James Sanford's heirs and Joshua Turner's heirs, &c., being the same land where the said James S. Turner lived at the date of the said deed--------that the said James S. Turner on the __day of January, 1826, departed this life intestate, leaving a widow, Sally Turner, a mother, Margaret Nottingham, the wife of William Nottingham, and the following brothers and sisters, Jenny Ward, the wife of Alexander W. Ward, William Nottingham, Thomas Nottingham, Samuel Nottingham and Esther Nottingham,-------- 3 July 1826 - p. 364.

Jacob E. Nottingham and William Thomas and Fanny, his wife, vs. - Suit for sale and division.
Elizabeth Nottingham and Patsy Nottingham, infant children
      of Thomas Nottingham, deceased.
    That your complainants, Jacob Nottingham and William Thomas and Fanny, his wife, formerly Fanny Nottingham, of Northampton County, together with Elizabeth and Patsy Nottingham, sisters of the said Jacob E. Nottingham and Fanny Thomas, all of the County of Northampton aforesaid, are now seized in fee simple in possession as tenants in parcenary, in undivided one fourth part of said lands --------to-wit: a plantation or parcel of land containing 45 acres, more or less, lying in the lower part of the county aforesaid against Old Plantation Creek, adjoining the lands of William D. Stratton, Southy Goffigon, &c., and three slaves, which said land and slaves formerly belonged to Thomas Nottingham, deceased, father of parties aforesaid, &c. -------- 9 July, 1827 - p. 372

Lorenzo D., Mary and John Mears, infants, by John Arlington
      their next friend,
vs. - Suit for sale and division of land.
Alvin and Elizabeth Mears, infant children of William Mears, dec.
    That a certain Anna Colonna, formerly Anna Mears, departed this life intestate and childless in the year 1827, leaving as her next of kin and heirs at law brothers and one sister of the whole blood, viz: your orators and oratrix and one brother and one sister of the half blood, viz: Alvin and Elizabeth Mears. That the said Anna Colonna at her death was seized in her own right in fee simple of a tract of land situate near Matchepungo, in this county, containing, by estimation, 80 acres, be the same more or less, and adjoining the lands of Mary Mears and Edmund W. P. Downing and others, which land on the death of the said Anna Colonna descended in parcenary to her aforesaid brothers and sisters, giving the whole blood whole shares and the half blood half shares. 12 Nov. 1827 - p. 380

John Ker

vs - In debt.

Jacob G. Parker, et ux, et als.

That on the 14 day of September, 1826, a certain Edward Stratton, late of this county, being indebted to your orator in the sum of $3,750., in order to secure the same did by deed dated 14 September, 1826 convey to your orator all that certain tract or parcel of land in the county of Northampton, containing 977 acres, and bounded on the North by a branch of Hungars Creek called "The Gulph", and adjoining Peter S. Bowdoin's lot in Eastville, a lot belonging to the said Edward Stratton, the public lot, a lot belonging to the heirs of William E. Lyon, a lot belonging to John E. Nottingham and the main county road; on the South by Savage's Neck road which separates it from the Old Castle land lately purchased by Dr. Jacob G. Parker from John N. Stratton, Esq., and on the West by the land belonging to Thomas L. Savage and a tributary of Hungars Creek, and being all that certain tract or parcel of land except a 4 acre lot which the said Edward Stratton sold to the said John E. Nottingham and a certain Caleb B. Upshur, which was willed to the said Edward Stratton by his father-------that the said Edward Stratton on the ___ day of __182_ departed this life intestate, leaving a widow, Mary Ann Stratton and an only son _____ Stratton; that the said ____ Stratton departed this life on the __day of ___1828 intestate and under the age of 21 years, leaving as his next of kin and heirs at law Lucy Stratton, his grandmother on the father's side and Sally Wilson and Ann G. Parker, his aunts, the sisters of his deceased father, the said Edward Stratton - 1 June, 1829

17 March, 1831 - It appearing that the defendant, Jacob G. Parker is deceased, this suit abates as to him - p. 393

Samuel G. Carpenter & Betsy, his wife, formerly Betsy Nelson,
      Maria Nelson, infant heiress of Southy Nelson, dec.,
      and Margaret Nelson,

vs. - Suit for sale and division.

Polly Nelson

That a certain Southy Nelson departed this life on or about the __day of __ being at the time of his death seized in fee of a tract of land adjoining the lands of James Goffigon, William S. Williams' heirs, William Goffigon's heirs and others, containing by estimation ____ acres, more or less, and leaving the following children and heirs, to-wit: your oratrix Betsy, now the wife of your orator Samuel G. Carpenter, Maria Nelson, Margaret Nelson and Polly Nelson, who are the sole heirs at law; That he left a widow Sally Nelson now living - 17 Mar. 1832 - p. 401

George Savage, infant of George S. Savage, by Michael R. Savage,
      his guardian and next friend,

vs. - Suit for sale of land.

John T. Savage, infant of George S. Savage.

That the said George S. Savage, father of your complainant, departed this life about the year 1819 or 1820 intestate and seized of about ___ acres of land, about 30 of which have been assigned to your complainant and his infant brother, John T. Savage; that the said lands are very poor, and that your complainant and his said brother, John T. Savage, have no other funds or means of support than the rents and incomes of the lands aforesaid; that the said rents and incomes are very trifling and entirely insufficient for their support and education, &c. ---- 13 July, 1829 - p. 405

Nathaniel West
vs. - Suit for sale and division.
Sally Taylor, widow of George, and William Dalby, infant of John.

That a certain William Dalby, Sr., departed this life on or about the year ___ seized in fee simple of a small piece of land containing, by estimation, five or six acres with a small house thereon, adjoining the lands of William West, John Simkins and Abel Powell's heirs, on the seaside county road in this county. That the said William Dalby, Sr., left three children, to-wit: John, Mary and William, and a widow, now Sally Taylor. That John, the son of William Dalby, Sr., conveyed by his deed dated 17 February, 1812, all his right and interest to the aforesaid tract to your orator; that Mary married with your orator and is since dead leaving one child who is since dead, and that your orator has an estate for life in her share as tenant by the curtesy. That William is since dead leaving no child or widow. That John, aforesaid, died leaving a son named William now an infant, who, as your orator is advised, is entitled to his uncle William's share in said land, and that Sally Taylor, formerly widow of the said William Dalby, Sr., has a title to dower in said land------ 10 Aug. 1827 - p. 408

John Fox and wife's lessee,
vs. - Ejectment proceedings.
Ferdinando Dreadnought.

Jury impanelled and returned the following verdict:
We find that Josiah B. Heath died intestate seized and possessed of the land and tenements in the plaintiff's declaration mentioned, in the month of December, 1815. We also find that at the time of his death he left William Heath and Nancy Heath his only children and his only heirs at law, and Priscilla Heath his widow who is the mother of the said William and Nancy. We also find that the said Nancy died in the year 1816 under age, intestate, unmarried and without issue, and that her mother, the said Priscilla and her brother, the said William, survived her. We also find that the said William Heath died in the year 1824 under age, intestate, unmarried and without issue, and that his mother, the said Priscilla (the female lessor of the plaintiff) survived him. We also find that the said Priscilla who was the widow of the said Josiah B. Heath, in the year 181_ intermarried with a certain John Widgeon who died in the year 18__. We also find that after the death of the said John Widgeon the said Priscilla intermarried with the said John Fox, the lessor of the plaintiff, in the year 1824.

We also find that at the death of the said William his paternal uncle, John S. Heath, entered upon the land and tenements aforesaid, and the said John S. Heath by deed on the 11 day of October, 1824, conveyed the said property, being four acres, more or less, in Bridgetown, in the county aforesaid, and one other lot of land in the said village containing ten acres, to John E. Nottingham in order to secure Littleton Upshur and Abel P. Upshur, administrators of John T. Elliott in the sum of $60.64 and $109.93, respectively, the said lots being described as subject to the dower of Mrs Priscilla Fox, and owned by the said Heath in common with the other heirs of William Heath.

That the said John S. Heath on the 8 November, 1824, conveyed the said property to Jacob G. Parker, High Sheriff, in order to avail himself of the benefit of an act of the General Assembly of the State of Virginia entitled "An Act to Reduce into one the Several Acts concerning Executions, and for the relief of Insolvent Debtors" passed February 25, 1819; That Jacob G. Parker, as sheriff of the said county, by virtue of the said deed, by his deed dated ___ day of ___ 1825, conveyed the lands and tenements in the plaintiff's declaration mentioned to Abel P. Upshur, he being the purchaser at the sale thereof.

We further find that the said Abel P. Upshur, of Vaucluse, and Elizabeth A. B., his wife, by deed dated 1 October, 1826, conveyed to David C. Taylor all his interest in said promises, being 2/3 parts of the said two lots lately owned by Josiah Heath, which said 2/3 interest was inherited from the infant son of the said Josiah by John S. Heath, his uncle, and was purchased by A. P. Upshur at a sheriff's sale thereof subject, nevertheless, to the dower of Mrs Fox, wife of John Fox and late widow of the said Josiah. We also find that the said David C. Taylor, of the county of Accomack, and Margaret, his wife, by deed dated 13 October, 1829, coveyed the said interest in said lots to William Jarvis, Sr., of the county of Northampton. We further find that the said William Jarvis, Sr., of Northampton, made his last will and testament in the following words: (Abstract) To daughter Elizabeth Kendall my King's Creek farm and so much of timber on the land purchased of William and Thomas Wilkins as may be necessary for the use of said farm; slaves; cattle &c. I request my daughter Elizabeth to find Leah Jarvis a home or pay her $10. annually during her life or widowhood. No accounts which I have against my daughter Elizabeth to be collected, but she is debarred all claims against me under penalty of forfeiting the above donations. I lend to my son Thomas Jarvis when he arrives to the age of 21 years, my Hungars farm and my lot at Bridgetown during the life or widowhood of his mother, and at her death I give to my son Thomas the privilege of keeping said farm and lot as his portion of my estate or of throwing up his right in the same and coming into equal division with his brothers and sisters, to-wit: Laura, George, Maria, Jesse and William Simkins. To wife Elizabeth all the balance of my estate, real and personal, during her life or widowhood, she to raise up and support her five youngest children, to-wit: Laura, George, Maria Ann, Jesse and William Simkins, and should any of the said five children marry before the death of their mother they shall be paid at the time of marriage $1000. to be deducted from their portion of my estate.

117

Friends John Goffigon, Sr., and Jesse J. Simkins, with the assistance of my son Thomas when he shall arrive at lawful age, my sole executors. Witt: Jesse J. Simkins, Temple N. Robins, Thomas Fitchett, Jr., James Goffigon, Peter Williams, Jr. - Dated 18 Aug. 1830 - Prob: 10 Jan. 1831.

We find that the defendant, Thomas Jarvis, attained his full age of 21 years on or about the 19 day of November, 1830. We also find that the widow of the said William Jarvis is still alive, &c. -------- 11 Sept. 1832 - p. 414

James Isdel and Lovea, his wife, Henry Mears and James Mears vs. - Suit for sale and division.
Susan Mears, widow of William Mears, dec., Susan Mears, George Mears, Littleton Mears, three of the children of the said William Mears, dec.

That a certain John Mears the first, late of this county, died on the __day of __ 18, __, having first made and published his last will and testament for passing real estate, in which among other things he devised as follows: viz: I leave to my wife Abi Mears all my land on which I now live during her life, at her death to be divided equally between my three sons Littleton Mears, John Mears and William Mears. That the said John Mears at his death left four children, viz: his said sons and a daughter named Tabitha and a widow, the said Abi, alias Abby Mears, surviving him; That the said Littleton Mears sometime after the death of the said John Mears the first, viz: on the __ day of __ A. D. 18__ also died of full age, intestate and without issue, leaving his said mother, Abi Mears, his said brothers John and William Mears and his said sister, Tabitha Mears, surviving him. That since the death of the said Littleton Mears, viz: on the __ day of __ A. D. 18__, the said Tabitha Mears also died of full age, intestate and without issue, leaving her said brothers John and William Mears and her said mother, Abi Mears, surviving her; that since the death of the said Tabitha Mears, viz: on the __ day of __, A. D. 18 __, the said William Mears also departed this life, leaving the following children, viz: your oratrix Lovea Isdel and your orators Henry Mears and your orator James Mears and other children, viz: Susan, George and Littleton Mears, surviving him; that since the death of the said William Mears the said Abi Mears has also departed this life intestate, leaving the said John Mears and the said children of the said William Mears surviving her; That the land of which the said John Mears, the first, died seized and which he disposed of by his said will as aforesaid, is a small tract of land situate in this county, containing, by estimation, 81 acres, more or less, and adjoining the land of Archibald Dennis and others; that since the death of the said Abi Mears the said John Mears and ____, his wife, by deed dated __day of ___, A. D. 18__, coveyed to a certain John W. Leatherbury of this county all their right, title and interest in said tract. That the undivided one half of the tract of land aforesaid to which the said children of the said William Mears, deceased, are entitled is of less value than $300. &c. ------ 13 Nov. 1833 - p. 437

118

William Elliott, Thomas Leatherbury and Nancy, his wife,
formerly Nancy Elliott; Robins Bell and Thomas Bell, infant
children of Geodiah Bell, dec., by George H. Bell their next
friend; William, John, James, Margaret, Juliet and Arinthia
J. Bell, infant children of William Bell, dec., by George H.
Bell their next friend; Hannah, Mary, Nancy and William
Kelly, infant children of John Kelly, dec., by John S. Beach
their next friend; John G. Joynes, Thomas R. Joynes, John
W. Leatherbury and John R. Fisher,

vs. - Suit for division of land.

John Turner, William Andrews and Margaret, his wife; William
Taylor, William G. Pitts, Margaret Pitts, Elizabeth Pitts,
Edward Pitts and Washington Pitts; James Ross, Susan
Ross, Severn Ross, Edward Savage, James Bunting and
Delight Bunting.

That a certain John T. Elliott, late of this county, died intestate on
the __ day of __, 182_, leaving neither child nor children nor the descendant of a child or children, nor father nor mother, nor brother or
brothers, nor sister or sisters, nor the descendant of a brother or sister, nor grandfather or grandmother, neither paternal or maternal, but
the following maternal and paternal kindred, viz: John Elliott and your
orator William Elliott, paternal uncles of the whole blood; Elizabeth,
George, John, Charles and James Elliott and Margaret Elliott and your
oratrix Nancy Leatherbury, children of Charles Elliott, dec., an uncle
of the whole blood who died in the lifetime of the said John T. Elliott,
dec.; Elizabeth, Abel and Molly Elliott, children of William Elliott,
dec., who was a son of the said Charles Elliott and died in the lifetime of the said John T. Elliott, dec.; Timothy, Jesse and Stephen
Kelly, children of Isaiah Kelly and Hannah, his wife, who was formerly
Hannah Elliott, a paternal aunt of the whole blood of the said John T.
Elliott, dec. who died in the lifetime of the said John T. Elliott, dec.;
George and Samuel Parker, two of the children of __ Parker and Anna,
his wife, who was formerly Anna Kelly and a daughter of the said
Isaiah and Hannah Kelly; Edward Turlington, Sally Turlington and
Maria Savage, formerly Maria Turlington, and now the wife of Major
Savage, the said Edward, Sally and Maria being three other children of
the said Anna Parker who after the death of her said husband, __
Parker (who died on the __ day of __ 18_) intermarried with a certain
Joseph Turlington and afterwards had the three children last named
and died in the lifetime of the said John T. Elliott; Molly Savage, now
the wife of Bagwell Savage and a daughter of __ Rogers and Sally, his
wife, the said Sally Rogers was also a daughter of the said Isaiah and
Hannah Kelly, and died in the lifetime of the said John T. Elliott;
Eliza and Thomas Elliot, also children of the said Sally Rogers who
after the death of the said Rogers, her first husband, intermarried with
a certain James Elliott who also died previously to the said John T.
Elliott; Susan East, wife of John East and a daughter of Sophia Kelly,
dec., who was a daughter of the aforesaid Isaiah and Hannah Kelly,
dec.; your oratrixes and orator Hannah, Mary, Nancy and William
Kelly, who are children of John Kelly who was a son of the aforesaid
Isaiah and Hannah Kelly, dec., and died in the lifetime of the said

119

John T. Elliott, dec.; Anne Kelly the only daughter of Charles Kelly, dec., who was a son of the said Isaiah and Hannah Kelly, dec.; William Bell, who was a son of ___ Bell and Nancy, his wife, which said Nancy was a paternal aunt of the whole blood and died in the lifetime of the said John T. Elliott; Betsy, George, Jesse and William Mears and Nancy B. Turlington, the wife of John Turlington, the said Betsy, George, Jesse, William and Nancy being children of Hillars Mears and Euphemia, his wife, which said Euphemia was a daughter of the said ___ Bell and Nancy and died in the lifetime of the said John T. Elliott; John and Anthony Bell, also children of the said ___ Bell and Nancy, his wife; Catharine, Margaret, Lorenzo, James, Mahala, Sally, William H. and George H. Bell and your orators Thomas and Robins Bell, all of whom are the children of Geodiah Bell, dec., who was a son of the said ___ Bell and Nancy, his wife and died in the lifetime of the said John T. Elliott; Geodiah, Thomas and George Bell, the children of George Bell, dec., who was a son of the said ___ Bell and Nancy, his wife, and died in the lifetime of the said John T. Elliott, dec.; William Oague, son of ___Oague and Esther, his wife, who was formerly Esther Turner and a maternal aunt of the whole blood and died previously to the death of the said John T. Elliott; William Broughton, only son of ___ Broughton and Sally, his wife, who was formerly Sally Oague, a daughter of the said ___Oague and Esther, his wife, and died in the lifetime of the said John T. Elliott; Hetty Gladding, wife of George Gladding, and a daughter of ___Wheatley and Rebecca, his wife, which said Rebecca was a daughter of the said ___ Oague and Esther, his wife and died in the lifetime of the said John T. Elliott; Richard and George Addison, who are also the children of the said Esther Oague, who after the death of the said Oague intermarried with a certain ___Addison; George Turner, a maternal uncle of the whole blood; John, William and Littleton Dowty and Margaret Andrews, formerly Margaret Dowty, and now the wife of William Andrews, which said John, William and Littleton Dowty and Margaret Andrews are the children of ___ Dowty and Susan, his wife, who was formerly Susan Turner and a maternal aunt of the whole blood and died in the lifetime of the said John T. Elliott; William Taylor, the only child of ___ Taylor and Caty, his wife, who was formerly Caty Dowty, a daughter of the said ___ Dowty and Susan, his wife, and died in the lifetime of the said John T. Elliott; John, Joshua and Teackle Turner and Polly, wife of Nathaniel West, and formerly Polly Turner, the said John, Joshua and Teackle Turner and Polly West are the children of John Turner, dec., who was a maternal uncle of the whole blood and died in the lifetime of the said John T. Elliott; Jane, wife of Bezeal Watson, and a daughter of ___ Bunting and Priscilla, his wife, who was formerly Priscilla Turner and died in the life time of the said John T. Elliott, and was a materanl aunt of the said John T. Elliott; James and Delight Bunting, children of Shepherd Bunting, dec., who was a son of the said ___ Bunting and Priscilla, his wife, and died in the lifetime of the said John T. Elliott; Nancy Savage, formerly Nancy Turner, a maternal aunt of the whole blood; Hetty, the wife of Henry Cook and daughter of ___ Ross and Rosey, his wife, which said Rosey Ross was formerly Rosey Turner, a maternal aunt of the whole blood, and died in the lifetime of the said John T. Elliott; James Ross, only child of Rosey Ross, dec., who was a daughter of the said __Ross and Rosey, his wife, and died in the lifetime of the said John T. Elliott; Susan and Severn Ross, only children of David Ross, dec., and who was a son of the said __Ross and Rosey, his wife, and died in the lifetime of the said John T. Elliott; John and Polly Ross and Peggy Belote, wife of George T. Belote, and formerly Peggy Ross, which said John and Polly Ross and Peggy Belote are children of John Ross, dec., who was a son of the said __Ross and Rosey Ross, his wife, and died in the lifetime of the said John T. Elliott;

that the said John T. Elliott left surviving him no more uncles or aunts either maternal or paternal than those above mentioned, who are the only heirs at law of the said John T. Elliott, and that the said John T. Elliott left a widow, Mrs Juliet Elliott who is now living.

That the said John T. Elliott was at the time of his death seized in fee simple of several different tracts or parcels of land, situate in the neighborhood of Franktown in this county, and of several different houses and lots in the said town containing on the whole, by estimation, 1200 acres, be the same more or less. That a tract of land containing 300 acres by actual survey, being part of the aforesaid tract, has been assigned to the said Juliet Elliott as and for her dower in the whole of the said real estate of which the said John T. Elliott died seized;

That since the death of the said John T. Elliott, viz: on the ___ day of __ 18__, the aforesaid Margaret Elliott, one of the children of the aforesaid Charles Elliott, dec., who was as aforesaid a paternal uncle of the whole blood of the aforesaid John T. Elliott, dec., departed this life unmarried, intestate and without issue, leaving the following descendants of the said Charles Elliott, dec. surviving her, three of whom, viz: the aforesaid John, George and Charles Elliott are brothers of the half blood, and the remaining descendants aforesaid brothers and sisters, and the descendants of a brother of the whole blood; that the aforesaid William Dowty, one of the children of the aforesaid Thomas Dowty and Susan, his wife, has also died since the death of the said John T. Elliott, dec., of full age, unmarried, intestate and without issue, and leaving the said Thomas Dowty, his father, surviving him; that the aforesaid Nancy Savage, a maternal aunt of the whole blood of the said John T. Elliott, dec., as aforesaid, hath also departed this life since the death of the said John T. Elliott, having first duly made and published her last will and testament, which after her death was duly admitted to record, a copy of which is herewith filed marked "A" as a part of this bill, by which said will the said Nancy Savage devised as follows: "3rd – I give to my sons John R. Savage, George Savage, Thomas D. Savage and Edward C. Savage, the whole of the real estate which I heir from John T. Elliott, dec., subject to the restrictions & limitations hereinafter mentioned, that is to say, if either of my sons die without lawful issue that the surviving brother or brothers have and enjoy the share or shares of those deceasing". That since the death of the said Nancy Savage the aforesaid John Savage, one of her aforesaid children, has also died unmarried and without issue, leaving his brothers, the aforesaid George, Thomas and Edward surviving him, and having first duly made and published his last will and testament, a copy of which is filed herewith marked "B", by which will the said John Savage devised his "right in the whole estate of John T. Elliott, dec., to his said brother Edward Savage.

That the aforesaid George Turner, one of the maternal uncles of the said John T. Elliott as aforesaid, has also departed this life since the death of the said John T. Elliott, having first duly made and published his last will and testament, a copy of which is herewith filed marked "C" as a part of this bill, by which said will the said George Turner devised the whole of the proportion to which he was entitled of the real and personal estate of the said John T. Elliott to his wife, Lavinia, during her life, with remainder to his two sons William G. Turner and Thorowgood West Turner, after the death of the said Lavinia; That the said Thorowgood West Turner has since died intestate and without issue, leaving as his heirs at law his brothers and sisters, viz: William G. Turner, John R. Turner, Mary Belote, Bridget Peyton, wife of William Peyton, Elizabeth Garrison, wife of Jeremiah Garrison, and Narcissa M. Nurse, wife of Uri Nurse, and since his death, viz: on the 10 day of November, 1832, the said William G. Turner was devisee of the said George Turner, dec., and the said William G. Turner, John R. Turner, Mary Belote, William Peyton and Bridget, his wife and Uri Nurse and Narcissa M. Nurse, his wife, as heirs at law to the said Thorowgood West Turner, dec., and as heirs at law of the said George Turner, dec., and also of his widow, the said Lavinia Turner, dec., by deed of that date conveyed all their right, title and interest in the real and personal estate of the said John T. Elliott to your orator, Thomas R. Joynes, a copy of which is herewith filed marked "D"; That since the death of the said John T. Elliott, viz: on the 22 January, 1833, the aforesaid Elizabeth Elliott, who was as aforesaid one of the children of the aforesaid Charles Elliott, dec., a paternal uncle of the whole blood of the said John T. Elliott, by deed of that date conveyed to your orator, Thomas R. Joynes all the right, title and interest to which she was entitled as one of the heirs of the said John T. Elliott, and as one of the heirs of her deceased sister, the aforesaid Margaret Elliott, in and to the real estate of which the said John T. Elliott died seized as aforesaid; that on the 25 day of January, 1829, the aforesaid Thomas Bell and Geodiah Bell and Elizabeth, his wife, by deed of that date, and afterwards, viz: on the 29 December, 1830, the aforesaid George Bell by deed of that date (which said Thomas, Geodiah and George Bell are, as aforesaid, the children of George Bell, dec., who was a son as aforesaid of the aforesaid ____Bell and Nancy, his wife, who was a paternal aunt of the whole blood of the said John T. Elliott, dec.) conveyed to George H. Bell and Lorenzo D. Bell all the right, title and interest to which they were entitled of, in and to the aforesaid real estate of the said John T. Elliott, dec; that since the date last mentioned, viz: on the 8 February, 1833, the aforesaid George H. Bell and Margaret, his wife, Lorenzo D. Bell and Alice Ann, his wife, William H. Bell and Margaret, his wife, James Bell and Charlotte, his wife, Benjamin Bradford and Catharine, his wife (who was formerly Catharine Bell and is the same Catharine Bell above mentioned), Jesse Phillips and Mahala, his wife (who was formerly Mahala alias

Mehaley Bell, and is the same Mahala Bell above mentioned), Sally Bell, alias Sally H. Bell, and Margaret Bell, by deed of that date conveyed to your orator Thomas R. Joynes the interest to which they became entitled as heirs at law of the said John T. Elliott, and to which the said George H. Bell and Lorenzo D. Bell became entitled under the conveyances aforesaid from the aforesaid Thomas Bell and Geodiah Bell and Elizabeth, his wife, and the said George Bell , of, in and to the aforesaid real estate of the said John T. Elliott, dec.; That since the death of the said John T. Elliott, viz: on the 28 September, 1827, the aforesaid Richard and George Addison, together with Matilda, the wife of the said Richard and Elizabeth, the wife of the said George, by deed of that date, and afterwards, viz: on the 31 January, 1831, the said William B. Broughton by deed of that date, and the 31 day of January, 1831, the said George Gladding and Hetty, his wife, by deed of that date, conveyed to your orator Thomas R. Joynes all the right, title and interest to which they were entitled, of, in and to the real estate aforesaid of the said John T. Elliott; That since the death of the daid John T. Elliott, viz: on the 18 January, 1829, the said Joshua B. Turner, by deed of that date; on the 20 January, 1829, the aforesaid Nathaniel West and Mary, his wife, by deed of that date, on the 7 February, 1829, the aforesaid Teackle J. Turner, together with Ann, his wife, by deed of that date, on the 14 December, 1829, the aforesaid Thomas S. Dowty by deed of that date, and on the 29 October, 1830, the aforesaid Thomas D. Savage by deed of that date, conveyed to a certain Littleton Upshur all their right, title and interest to which they were entitled, of, in and to the real estate aforesaid of the said John T. Elliott, dec.; That since the said conveyances the said Littleton Upshur has departed this life, having first made and published his last will and testament; that since his death, viz: on the 14 January, 1833, Abel P. Upshur, the executor of the said Littleton Upshur, in pursuance of the aforesaid will of the said testator, by deed of the date last mentioned, conveyed to your orator, Thoms R. Joynes, all the right, title and interest to which the said Littleton was entitled in said tract of land by virtue of the above mentioned conveyances; That since the death of the said John T. Elliott, viz: on the 27 January, 1824, the aforesaid Jesse Kelly, one of the children of the aforesaid _____and Hannah Kelly, dec., by deed of the date last mentioned conveyed to a certain Thomas W. Smith all the right, title and interest to which he was entitled in said estate, and that since the said conveyance was made to him, the said Smith, he, the said Thomas W. Smith by deed dated 28 January, 1833, conveyed to your orator Thomas R. Joynes all his interest in said estate; That since the death of the said John T. Elliott, viz: on the 12 December, 1828, the aforesaid John Elliott and George Elliott, (two of the children as aforesaid of the said Charles Elliott, dec., who was a paternal uncle of the whole blood of the said John T. Elliott, dec.), by deed of that date conveyed to your orator John G. Joynes all their right in said estate as two of the heirs of their sister, the aforesaid Margaret Elliott, dec., and on the 11 December, 1827, the aforesaid Charles Elliott, one of the children of the aforesaid Charles Elliott, by deed of that date conveyed to your orator, John G. Joynes all his right in said estate as heir of the said

John T. Elliott, and as one of the heirs of the said Margaret Elliott, dec., and on the 14 June, 1828, the aforesaid James Elliott, who is also a son of the aforesaid Charles Elliott, dec., together with Betsey, his wife, conveyed to your orator John G. Joynes all his right as one of the heirs of the said John T. Elliott and as one of the heirs of Margaret Elliott, dec., and on the 1 day of May, 1833, the aforesaid Elizabeth and Molly Elliott, two of the children as aforesaid of the said William Elliott, dec., who was one of the children as aforesaid of the aforesaid Charles Elliott, dec., by deed of that date (the aforesaid Margaret Elliott being at that time dead), conveyed to your orator, John G. Joynes, all their right, title and interest in said estate, and on the 19 December, 1828, the aforesaid Abel Elliott, who was a son of the last named William Elliott, dec., (the said Margaret being then dead), conveyed to the said John G. Joynes all his right, title and interest in said estate, and on the 1 May, 1833, the aforesaid Edward Turlington and George S. Parker, together with Polly, the wife of the said George S. Parker, which said Edward and George are two of the children of the aforesaid Anne Turlington who was formerly Ann Parker as above mentioned, conveyed to the said John G. Joynes all their right, title and interest, of, in and to the real estate of the said John T. Elliott, dec, and on the 18 February, 1828, the aforesaid Major Savage and Maria, his wife, conveyed to the said John G. Joynes all their right, title and interest in said estate, and on the 17 December, 1827, the aforesaid Sally, Alias Sarah Turlington coveyed to the said John G. Joynes all her right, title and interest in said estate; that on the 9 February, 1828, the aforesaid Samuel Parker conveyed to the said John G. Joynes all his interest; that on the 3 August, 1828, the said Timothy Kelly, together with Betsey, his wife, conveyed to the said John G. Joynes all their right, title and interest in the said estate; that on the 8 February, 1828, the aforesaid Bagwell Savage and Molly, alias Mary, his wife, conveyed to the said John G. Joynes all their right, title and interest in said estate; that on the 13 May, 1833 the said Eliza Elliott conveyed to the said John G. Joynes all his right, title and interest in said estate; that on the 12 December, 1828, the aforesaid Thomas Elliott conveyed to the said John G. Elliott all his right, title and interest in said estate; that on the 11 December, 1827, the aforesaid Stephen Kelly, together with Margaret, his wife, conveyed to the said John G. Joynes all his right, title and interest in said estate; that on the 5 June, 1828, the said John East and Susan, his wife, conveyed to the said John G. Joynes all their right, title and interest in said estate; that on the 12 July, 1828, the aforesaid Jesse, George, William B. and Betsey, alias Elizabeth Mears, and the aforesaid Nancy B. Turlington, together with Betsey, the wife of the said Jesse, Patsy, the wife of the said George, Molly the wife of the said William B. Mears, and the aforesaid John Turlington, the husband of the aforesaid Nancy B. Turlington, conveyed to your orator John G. Joynes all their right, title and interest in said estate; that on the 15 July, 1828, after the death of the aforesaid Nancy Savage, and also after the death of the aforesaid John Savage, the aforesaid George Savage conveyed to the said John G. Joynes all the right to which he was entitled; that on the 30 day of July, 1828, the aforesaid William

124

Oague, and afterwards on the 5 September, 1828, the said William Oague and Ann, his wife, conveyed to the said John G. Joynes all their right, title and interest in said estate; That on the 11 August, 1828, the aforesaid John Dowty conveyed to the said John G. Joynes all his right, title and interest in said estate; that on the 22 February, 1825, the aforesaid George Elliott conveyed to the said John G. Joynes and a certain Walter D. Bayne all his right, title and interest in said estate; that on the 1 March, 1821, the aforesaid John Elliott, a brother of the said George, conveyed to the said John G. Joynes and the said Walter D. Bayne all his interest in said estate; that on the 20 May, 1833, the said Walter D. Bayne, together with Harriet E. R., his wife, conveyed to the said John G. Joynes all his interest in said estate; that on the 9 July, 1830, the aforesaid Anne Kelly, who is a daughter of the aforesaid Charles Kelly, dec., who was as aforesaid one of the children of the aforesaid Isaiah and Hannah Kelly, dec., conveyed to a certain Vespasian Ellis all her right, title and interest in said estate, and afterwards, on the 22 October, 1830 the said Vespasian Ellis, together with Sophia H., his wife, conveyed to the said John G. Joynes the said interest; that on the 27 January, 1824, the aforesaid John Bell, one of the children as aforesaid of the aforesaid ____and Nancy Bell, dec., together with Lucretia, his wife, conveyed to a certain Jacob Bell all his interest; that on the 6 April, 1825, the aforesaid Anthony Bell, one of the children as aforesaid of the aforesaid ____Bell and Nancy, his wife, conveyed to the said Jacob Bell and a certain John Kelly (of S., all his interest in said estate; that on the 4 August, 1827, the said John Kelly (of S.) and Jacob Bell, together with Margaret, the wife of the said Jacob Bell, conveyed to the said John G. Joynes all their right, title and interest in said estate; that on the 12 February, 1824, the aforesaid John Elliott, who was as aforesaid one of the paternal uncles of the aforesaid John T. Elliott, dec., conveyed to the aforesaid George H. Bell all his right, title and interest in said estate; that on the 22 August, 1827, the said George H. Bell, together with Margaret, his wife, conveyed to the said John G. Joynes all the said interest.

That since the death of the said John T. Elliott on the ___ day of __, 182_, the aforesaid William Bell, who was one of the children as aforesaid of the above named ___ Bell and Nancy, his wife, has departed this life intestate, leaving a widow, Rachel Bell who is still living, and nine children, viz: Catharine, Eliza and Nancy Bell and your orators and oratrixes Arinthia J., Juliet, Margaret, James, John and William Bell, and since the death of the said William Bell, dec., his said widow Rachel and three of his said children, viz: the said Catharine, Eliza and Nancy Bell on the 9 January, 1829, conveyed their interest to the said John G. Joynes.

That on the 7 April, 1827, the aforesaid Henry Cook and Hetty, his wife, conveyed to a certain Major S. Pitts all their interest in said estate; and on the ___day of __, 182_ the said Major S. Pitts departed this life having first duly made and published his last will and testament, by which he did not specifically devise the aforesaid interest, but which passed and was disposed of under the residuary clause of said will to all the children of the said Major S. Pitts; that the said Major S. Pitts left surviving him the following children, William G.

Pitts, Margaret Pitts, Elizabeth Pitts, Edward Pitts and Washington Pitts.

That on the 11 December, 1824, the said Bezeleal Watson and Jane, his wife, coveyed by mortgage to your orator John W. Leatherbury all their right, title and interest in said estate; that on the 2 February, 1827, the said John W. Leatherbury assigned the mortgage deed to a certain William W. West; that on the 2 July, 1827, the said William W. West filed his bill for the purpose of foreclosing the said mortgage; that the said interest was sold by decree of court, at which sale a certain John C. Jacob became the purchaser as agent for your orator John W. Leatherbury; that on the 20 May, 1833, the aforesaid James Ross conveyed to the said John W. Leatherbury his interest in said estate, and that on the ___day of __1833 the aforesaid John Ross and George T. Belote and Peggy, his wife, the said John Ross and Peggy Belote being two of the children as aforesaid of the aforesaid John Ross, dec., who was one of the children as aforesaid of the aforesaid_____Ross and Rosey, his wife, conveyed to the said John W. Leatherbury all the interest to which they were entitled, and on the 19 February, 1824, the aforesaid Littleton Dowty, one of the children as aforesaid of the aforesaid_____Dowty and Susan, his wife, to which said deed Susan the wife of the said Littleton was a party, conveyed to the said John W. Leatherbury all their right, title and interest in said estate; that on the 20 March, 1833, the aforesaid Polly Ross, by the name of Mary M. Ross, conveyed to your orator John R. Fisher all her right, title and interest in said estate &c. ------- 29 May, 1833 - p. 445 et seq.

THE FOLLOWING CAUSE IS NOT RECORDED IN THE REGULAR SERIES BUT WILL BE FOUND IN VOLUME MARKED "MARRIAGE RECORDS NO. 1 1791-1854"

Be it remembered that heretofore, to-wit: at a Quarterly Court held in and for the said county at the Court House thereof, by adjournment, on Tuesday, the 14 day of June, in the year 1836, came the plaintiffs, by their attorney, and field their bill and an exhibit, which bill, with the proof thereof and the exhibits therein referred to marked "A", are in the following words and figures, to-wit:

Humbly complaining--show to your worships your orators Nathaniel Holland, guardian of Lafayette Harmanson, John Simkins, guardian of John L. Harmanson and George S. Christian, guardian of Caroline E. Harmanson:

That a certain John H. Harmanson late of the said County of Northampton departed this life of the ___day of August, 1825, leaving nine children, Mary C. Harmanson, Margaret Harmanson, Elizabeth Sabra Harmanson, Sarah Harmanson, Maria Anne, now the wife of Montcalm Oldham, William T. Harmanson and your orators wards aforesaid, and a widow, Juliet B., now the wife of Miers W. Fisher. That the said John H. Harmanson previous to his death duly made and published his last will and testatment for passing real and personal estate, and after his death, viz: on the 12 day of September, 1825, the same was duly proved and admitted to record in this Court: That the said John H. Harmanson was at the time of his death seized in fee simple of six several tracts or parcels of land situate in the said county of Northampton, the first called Federal Hall, containing, by estimation, 640 acres; the second called Martins & Coursers place, containing, by estimation, 200 acres and adjoining the tract called Federal Hall; the third called Goshen & Belotes place, containing ___acres, more or less; the fourth called Hungars Plantation, containing, by estimation, ___ acres, more or less; the fifth called Castle Ridge, containing, by estimation, 150 acres; the sixth, containing, by estimation, ____ commonly called by the name of Fowling Point and Brickhouse's Neck. That by his last will the said John H. Harmanson devised to his son William T. Harmanson 150 acres of pasture land commonly called and known by the name of Castle Ridge &c., he to pay to each of his children the sum of $30. when they arrived to the age of 21 years. That the said John H. Harmanson also devised to his daughters Mary, Margaret, Elizabeth, Sarah, Caroline and Maria, and to his son John, each 50 acres of pasture land commonly called and known by the name of Fowling Point & Brickhouse's Neck, and by his said will devised all the remaining part of his estate, real and personal, to be divided as the law directs, &c. That since the death of the aforesaid John H. Harmanson the said William T. Harmanson, his son, hath also departed this life intestate, under age and without issue, leaving the aforesaid Mary, Margaret, Elizabeth, Sarah, Caroline and John L. Harmanson and Maria Ann Oldham his sisters and brother of the whole blood, and the aforesaid Lafayette Harmanson his brother of the half blood, his heirs at law-------that the said Lafayette Harmanson is under the age of 14 years, &c. ---- Pages not number - Immediately follows marriage records.

COMPLETE RECORDS
IN CHANCERY
OCT. 1831 TO ----

James D. Williams, guardian of William P. Fitchett,
vs. - Suit for sale and division.
William P. Fitchett, William W. Dixon and Mary P., his wife,
Thomas K. Dunton and Emeline P., his wife and Sabra P. Fitchett.
    That on the ___day of __18__, a certain Joshua Fitchett, late of the said county, departed this life having first duly made and published his last will and testament, in which the said testator loans the whole of his estate, real and personal, to his widow, Patsy Fitchett, during her life or widowhood, and at her death gives the same to be equally divided between his four children, viz: the said William P. C. Fitchett, now deceased, Mary Fitchett and Emeline and Sabra P. Fitchett; since the death of the said Joshua Fitchett his daughter, Mary Fitchett, has intermarried with a certain William W. Dixon, and his daughter Emeline has intermarried with a certain Thomas K. Dunton; that the said William P. C. Fitchett, the son of the said Joshua, departed

this life on or about the __day of __,184_ intestate, after he had arrived to his full age, leaving as his only heir at law and child your orator's ward, William P. Fitchett, who is now about 30 months old; that the said Patsy Fitchett, the widow of the said Joshua, departed this life on or about the __day of December, 1841 unmarried, and that at the time of his death the said Joshua Fitchett was seized and possessed of three tracts or parcels of land situate, lying and being in the said county of Northampton, one of which tracts contains 578 acres, more or less, another contains 445 1/2 acres, more or less on the bayside, and the other tract containing 105 acres adjoining the last above named tract - 25 May, 1842 - p. 1

Catherine P. Parker, an infant, by Chess ___Purnell, her next friend, vs. - Suit for dower and division.
Catherine G. Parker, George P. Upshur and Peggy E. Upshur, his wife, and George P. Upshur, adminstrator of Severn E. Parker.

That in the month of October A. D. 1836, Severn Eyre Parker, father of your oratrix, departed this life intestate, leaving a widow, Catherine G. Parker, and two children, your oratrix and Peggy Eyre, wife of George P. Upshur his only heirs at law; that the said Severn Eyre Parker at the time of his death was seized and possessed of a large real and personal estate, and at the November term of this Court letters of administration were granted to the said George P. Upshur upon the estate of the said Severn Eyre Parker; that the said Severn Eyre Parker at the time of his death was engaged in the cultivation of all his lands in this county, and that none of the slaves will be required for the payment of his debts; your oratrix further shows that the said Severn E. Parker was seized and possessed of the following tracts of land and slaves; A tract of land in the County of Accomack called the Stringer Farm, containing 390 acres, adjoining the land of James Bell and others; a tract in this county call Kendall Grove on which he resided containing 500 acres, more or less, adjoining the lands of John Simkins; a tract adjoining the Kendall Grove tract called Purnells, containing 173 acres; a tract called the Poulson land adjoining the Purnell land, containing 320 acres, and a tract near Eastville adjoining the land of Harriet B. Parker, Nathaniel Winder and others containing 200 acres, also a house and lot in Eastville; 43 slaves, "six of which were house servants" &c. 13 Feb. 1837 - p. 14

Robert C. Jacob, guardian of William R. Hallett, vs - Suit for dower and division.
Edward M. Hallett, Robert J. Hallett, Eliza Hallett and William R. Hallett.

That Michael Hallett, late of this county, departed this life on the ___ day of __, 184_, leaving three children, viz: Edward M. Hallett, Robert Hallett and the aforesaid infant child William R. Hallett, the ward of your orator, as his heirs at law; that the said Michael Hallett left a widow, Eliza Hallett who is entitled to dower in the real estate of which the said Michael died seized and possessed; that the said

Michael Hallett at the time of his death was seized and possessed of considerable real and personal estate; that the whole of the personal estate except certain slaves, 19 in number, which have been divided among the heirs entitled to same, has been sold; that the real estate consists of a tract of land situate, lying and being in the lower part of Northampton near Capeville, containing 507 acres, more or less, adjoining the lands of Robert J. Poulson, John T. Collins, Benjamin Hailey, Henrietta Scherer and others &c., ----- 24 Apr. 1856 - p. 38

LAND CAUSES APRIL 1854-1868

John H. Powell, assignee of John B. Carpenter,
vs. - In Chancery.
Nathan F. Cobb and Esther, his wife, James Fletcher and Sally
Fletcher.
Suit for dower of Esther Cobb, the wife of Nathan Cobb, in the lands
of William Fletcher, dec., situate on Hog Island, containing 14 acres,
more or less - 18 Apr. 1854 - p. 1

Edward C. Fitchett and Mary W., his wife, formerly Mary W. Dunton,
George B. Taylor and Patsy, his wife, formerly Patsy
Dunton, Joshua F. Dunton and Samuel H. Dunton, the last
being an infant who sue by Edward C. Fitchett, his
next friend,
vs.
Sally Dowty.
Suit for division of land (Bill not recorded) - 18 Apr. 1866 - p. 6

Stewart J. Saunders and Laura C., his wife,
vs. - Suit for division of land.
Nancy Griffith, Elizabeth S. Griffith, John H. Griffith, Catharine
Griffith, Sarah Griffith and Nathaniel G. Downes,
administrator of John H. Griffith -
It appearing to the Court that since the last decree and continuance
in this cause, the defendant, Elizabeth S. Griffith, has intermarried
with a certain William G. Costin, on motion of the plaintiffs the said
William G. Costin is ordered to be made a party defendant to this
cause --------1866 - p. 12

---- Alicia, 35 Benjamin 84
Betsey 86 Betty 6 Cassey 95
Edward 102 Elizabeth 90
Esther 66 67 George 111
Hannah 65 James 69 Jennet
102 John 69 116 Jonathan 70
71 Levin 90 Lucretia 90
Maragaret Ann Meredith 27
Margaret 84 Maria J 27 Molly
124 Patsy 124 Peggy 90 Rose
90 Sally 84 90 94 Susan 90
Susanna 65 Tab 5 William 94
ABBOT, John 45
ABBOTT, William 68
ABDELL, Rachell 105
ABEL, Hendrick 55 68
ABELL, Hendrick 45
ADDISON, 120 Elizabeth 123
George 120 123 John 99 113
Matilda 123 Richard 120 123
Thomas E 114
ADOLFE, 69
ALDERSON, James 7 17 Richard
8
AMES, Ann 98 Bridget 95 96
Jesse 98 John G 89 Mahala 98
Margaret 98 Nancy 89 Richard
98 Sally 98 Shadrack T 98
Tabitha 98 Teackle 95 96
Thomas 98 William 95 96
AMULE, Dennis 51 53
AMULL, Dennis 51
ANDERSON, Mildred 7 8 Nathan-
iel 7
ANDREWS, 62 Elizabeth 74 John
74 Margaret 120 William 60-
62 120
ANGELL, John 12 Sarah 12
ARLINGTON, John 114
ARMISTEAD, Edward 94 Ellison
102
ATKINS, John 4

AYRES, Edmund 105 Kessy 105
BAGWELL, Alexander 37 Eliza-
beth 37 Henry 37 John 56
Thomas 36 William 37
BAKER, Mary 45
BALL, Alice Olivia 18 James F
18 30 Lucy 30 Lucy Olivia 30
BALY, Elisha 35 Isaac 35
BANKES, Thomas 45
BANKS, Thomas 55
BARNETT, Achilles 1 Ann 1
William 32
BARTLETT, James 1
BASYE, Elizabeth 14 33 Harriett
C 33 Henry 33 Joseph 33
Lewis O 33 Mary M D 33
Novella J 33 Richard F 33
Thomas 33 William 33
BATSON, Anne 50 Bridget 50
Elizabeth 49 50 Francis 50
John 50 Leah 50 Luke 79 Mary
50 Rachel 50 Ralph 52 Sarah
52 79 Tabitha 49 50 Thomas
50 William 49 50
BAYNES, Harriet E R 125 Walter
D 125
BEACH, John S 119
BEALE, Alice Olivia 18 Milly 18
BEANE, 15 Leannah 14 Peter 14
15 Peter Sr 14 15 Thomas J 14
15
BEATTY, Betsy 15 James 15
BELL, 120 122 125 Alice Ann 122
Ann 7 92 Anthony 120 125
Arinthia J 119 125 Catharine
120 122 125 Charles 7 8 Char-
lotte 122 Eliza 125 Elizabeth 7
8 122 123 Euphemia 120
Geodiah 119 120 122 123
George 36 71 122 123 George H
119 120 122 123 125 Hannah 36
Jacob 125

BELL (continued)
James 7 8 119 120 122 128
Jeodiah 36 Jesse 92 John 119
120 125 Jonathan 36 Juliet 119
125 Lorenzo 120 Lorenzo D
122 123 Lucretia 125 Mahala
120 123 Margaret 119 120 122
123 125 Mehaley 123 Mildred 7
Nancy 86 120 122 125 Rachel
125 Robert 86 Robins 119 120
Sally 120 123 Sally H 123
Thomas 7 8 75 119 120 122
123 William 119 120 125
William H 120 122
BELOTE, 127 Abel Jr 108 Daniel
Jr 108 Edward 71 George Sr
108 George T 126 Hezekiah
108 Mary 122 Peggy 121 126
Susan 108
BENSON, Betsey 98 99 John 76
Samuel 76
BERRYMAN, Richard 17
BEURY, John 45
BIGGS, John 88 Molly 88 Nancy
88 Thomas 88
BIRT, Frances 75 John 75 John Jr
75
BISCOE, Henry L 31 Sarah 31
BISHOP, 72 George 87 112 Grace
72 Jacob 45 John 72 Nathaniel
87 112 Sally 87 112 Sarah 87
112 Sylvester 87 112 William
87 112
BLACKERBY, Catharine 12
Catharing 12 Elizabeth 12
Joseph M 12 Richard 12
Thomas 12 William 12 13
BLACKWELL, John 48 49 Joseph
49
BLAIR, Thomas 65
BLAKEMORE, Eliza 31 John E
31 Mary 31 Sarah 31 Tomze 31
William 31
BLOXOM, 48 Grace 48 Savage 48
BOOTH, George W 22 Mildred B
21 22
BOWDOIN, Elizabeth 66 Peter 52
65 66 Peter S 111 115 Preeson
66 Susanna 65 66
BOYD, Ellen 29 John 29 Lucy 29
Mary 29 Thomas 29

BOYD (continued)
William 29
BRADFORD, Benjamin 122
Catharine 122
BRAMHAM, Benja 9 John B 26 27
Margaret E Y 26 27
BRENT, Alice 26 Hugh 26 Isaac
26 Judith N 26 Kenner 26 Sarah
N 18 Vincent 18 William 26
BRICKHOUSE, 127 Elem 85 Elem
L 85 George 36 John 71 85
John N 85 Mahala 85 Smith 85
Thomas S 85
BROUGHTON, 120 Sally 120
William 120 William B 123
BROUN, Charles Lr 27 James P
27 Maria J 27
BROWN, Jane 16 Thomas 65
William 16
BULLOCK, Sarah 52 Thomas 52
BUNTING, 120 Delight 119 120
Dicky 111 112 James 120
Lishea 111 112 Priscilla 120
Shepherd 120 Solomon 34
BURRIS, Nathaniel 87
BURROUGHS, John 68
BURTON, John 63 64 Margaret 36
William 36
BUSH, Alice 30
CABLE, Sarah 50 Sorrowful
Margaret 50 S Margaret 56
Thomas 38 50 56
CALLAHAN, Ann M 31 Ann Maria
31 Eliza 31 Elizabeth 31 Sarah
J 31 Sarah Jane 31 Thomas C
31 William E 31
CAPELL, Nathaniel 51 53
CARPENTER, Betsy 115 John B
130 Samuel G 115 Susanna 75
CARTER, 10 Addison L 26 27
Adelina S 27 Althea R 27 Ann
C 22 Catharine 5 Dale 4 21
Edward 4 5 52 54 Edward Jr 4
Edward Sr 5 Elizabeth L 22
Fanny 11 22 Frances E 11
Frances M 11 George 4 James
4 5 94 John 4 John A 22 John
M 11 John Miller 11 Joseph A
11 14 26 27 Joseph Addison 11
Judith 21 Landon Jr 22 Landon
Sr 22 Margaret E Y 26 27

CARTER (continued)
Marietta E 27 Martin 4 5 Mary
L 22 Paul 52 54 Polly 11
Rawleigh 4 Robert A 11 Robert
Alexander 11 Robert W 22
Thomas 4 5 21 W L S 27
Warren 11 William H 11
William Henry 11
CASEY, Ann 107 John 107
CAUL, Daniel 72 Elizabeth 72
CHARLES, King 36
CHICHESTER, Caty 3 Doddridge
Pitt 2
CHILTON, Betsy 30 Charles 4
Cordelia 16 Cyrus 14 15 David
29 30 Edward 30 Fauntleroy N
16 Judith 4 Leannah 14 15
Louisa 16 Merryman 4 5 Polly
30 Robert N 16 Sally 16 Ste-
phen 30 Thomas 4
CHRISTIAN, George E 98 George
S 126 John 98 William 98
William A 95 98
CHRISTOPHER, Achsah 17
George 17 John F 17 Thomas
17 William 17
CHURCH, Samuel 45
CHURCHES, Thomas 45
CLARKE, Anne 42 George 42
Sarah 42
CLAY, 104 Benjamin 87 104
Eliza 87 104 Elizabeth 87 104
James 87 John 87 104 Nancy
104 Sally 86 87 Sukey 87 104
Susan 87 Thomas 87 104
William 87
CLAYTON, George 9
COBB, Esther 130 Nathan F 130
COBLE, Edward 45
COCKERRALL, Nancy 28
COCKRALL, Nancy 28
COCKRELL, Elijah 10 Jane 10
Presley 10
COFFIN, John 70
COLES, Amanda 25 Lavala 24
COLLINS, Gracy 103 John 103
John T 129 Molly 85 Nathaniel
85 Sally 103 William 103
COLONNA, Anna 114
CONWAY, Eustace 30 Maria T 30

COOK, Henry 120 125 Hetty 120
125
COPES, 99 Levin 99 100 Sarah 91
Thomas 91 94 Thomas P 34
CORBIN, George 45 46 48 Grace
45 48
COSTEN, Francis 38 Stephen Sr
38 Thomas 38
COSTIN, 67 Abraham 103 Abram
90 Bowdoin 90 Charlotte 90 92
Coventon 90 Elijah 92 Eliza-
beth 90 Elizabeth S 130 Fran-
cis 90 103 John 90 Lucretia
108 Margaret 67 Nathaniel 90
Patsey 103 Polly 90 Ralph P
90 Samuel 90 William 103
William G 130
COWDRY, William 45
COWLES, Rachel 95
COX, Peter 13
CUGLEY, Daniel 39
CULPEPPER, John 75
CUMMINGS, Mellicent 4
CUNDIFF, John 8 14 Richard 14
CURRIE, Ellyson 4
CURTIS, Henry 75 John 75 John
Jr 75 Anne 75 George Wash-
ington Park 91 John 65 67
Peggy 67
DALBY, Hezekiah 101 Isaac 98
James 101 Severn 97 William
116 William Sr 116
DALE, Chloe 21 Elizabeth W 21
Joseph 21 Mildred B 21
Thomas J 21 22
DAVENPORT, George 7
DAVIS, John 45
DEGGES, Eliza A 28 James B 27
28
DENNIS, Archibald 101 118
Pamelia 101 Reubin 71
DEWEY, Beautifila 59 Jacob 59
Matilda 59 Tabitha 59
DIMMER, Thomas 46 54
DINES, Mary S 29 Tyson 29
DIX, Catharine E S 20 James T M
20 Levin 112 Lewis H 20 Lucy
20 Thomas 20
DIXON, Elizabeth 105 Joanna 105
Mary 127 Mary P 127

DIXON (continued)
Polly 105 William 105 William Sr 105 William W 127
DOGGETT, 29 30 Benjamin 29 Coleman 30 Eliza 29 Elizabeth 29 Griffin 10 Hugh 29 30 James 30 Jane 29 Joseah 29 Judith 33 Lucinda 29 Mary 30 Samuel 30 Sarah 29 William 29 William S 29
DOLBY, Thomas 67 71
DOUGLAS, George 66
DOWNES, Daniel 99 Nathaniel G 130
DOWNING, Catherine E 27 Comfort 110 Edmund W P 94 114 Samuel 27
DOWNMAN, Frances 18 George W 18 Harriet Jane 18 James W P 18 Jane E 18 John B 18 Joseph B 18 Milly 18 Sarah 18
DOWNS, Daniel 100 Eliza 99 Henry 99 100 Thomas 71 William 99
DOWTY, 120 126 John 120 125 Littleton 120 126 Margaret 120 Susan 120 121 126 130 Thomas 112 121 123 Thomas S 123 William 120 121
DREADNOUGHT, Ferdinand 8 Ferdinando 116
DRUMMOND, Barbary 66 Elizabeth 66 Hill 65 66 Tabitha 66
DULANY, Fanny 22 Henry R 22 Rebecca 22
DUNAWAY, Frances E 11 Robert T 17 William 5
DUNNAWAY, 10 Frances E 11 Rawleigh 11
DUNTON, 74 Ann 86 102 Anne 86 Daniel 67 Elias 74 105 Elias Jr 74 Elias Sr 67 Emeline 127 Emeline P 127 Friend William 112 Isaac 67 Isabell 37 Joshua F 130 Leah 74 Lovin 74 Mary W 130 Matthew H 112 Michael 74 Patsy 130 Polly 86 102 Richard 89 Rickards 88 Robert 86 102 Rose 74 Sally 86 Samuel H 130 Southy 74 Stephen 37 Sukey 86

DUNTON (continued)
Thomas 86 102 Thomas K 112 127 William 74
DUPARKS, Peter 45 Thomas 45 55
EAST, John 119 124 Susan 119 124
EDMONDS, Elias 12 Elizabeth 12 Janella P 12 John W A 12 Margarett M 12 Olivia 18 Phillip 12 Ralph 12 Robert 12 Susanna 11 12 Thomas M 18 William 12
EDMUNDS, Sarah 40 Thomas 40
ELIASON, 75 Cornelius 75 Elias 75 Mary L 22 William A 22
ELICOT, Catharine 34 Littleton T 34 Teackle 34 William 34
ELLIOT, Eliza 119 Thomas 119
ELLIOTT, Abel 119 124 Charles 119 121-123 Eliza 124 Elizabeth 119 122 124 George 119 121 123 125 Hannah 119 James 119 124 John 101 102 110 119 121 123 125 John G 124 John T 83 117 119-125 Juliet 83 121 Lavinia 122 Margaret 119 121-124 Molly 119 124 Nancy 119 Polly 101 102 110 Rosey 101 102 Sally 90 111 Thomas 110 124 William 110 119 124
ELLIS, Sophia H 125 Vespasian 125
ESHON, Ann 108 Daniel 108 George Jr 108 Harriet 108 Harriot 108
ESHON, Samuel 108 William 108
EUSTACE, John 13 Mary 22 Mary Ann 13 William 13 22 William C 30
EVANS, Caroline 106 I 88 John 106 Molly 90 Nancy 106 Nelly 90 Sarah Ann 106 William 106 William S 106
EYRE, Daniel 62 John 85 104 113 Littleton 56 Neech 56 Peggy 128 William L 90
FENN, Dick 80
FINNEY, Louis C H 34
FISHER, 40 77 James 98 John 40 John R 99 119 126

FISHER (continued)
Juliet B 126 Miers W 126
Philip 40 Rosey 98 Sally 83
Sarah 40 Thomas 40 76
FITCHETT, Charles 112 Daniel
108 Emeline 127 Hannah 111
112 Joshua 127 128 Margaret
111 112 Mary 127 Patsy 127
128 Sabra P 127 Sally 89
Thomas 87 112 Thomas Jr
118 Thomas Sr 112 William 89
William P 127 128 William P
C 127
FLEET, John 17
FLETCHER, Edward C 130
James 130 Mary W 130 Robert
48 Sally 130 William 130
FLIPPO, Eliza P 33 Joseph P 33
FLOOD, Catharine 9 Elizabeth 9
Nicholas 8-10 William 9
William Pinkstant 9
FLOY, John 71
FLOYD, James 91 John K 107
Matthew 87 Sally 87 Shepherd
B 86 87 Susan 87
FORD, William 26
FORESTER, Patsy 29 Thadeus 30
FOX, John 116 Mrs 117 Priscilla
116 117
FRESHWATER, Christopher 86
87 Nathaniel 87
GALLOWAY, Judith 8 William 8
10 William Sr 8
GAMBLE, Ann 7 8
GARLAND, Frances 22
GARRISON, 42 Cantwell 42
Elizabeth 122 Jeremiah 122
Margaret 42
GAYLE, Christopher 95 John S 95
GEORGE, 34 Benjamin 33 34
Benjamin G 19 Eleanor 34
Eliza 33 34 James S 32 Judith
28 33 34 Judith Ann 34 Julia
25 King 37 59 Lamoth Jeter 34
Margaret 32 Newton 32 Susan
P 19 Thomas 32 William 34
William H 33
GIBBONS, Sarah 65
GIBSON, 64 James 66 John 65 66
GLADDING, George 120 123 Hetty
120

GLASCOCK, Frances F 12
GODWIN, Archibald 38 72 Dever-
ex 38 Joseph 38 68 Susanna 38
GOFFIGON, James 84 113 115
118 John 86 112 John Sr 118
Nancy 86 Polly 90 Southy 84
114 William 90 113 115
GOOCH, William 37
GOODRIGHT, 50 52 54 58 59 74
76 Henry 38 39 Jacob 78 John
81 Thomas 35 41 43 45 52 53
GORDON, James 5
GOSHEN, 127
GRAY, Benjamin Dingly 59 60
GREAR, Frances 90
GREEN, 36 George 72 Sarah 72
Thomas 72
GRESHAM, Betsy 32 George 32
James W 32 Mary 32 Polly 32
Sally 16 Sally G 21 Samuel 16
21 William 32
GRIFFIN, Littleton 103 Polly 103
GRIFFITH, Ann 93 Anne 80 81
Benjamin 80 81 93 Catharine
130 Elizabeth S 130 Jeremiah
80 81 93 John 80 81 93 John H
130 Louisa 80 81 93 Major 81
93 Moses 80 81 93 Moses Sr
93 Nancy 130 Nathan 80 81 93
Polly 103 Rachel 80 Sarah 130
Thomas 80 81 93 William 80
81 90 93
GRIGGS, Alice 4
GROTEN, Edmund 89 Eliza L 89
William 89
HADLOCK, Robert 98
HAGGOMAN, William 67
HAILEY, Benjamin 129
HALEY, Peggy 90 Robert 90
HALL, Abraham 56 57 Absolum
47 Addison 12 20 Ann Mary 56
57 Anne Mary 47 Daniel R 80
Elizabeth 37 Eppa 10 John 37
Susanna 12
HALLETT, Edward M 128 Eliza
128 Michael 128 129 Robert J
128 William R 128
HAMMOND, Charles 9 Louis 32
HAMMONDS, Catharine 20 Eliza-
beth 20 Gawin 23 John 23
Lewis 23 Lucy 23

HAMMONDS (continued)
Patsey 20 Sarah Ann 20 William 20
HARCUM, Emeline L 32 James 32 Joseph 32 33 Marrietta 32 Polly 32 Samuel 32 33 Willie Ann 32
HARDING, Frances J 19 J H 19 John H 19 Lavala 24 William H 24
HARMAN, Elizabeth 68
HARMAN-SON, Gertrude 46
HARMANSON, 106 Caroline 127 Caroline E 126 Catharine 63 Elishe 62-64 Elizabeth 62 63 106 127 Elizabeth Sabra 126 Esther 62 63 George 56 Gertrude 46 55 Henry 46 55 56 61 Joane 60 61 John 45 61 62 John H 81 105 112 126 127 John L 126 127 John M 81 Katharine 62 Lafayette 126 127 Margaret 126 127 Margaret M 81 Maria 127 Mary 127 Mary C 126 Matt 65 Matthew 48 55 56 65 106 Patrick 63 64 Sally 82 111 112 Sally W 112 Sarah 126 127 Sophia 47 Susan 61 Thomas 46 60-62 Thomas Jr 61 Thomas Sr 60-62 William 61-63 81 William P 81 82 William T 126 127
HARRIS, 11
HARRISON, Robert 45 55 Salathiel 38
HATHAWAY, Lawson 1 2 17
HAWKINS, William 56
HAYDEN, Alice 31 Hiram 31
HAYDON, Polly 28
HAZZARD, Cyrus 22 23
HEADLEY, A Y 33 Elizabeth 33 Juliet 26 William Walton 26
HEATH, John 8 9 John Jr 10 John S 109 117 John Sr 10 Josiah 108 109 117 Josiah B 116 Judith 8 Nancy 116 Priscilla 116 Sally 10 William 116 117
HENDERSON, Catharine 109 110 William 109
HENNING, Lucy 4 Robert H Jr 4
HENRY, James 63 67 77

HICKMAN, Louisa 80 93 Nathaniel 80 93 110 111 Sally 110 111
HILL, Elizabeth 10 Eppa 22 23 Humphrey C 23 Humprey C 22 James H 22 James Monroe 22 23 Jane 65 John 10 John M 22 23 Lucy Pollard 10 Mary 10 Mary C 22 Milly 10 22 23 Nancy Morris 10 Thomas Pollard 10 William 10
HODGES, 42 Adah 42 Edward 42
HOLBROOKE, Edward 59
HOLDEN, George 38 50
HOLDFAST, 60 75 Thomas 60
HOLIDAY, Amanda 19 Needham 19
HOLLAND, Nathaniel 126 nWilliam 71
HOLLIDAY, Amanda 19 Needham 19
HOW, Elizabeth 12 13
HUDSON, Anne 45
HUGBIN, John 75
HUNT, 51 53 John 51 53 John G 89 Nancy 89 Obediah 89 Thomas O 89
HUNTON, Alexander 6 7 Ann 4 6 Betty 6 7 Caty 6 7 Elizabeth 7 George 6 7 Hannah 5 Jane 16 John 5-7 Lucy 6 7 Mary 6 7 Molly 6 Nancy 6 7 Robert 6 7 Sally 6 7 Susan 16 Susanna 6 7 Thomas 6 7 Thomas H 16 Thomas Y 16 William 6 7 William W 6
HUTCHINGS, Frances J 25 26 John 25 26 Mary E 25 26 Polly 26 26 William R 25 26
HYSLOP, John 99 Nancy 99
ISDEL, James 118 Lovea 118
JACOB, Anne 95 Esau 64 78 Hancock 74 95 John C 126 Lazarus 52 54 Philip 58 Robert C 128
JAMES, 3 75 Benjamin 84 Elizabeth 1 Jack 92 Jeduthan 4 John 1 2 Margaret 95 Mary 1 Nancy 1 Robert 95 Thomas 18 76 95 William 2 98 William D 95
JARVIS, Elizabeth 117 Leah 117 Margaret 84 113

JARVIS (continued)
  Thomas 117 118 William 84
  92 118 William B 113 William
  Sr 117
JEFFERSON, Peter 87 Polly 87
  Thomas 112
JOHNSON, 59 76 A B 105 Abel B
  105 110 Ann 98 Benjamin 50
  Catherine 98 Edmund 76 Harri-
  et 110 Ismey 94 James 94
  Jeptha 95 John P 96 Joshua 60
  Kitty 110 Laban 101 Luke 36
  Margaret 110 Mary 110 Moses
  112 Obedience 76 Polly 110
  Richard 59 60 98 105 110
  Rosey 95 Tabitha 59 60 Wil-
  liam P 105 110
JONES, Ann Mary 56 Anne Mary
  47 Athalia A 21 Evelina 90
  Frances 47 56 John 47 56
  Richard 90 Sarah 47 56 Walter
  9 Walter Flood 9 William 9
  Williamson C 21
JOURDAN, George 72 Susanna 72
JOYNES, 105 Edward A 94 John
  107 John G 119 123 124 125
  Kendall 105 Letitia 107 Livia
  95 Melinda 94 95 Nancy 94
  Sally 94 Thomas R 91 103 122
  123 Tully 94 95 Watkins 98
  William 94 95
JUSTICE, 60 63 Catharine 63
  Catherine 63 Ralph 63 William
  63 64
KELLAM, Elizabeth 110 Harriet
  97 Juliet 97 Margaret 97
  Samuel 110 Shadrack 97
  Walter 97
KELLUM, Custis 92 Margaret 92
KELLY, Anna 119 Anne 120 125
  Betsey 124 Charles 120 125
  Hannah 119 120 123 125 Isaiah
  119 120 Jesse 119 123 John
  119 125 Margaret 124 Mary 119
  Nancy 119 Sophia 119 Stephen
  119 124 Timothy 119 124
  William 119
KEM, John 29
KEMM, John 30
KENDALL, 60 63 Custis 71 107
  Elishe 63 Elizabeth 62 63 117

KENDALL (continued)
  Elizabeth Custis 107 George
  39 63 John 45 46 62 63 68
  Lucretia 106 Susanna 45
  Thomas 45 William 46
KENT, Elizabeth 1 William 1
KER, John 115
KING, Charles 37 George 37 59
KIRK, Catherine 5 Elizabeth M 24
  25 Mary 5 William H 24 25
LANSDELL, Nancy 21
LAWRENCE, William 45 55
LAWSON, Elizabeth C 26 Henry
  C 17 Judith N 26 Margaret 17
  Margarit 17 Marian L 26
  Thomas L 26
LEATHERBURY, 99 John W 118
  119 126 Nancy 119 Thomas
  119
LECATT, Stephen 45
LEE, Ann 17 Elizabeth 7 8 John
  17 Margaret 17 Margarit 17
  Thomas 17
LELAND, Charles 1
LEMOINE, Feriol 19 Frances B
  19 Frances Ellen 19 Frances J
  19 Louisa 19 Moreau 19 Vir-
  ginia 19
LEWER, Ann 109 110 Anne 109
  George 109 110 Hannah 109
  110
LILLISTON, 90 Edmund 90 Sukey
  90 Southy 56
LOCKE, Joseph 14 15 Thomas M
  14 15
LOWRY, David 23 David 23
  Fanny 23 Gawin 23 James 23
  Jeremiah 23 John 23 Lucy 23
  Mary 23 Polly 23 Stokely 23
  Stokely D 23
LUKER, Walter 91 94 101
LUNSFORD, John 4 11 Lettice 11
  Nancy 30 Seth 12 13 Warner C
  30
LYON, James 81 104 106 Marga-
  ret 81 104 William 81 William
  E 81 104 113 115
LYTT, Thomas 91
MAJOR, John 35 Littleton 102
MALL, Addison 20
MAPP, John C 93 95 Kessey 95

MARSH, Charles 8
MARSHALL, Thomas 36 48
MASON, James 28 John 28
Margaret 28 Mary 28 Nancy 28
Thomas 28 William 28
MATTHEWS, John 67 Samuel 96
97 Vianna 96 97
MCCALL, Archibald 9 Catharine
8 Catharine Flood 9 10 Eliza-
beth 9 10 Katharine Flood 9
MCCARTY, Charles 9
MCTYRE, Sarah 4
MEARS, Abby 118 Abi 118 Alvin
114 Anna 114 Betsey 124
Betsy 120 Elizabeth 114 124
Euphemia 120 George 118 120
124 Henry 118 Hillars 120
James 118 Jemima 96 97
Jesse 120 124 John 114 118
Littleton 118 Lorenzo D 114
Mary 114 Molly 124 Nancy 120
Patsy 124 Shadrack 97 Susan
118 Tabitha 118 Thomas W 94
William 114 118 120 William
B 124
MEREDITH, Ann 17 Ann S 18
John 17 18 Maragaret Ann 27
Margaret 17 18 Margaret S 18
Thomas 17 18 Thomas James
18 Thomas W 28 William V
18
MICHAEL, Comfort 52 John Sr 46
Sally 110 Thomas 52
MILBY, 76 Betsy 98 Gilbert 76
MITCHELL, Athalia A 21 Julius
18 Littleton D 18 Margaret 18
Mary M K 21 Nancy 21 Ricahrd
B 18 Richard 16 21 Richard B
21 Robert 3 18 Sally G 21
William G 18
MONGOM, Philip 45
MONK, Elizabeth 44 George 41 43
44
MONTAGUE, Frances 18 William
D 18
MOOR, 58 John 58 Jonathan 58 77
Levi 40 Margaret 58 Sarah 40
Thomas 77
MOORE, John 58 77 Margaret 58
77 William 77

MUSE, Frances 12 John 12 Sarah
30
MYERS, Amanda 24 25 Elizabeth
M 24 George F 25 Mary Ann 24
Pleasant 24 25 William 24 25
NASH, Fanny 23 George 23
NEGRO, Abel 85 Agnes 85 Alice
5 Ann 56 Bridget 88 Charles 4
5 Comfort 85 Daniel 4 5 83
Darkey 6 Dick 6 Dolly 85
Edath 85 Edward Carter 52 54
Eliza 85 Esther 4 Fanny 85
Frank 4 6 George 83 George
the elder 85 Hannah 4 Harry 4
Jack 5 Jacko 65 Jacob 85
James 6 Jenny 5 Jim 88 Jinny
4 Jude 7 Judith 6 Judy 6
Kesiah 65 Leah 85 Leety 5
Lette 6 Lity 88 little George
85 little James 85 Mark 4 85
Martha 5 Martha's child 5
Mary 85 Meina 6 Mingo 4 5
Mingoe 5 Minon 4 Myma 5
Nancy 85 Nanny 85 Nat 85 Ned
6 Nell 5 Old James 85 old
Rachel 88 Pat 6 Paul Carter 52
54 Pete 74 Pleasant 5 Rose 90
90 Sam 85 Sarah 4 85 88 Siller
4 85 Stephen 85 Sue 4 5 Tom 6
Tony 85 Winney 6 Winny 4
Young Harry 5 young Rachel 88
NELSON, Betsy 115 John 84
Margaret 115 Maria 115 Polly
115 Sally 115 Southy 113 115
NEWBY, Ann 6 Cyrus 6 Elizabeth
6 7 William 6 7
NICHOLLS, William 51 53
NIVISON, John 103
NOTITLE, John 35
NOTTINGHAM, 83 Addison 74
Betsey 86 Elizabeth 103 104
113 114 Esther 113 114 Fanny
103 104 114 Jacob 85 103 104
114 Jacob E 114 Jacob Sr 86
John 113 John E 115 117
Joseph 90 Juliet 113 Margaret
113 114 Maria 90 Patsey 103
104 Patsy 114 Polly 86 Rich-
ard Jr 68 Sally 84 86 113
Samuel 113 114 Severn E 86
Smith 84 113 Sukey 88

138

NOTTINGHAM (continued)
Thomas 88 103 113 114 William 85 90 113 114 William E 83 84 91 William J 90 William Sr 86
NURSE, Narcissa M 122 Uri 122
OAGUE, 120 Ann 125 Esther 120 Rebecca 120 William 120 124 125
OBEN, Obedience 75
OLDHAM, Maria Ann 127 Maria Anne 126 Mary J 31 Montcalm 126 Thomas 31
ORREL, Polly 23 William 23
OWENS, Thomas M 12
PALMER, Betsy 32 Charles 32 Chloe 21 James A 27 John 21 Judith 21 Margaret Ann 27 Thomas 21 Thomas Jr 21
PARKER, 59 119 Ann 124 Ann G 115 Anna 119 Caleb 60 Catherine G 128 Catherine P 128 Edward 119 George 88 119 George S 124 Harriet B 128 Jacob Dewey 59 Jacob G 115 117 Maria 119 Philip 59 Polly 124 Sally 119 Samuel 119 124 Severn E 91 102 106 128 Severn Eyre 128 Tabitha 59 Thomas Hall 60 Thomas L 106
PARRAMORE, John C 95
PARROT, Capt 106
PARSONS, John 72 Mariot 52 54 Thomas 88
PATRICK, Agnes 40 41 43 68 78 Anges 68 Elizabeth 40 41 43 44 68 69 73 78 Richard 40-44 68 69 72 73 78 Richard Jr 41-44 Richard Sr 41-44 Ursly 68 69 Ursula 40 41 43 44 73 78
PAYNE, Catherine E 27 Harriot 13 John 13 Maria 27 Maria J 27 Richard 27 Richard H 27
PEACHY, Leroy 9 Thomas Griffin 9 William 9 William Travers 9
PEDE, Susan 113
PENDENDEN, Henry 36 37 Henry Jr 37
PENDENDENS, Henry 37
PERCIFUL, Elijah 10

PERKINSON, Edward 45
PETTIT, Fanny 109 110 William 109
PETTITT, Henry 70 John 70 71 Peter 71 William 71 78
PEYTON, Bridget 122 William 122
PHILLIPS, Bryant 7 Jesse 122 Mahala 122
PIERCE, Daniel 20 Nancy 20
PIGOT, Francis 69 Ralph 36 52 54
PIGOTT, Francis 36 Ralph 36 Thomas 36
PINCKARD, Thomas 11
PITMAN, Emily 30 Leroy 10 Polly 10 Sally 10 Thomas 30 William 10
PITT, Robert 78
PITTS, Ann 96 Anne 96 Edward 119 126 Elizabeth 119 126 John 96 John R 96 Major S 97 101 125 Margaret 119 Washington 119 126 William G 119 125 126
POLLARD, Lancaster William 17
POULSON, 128 Elizabeth 95 James 95 Robert J 129
POWELL, Abel 86 116 Betsey 112 Betsy 111 Frances 47 56 George 91 111 112 John 47 56 John H 130 Margaret 88 Molly 111 112 Nancy 111 112 Nathaniel 111 112 Pamela 85 86 Sally 111 112 Sally Sr 112 Samuel 45 47 56 Susanna 38 Thomas 91 111 112
PRATT, Martha 80
PREESON, 64 Brown 65 Elizabeth 64 65 Susanna 65 Thomas 64 66 Zerobabel 64-66
PRESTON, Alice 31 Thomas J 31
PURNELL, Chess 128
PURNELLS, 128
PURSELL, Joseph 25 26
RAMSEY, Nathaniel 78
READ, Edmond 109 Hannah 49 Ishmael 49 John 48 49 Major 48 Mary 49 Nancy 109 Nancy B 110 Thomas 49
RESPESS, Esther 63 67

SLAVE (continued)
Sarah 107
SMAW, 50 52 101 Abbigall 39
Abigail 40 52 Daniel 101 Luke
39 40 52 Nancy 101 102
SMITH, Abraham 50 Ann 108
Elizabeth 108 Esther 108
George 103 George Jr 108
George Sr 108 Henry 108 John
37 52 99 108 John E 99 Juliet
99 Littleton 72 Lucretia 108
Merrywether 9 Richard 99
Sarah 108 Susan 108 Thomas
W 123 William 108 William
Sr 108
SMITHER, Lucy 4
SNEAD, Catharine 34 Charles S
34 Charles W 34 Henrietta W
34 Littleton L 34 Margaret A
34 Rachel B 34 William T 34
SOMERS, William 51 53
SPADY, Adad 100 Adah 101
Amelia 90 100 Ann 100
Benjamin 100 Betsey 100
Elizabeth 113 George 100
James 100 101 John 100 101
Mary 100 Sally 90 Samuel 100
Sarah 47 56 57 80 Sukey 100
101 Thomas 47 56 57 Thomas
S 113 William 100
SPANN, 29
SPEAKMAN, Thomas 71
SPILLER, Benedictus 11 12
Benjamin V 11 James 11
William 12
STAKES, Archibald S 29 Asa 29
Betsy 29 George 29 John F 29
Margaret 29 Mary S 29 Wil-
liam 29 William L 29
STAYTON, Elizabeth 66 Thomas
66
STEER, Timothy 68 69
STEPHENS, 30 Rich: 4 William 4
STERLING, Elizabeth 37 Richard
37 William 37
STEWART, James 94
STILES, Thomas 39
STONHAM, Betsy 14 Samuel 14
STOTT, Betsey 98 99 Elizabeth
W 22 Joanna 98 99 Jonathan
65 Keely 98 99 Laban 71 74

STOTT (continued)
Ralph 98 Robert 98 T C 22
Teackle 98 99 Thaddeus C 22
STRATTON, 115 Benjamin 81 82
103 Edward 115 Esther 56 John
36 56 John N 115 Lucy 115
Margaret M 81 Mary Ann 115
William 81 101 William D 114
William H 81
STRINGER, Alicia 39 Col 45 55
Elishe 46 Hillary 38 39 47 48
95 Jacob 39 John 46 54 55
John F 91 Kitty 95
STUBBENS, 51
STURGIS, Jacob 102 Margaret 102
SUMMERS, Hugh 20 Sarah Ann 20
SYDNOR, Ann 2 3 Caty 3 Ellen 2
3 Fanny 2 3 Fauntleroy 3
George 2 3 James 3 Moore 3
Richard 2 3 Samuel B 2 3
Samuel G 2 3 William 2 3
William F 2 3 William Faun-
tleroy 3
SYDNORBY, George 2
SYNDOR, Anne 3 James 3 Samuel
B 3 Samuel G 3 William F 3
TALLEY, Frances 30 James 15
Polly 30 Robert 30 Sarah 30
TALLY, James 15 Nancy 15
TANKARD, Amy 112 Azariah 78
Fanny 109 110 George L 109
110 George L E 109 Hannah
109 110 Mary 109 110 Zilla
110
TAPSCOTT, Joseph 29 Margaret
29
TAYLOR, 120 Caty 120 Daniel C
109 David C 108 117 George B
130 John 89 Margaret 117
Patsy 130 Philip 60 61 Prin-
cessa 89 Sally 116 Thomas 60
William 120
TAZEWELL, 54 Anne 56 Ger-
trude 56 Littleton 56 Sophia 55
56 William 46 56
TEACKLE, Thomas 68
TEACLE, Elicot 34 Elliot 34
TEAGUE, Jonathan 67
THOMAS, 58 Fanny 103 104 114
George 58 John 77 William
103 104 114

WATTS, 33 David 33 Elizabeth
33 Frances 39 Jane 33 John E
33 John Wilkins 39 Joseph L
33 Robert K 33 Thomas 39
WEBB, Hannah 45 Southy 97
WEBLEY, Widow 45 55
WEBSTER, John 45 55
WELBURN, Daniel 66
WELCH, Elenor 36 37
WESCOAT, Ann 97 Anne 96
Edmund 96 George 96 Hezeki-
ah 96 97 Hezekiah P 92 John
96 97 Joshua 96 Major 96
Polly 96 97 Rosey 96 97
Susanna 92 Vianna 96 William
96
WEST, John 55 66 Mary 123
Nathaniel 116 120 123 Polly
120 120 William 116 William
W 126
WHAPLES, Peter 51 53
WHEATLEY, 120 Rebecca 120
WHITE, Joseph 102 Sally 102
Teackle 98 William 102
WHITEHEAD, John 99 Stephen 38
99 Thomas 38 99 William 99
WIBLIN, Alice 12 Wmson 12
WIDGEON, Adah 85 Anne 85
George 85 John 90 113 114 116
Jonah 49 50 Maria 90 Mary 50
Nancy 85 Nathaniel 88 Patsey
85 Susan 90 Walter 85 West-
erhouse 85 William 90 Wil-
liam Jr 90 William Sr 90
WILKINS, Elizabeth 107 Frances
39 George F 107 John 39 69 71
78 85 John Sr 71 Jonathan 39
Judith 71 Major 71 Margaret
107 Nancy 92 Stockly 71
Thomas 117 William 71 92
101 117 William H 107

WILLIAMS, Anne 90 Azariah 80
84 104 Betsey 86 Betsy 85
Elizabeth 90 113 James 113
James D 127 John 84 90 John
Jr 84 113 John Sr 84 Margaret
84 85 113 Nancy 87 104 Peggy
90 Peter 87 104 Peter Jr 118
Polly 90 Samuel 84 Samuel S
113 Sukey 104 Susan 113
Thomas 6 7 84 90 Thomas Jr
113 Thomas Sr 113 William 84
William G? 90 William H 90
William S 84 113 115
WILLIS, A S 19 Comfort 107
Frances 107 Louisa 19 Marriot
107
WILLOTT, John 69
WILSON, 83 Ann 84 Bishop 83
James 100 John C 90 113
Letitia 83 Nancy 83 Peggy 83
Sally 115 Sukey 100 Susanna
100 Thomas 35 45 83 William
83
WINDER, Nathaniel 128
WINGATE, Amy 106 Daniel 106
107 Emily 107 Henry 106 Ira
106 Margaret 107 Sarah 106
Sarah Ann 107 William 106
WISE, Elizabeth 50 John 50
WYAT, George 36 Margaret 110
William 110
WYATT, Peggy 109 William 109
YERBY, Artimesia 16 Charles J
16 Cordelia 16 George 9 Maria
16 Sally 16 William 16
YOUNG, Betsy 92 Elizabeth 92
John 105 Susan 105 Thomas 92
YOUNGE, Samuel 45